Computational Neuroscience and Cognitive Modelling

Computational Neuroscience and Cognitive Modelling

a student's introduction to methods and procedures

Britt Anderson

Los Angeles | London | New Delhi
Singapore | Washington DC

Los Angeles | London | New Delhi
Singapore | Washington DC

SAGE Publications Ltd
1 Oliver's Yard
55 City Road
London EC1Y 1SP

SAGE Publications Inc.
2455 Teller Road
Thousand Oaks, California 91320

SAGE Publications India Pvt Ltd
B 1/I 1 Mohan Cooperative Industrial Area
Mathura Road
New Delhi 110 044

SAGE Publications Asia-Pacific Pte Ltd
3 Church Street
#10-04 Samsung Hub
Singapore 049483

Editor: Michael Carmichael
Editorial assistant: Keri Dicken
Production editor: Imogen Roome
Copyeditor: Neville Hankins
Proofreader: Audrey Scriven
Marketing manager: Alison Borg
Cover design: Wendy Scott
Typeset by: C&M Digitals (P) Ltd, Chennai, India
Printed in India at Replika Pvt Ltd

Library of Congress Control Number: 2013940255

British Library Cataloguing in Publication data

A catalogue record for this book is available from
the British Library

ISBN 978-1-4462-4929-1
ISBN 978-1-4462-4930-7

Contents

Contents ix

Preface

My own efforts to develop a little computational competency have followed a fairly standard path. Whenever I came across some research article with an intriguing title, I would try to read it, usually only be able to get through the introduction and conclusion, and be further convinced that it was just the ticket for some project I was working on. However, problems would begin when I tried to plow through the methods section. This would yield some blur of terminology and formulas that I did not understand. In trying to push on, I would look up a term and my efforts to answer one question would to lead to two others; my route would bifurcate and grow. An article on a model of memory using neural networks might lead me to read someone's MATLAB code. My ignorance of MATLAB would lead me to questions about programming. This could lead to questions about "vectorizing." And that might bring me to learn a bit about vectors and linear algebra. Occasionally, the loop would close. I would realize that vectors were the mathematical "things" at the heart of many neural network algorithms. I could envision how they needed to be manipulated, and then I could understand the MATLAB code that had been programmed explicitly for the purpose of making those manipulations. Finally, I could understand the article that had started the whole process.

What I am trying to write here, of course, is the book I wished I had had way back when. A book that defined common mathematical notation, covered the basics of computer programming terminology, and had enough elementary examples that I could see how things were supposed to work in the small, before trying to apply them to some larger problem. No book of any practical size can accomplish this for all the topics that are relevant for psychology and neuroscience, but I do believe that it can be done for a sample of topics, and thereby serve as an introduction and invitation to further study.

Who is this book for? It is for the undergraduate student, especially the undergraduate psychology student, who is intrigued by computational modelling as a method, but does not have the background to read the literature or conduct a computational experiment.

It is also for the scientist who trained, as I did, in an earlier era. Computational topics did not seem as relevant when computer programs were punched into cards, carried around in boxes, and executed on centralized resources. Now, the growth in computing power has put the capacity for major simulations on our desktops, but many of us are still at the stage where we need to contact tech support to upgrade our copy of Microsoft Office.

The book is for anyone who feels themselves intrigued, but excluded. They may feel excluded by the odd notation of the research literature. Or they may feel excluded by a perceived lack of time to take the courses necessary for achieving expertise in "differential equations" or "predicate calculus," mathematical topics with forbidding reputations. They may feel excluded by the recondite nature of computer programming and its plethora of languages ("Suppose I choose the wrong one?"). Lastly, it is for those who feel excluded by ability; mathematical ability is viewed by many as a natural endowment.

What is the purpose of the book? It is to assure each of these audiences that their concerns are unfounded.

Mathematical notation should not be a barrier. Mathematical notation is just another bit of technical jargon used to express complex ideas concretely and concisely. The use of mathematical notation does not necessarily mean that something deep is being expressed. The expression $6 = \sum_{i=1}^{3} i$ may look mysterious, but it merely states that the numbers one, two, and three sum to six. For each mathematical area covered in the book, I introduce some of the common notation's abbreviations. This is intended to make the scientific literature more accessible. It is also intended to convince people that most equational statements are straightforward once the symbols are understood. Equations may contain deep insights, but their depth does not come from their specialized vocabulary.

Computers, their programming, and their use, should not be a barrier to the use of computational models. This book intends to eliminate this objection by building a familiarity with computing terms and procedures. Programming a computer, or writing "code," is what we do when we download apps to our phones, schedule an appointment in a computer calendar, or set up a spam filter for our email. We use an application's programming interface to instruct a computer to do something. That is programming. Most of us have used a spreadsheet, but we have never regarded it as programming. It is. This book introduces computer programming through exercises that can be solved with spreadsheets, so that we can program without really feeling like that is what we are doing. At the same time, I gradually introduce the constructs and terminology of programming. When we can see the parallels between what we have done in our spreadsheet and an equivalent command in a programming language, we might feel emboldened enough to give conventional programming a try. Like speaking a foreign language, fluency comes with practice, and the book intends to give readers lots of opportunities for hands-on experience. In addition, I describe some of the types of computer languages and show how most are very similar. You cannot pick a bad one to learn. They will all do much the same thing, often using very similar techniques with a slightly different syntax. There are differences among programming languages, but those differences will not matter very much for our uses.

Mathematics is hard, and to become a mathematician requires years of dedicated study. But to use math for a particular purpose does not. We do not feel we have to be mathematicians to evaluate different cell phone plans; a few back-of-the-envelope calculations suffice, and we don't make references to Peano's axiomatization of arithmetic. Similarly, while differential equations, linear algebra, and the like can be deep areas of mathematics, they can also be employed for specific purposes. We do not need to approach them as the mathematician does. The book provides a brief, introductory, and selective survey of some mathematical topics used in computational neuroscience and cognitive modelling. For each, it demonstrates their use.

In the aggregate, I hope the above demonstrations eliminate the objection that the mathematical and computational methods are beyond one's natural ability. They are not. Any curious university student, regardless of background or whether their last math class was in grade 11, can do all the exercises in this book. I know that because I teach such students these materials, and I have yet to meet one who could not master them. This does not mean that it will be easy, but it is not impossible. The key, as with any new and challenging subject, is persistence, guidance, and encouragement. Computational modelling is like curling or piano. Competency comes with practice.

How the book is organized. To accomplish its goals, the book is graduated in its approach and strives to be self-contained. Topics are selected that highlight a particular computational theme and mathematical approach. I associate each with a neurological or psychological computational application. Where I talk about the mathematics, I introduce common notations and abbreviations. I demonstrate how very basic mathematical ideas serve us quite well in psychology. Much of the complicated mathematics, and all the challenging analytic solutions that mathematicians spend their time learning, are typically not necessary for the psychologist modeller. We can use the power of the computer to simulate or approximate the answers that we need. The book uses exercises that can be implemented in a spreadsheet. After some lessons an example of how the same effect could be accomplished in a conventional computer language is demonstrated. After implementing a "loop" by dragging and copying a few hundred rows in a spreadsheet, the student has an incentive to explore other methods and can appreciate the power of a few lines of computer code.

The selection of topics covered is idiosyncratic, but that is because the book's purpose is to develop the skills needed for more advanced study. I have sacrificed depth for breadth, and I favor material that gives beginning students a leg up.

How to use this book. For all users, I suggest starting with Chapter 1. It is important to understand the goals and limits of an approach before beginning to use it. If you are an independent reader you should be able to work though this book on your own, and while you can vary the order among parts, I think you will find it easier to proceed in the order written. There are a number of exercises available for you to try, and I have included answers or example figures of what the answers should look like so that you can evaluate your work. Undergraduates from engineering and computer science may find it instructive to implement some of the examples with a computing language of their choice to see how these techniques are useful to neuroscience and psychology. Advanced students in psychology, whether graduate or post-graduate, should simply start with the part that most interests them.

If you are an instructor using this book for a course, I think you can generally pick and choose to teach any or all parts in any order. Each part is relatively self-contained with its own mathematical emphasis, history, and exercises. I think any of the major parts could also be taught in isolation and used to extend an undergraduate psychological methods course with a computational component.

There are two schools of thought about whether to start with the section on the Hodgkin–Huxley model and differential equations or some other topic. One point of view is that the forbidding terminology, and near mythic difficulty of differential equations, will put off the very students that I most want to target. I understand this argument, and if the instructor does not personally feel comfortable with that section it is not a good place to start. The second point of view, which is the one I hold, wants to build confidence early. The neuron modelling section starts gradually and dryly, and there may be the need for extra coaching early on, but it is quite a boost for most students when they see how something familiar, like compounded interest, "is" an exponential equation, and that the very same structure turns up in the integrate and fire model. The Hodgkin–Huxley model is complex, but it introduces no new concepts beyond those of the integrate and fire model. I find the key is pace. Students who try to read the book like a novel usually get frustrated, but if you can convince them to pace themselves, and to spend a week or so working through each chapter, you can get them to the full Hodgkin–Huxley model in four to five weeks. It gives the less confident students quite a boost to see that they can progress over a month to the point where they can code in Microsoft Excel a complex partial differential equation whose discoverers received the Nobel Prize. The students may not go on to use computational models, but they no longer see them as magic.

The one exception to ordering based on preference is the intermezzos that introduce various programming information and ideas. These sections can be skipped entirely if all the work is to be confined to spreadsheet programs, or the reader or instructor will have to direct students to the appropriate sections as they arise in the course of a reordering of the principal parts.

As to the time each unit takes, I usually devote about two to three hours once a week to each chapter. I try to get students to read outside of class time, and then to use the class session for collaborative work on the exercises, or to explore and look at solutions the students found for the material from the week before.

Final comments. My principal goal is for the book to provide an entrance to a world of useful investigatory tools. It has taken me a long time and a lot of work to get to where I am today. I feel my understanding is only a fraction of what I aspire to, but it is still enough for me to appreciate the power and pleasure of computational modelling. You will not be a mathematician when you finish this book, but you should have a foundation, and you should be confident that the additional hard work required to become proficient is well within your grasp. You will be able to decide for yourself if the work required is worth your while, and if you decide not to pursue further studies along this line, you will know that you could have, you will have a deeper understanding of the work required by those who do, and you will be a better collaborator if you work with a computational modeller. Should you elect to pursue additional studies on any of these topics, I would be very pleased if you would take the time to share your progress with me. In any case, I look forward to receiving feedback on the book.

Chapter 1

An Introduction to the Ideas and Scope of Computational Methods in Psychology

Objectives

After reading this chapter you should be able to:

- understand the goals of computational modeling for psychology and neuroscience;
- describe the limits of computational models;
- describe the role played by computers in the growth of computational modeling; and
- describe how the success of a model can be evaluated.

1.1   Overview

My overall objective in this chapter is to introduce some of the motivations for using computational models in psychology and to suggest some of the limitations. It is often easier to sharpen one's thinking on these points if there is some form of dialogue. If you do not have the chance to discuss these ideas with someone else, you might first read one of a number of recent position papers (e.g., McClelland, 2009; McClelland et al., 2010; Griffiths et al., 2010) and try to come to your own personal opinion of their correctness. Try to form your own answers to the following questions:

- Why bother modelling at all?
- Can we make a brain? Should we try? Should we care? Is this important for computational psychology?
- What role should biological plausibility play in neural and psychological models?
- Do you need a computer to create a computational model?
- How do you evaluate a model?
- What is the importance of a model's assumptions?

1.2   Why Model?

One answer to this question might be because you believe that modelling is something that the brain itself engages in. By modelling you are trying to reproduce or discover the architecture of thought.

Mental models as a basis for cognition have their roots in the writings of Craik (1952). A more contemporary proponent for mental models as models of cognition is Johnson-Laird (e.g., Johnson-Laird, Byrne, & Schaeken, 1992). Just as a small mechanical model can be used to predict the oscillations of high and low tides, perhaps in our brains (or our minds) we have some small simulacra that reproduce the functional organization of our world. To model cognition then is to model our models of our world (Chapter 21 looks at one modelling platform for building mental models).

Modelling does not have to be justified so directly. Models can be viewed as simplified versions of complex phenomena. The phenomena may be too complex for us to directly grapple with, but by abstracting away some of the complications we can achieve a core set of features that we think are important to the phenomena of interest. This reduced, simpler set provides a more tractable basis for us to see how the pieces fit together and to understand better the causal relations.

This justification raises the question of how simple is too simple. How do we really know which features are unnecessary complications and which are core features? What are the criteria for making such a judgment? And doesn't this put us on the road to reductionism, where we reduce, ultimately, all the laws of thought to the models of particle physics? Would an explanation at that level, even if accurate, gain us a deeper understanding of human psychology?

1.3   Can We Make a Brain?

The trivial answer is that yes, we can make brains; and every parent has done so. A parent's actions lead to a new brain with all the attendant complexities and capacities. It is done with no insight into the process. We achieve no greater understanding. Therefore, we can argue that building a brain per se is not guaranteed to improve our understanding of the rules and procedures regulating human thought.

This example is not trivial. The tools of neuroscience are giving us an increasing understanding of neurons and their constituents. We know the make-up of many ion channels down to the level of genes and post-translational modifications. If we knew the position of every molecule in the brain, would we learn anything about how the brain as a whole functions? This can be restated as a question about whether we believe the brain and the mind to be merely the sum of their parts.

There are scientists pursuing this route to modelling the brain. The Blue Brain Project at the Ecole Polytechnique Federale Lausanne announces exactly these intentions on its website*:[1]

---

*Since website addresses change frequently, I use numbered page notes to refer to a URL, which is then listed in the back matter of the book. This will allow me to more easily update the links.

> Reconstructing the brain piece by piece and building a virtual brain in a supercomputer – these are some of the goals of the Blue Brain Project. The virtual brain will be an exceptional tool giving neuroscientists a new understanding of the brain and a better understanding of neurological diseases.

Do you share this conclusion?

A challenge to this approach claims that an understanding of the brain requires a consideration of scale. A sand dune is made up of individual grains of sand just as the brain is made up of individual neurons, but no amount of study of individual sand grains can explain the behavior of sand dunes. The behavior of a dune requires a large number of sand grains to interact. Is the same true of the brain?

Discussion: Are Psychological Concepts Experimentally Accessible?

We often use computational methods because something is experimentally inaccessible. This can be due to size or complexity or because, by its very nature, it is inaccessible to direct experimental manipulation. Do you agree that cognitive processes are inaccessible to direct experimentation? For example, can one *directly* manipulate working memory? And how does your answer to that question effect your position on the value of computational modeling?

1.4 Computational Models as Experiments

Another reason commonly given for using computational approaches in brain research is that they offer practical efficiencies. Generally, it is easier to run a computer program over and over again with minor variations than it is to repeat a behavioral task on numerous pools of subjects. In some cases it may not be possible to repeat behavioral investigations. Patient HM,[2] perhaps the most psychologically studied person of all time, had his problems as the result of surgery that will never be done again. The only way to repeat HM's lesion is by modelling.

Under what circumstances is the quest for experimental efficiency justifiable as the basis for computational modelling? Some authors suggest that it is sufficient that computational models enable exploration. We have an idea on some topic, and before doing more focused, expensive, or time-consuming research we can "play" with our computer model to decide if further experiments are warranted, and which ones we should do first. But doesn't this presume we have more confidence in the model than we should? Isn't there a danger that a poorly chosen model could direct us in the wrong direction or lead us not to explore lines of research that we should? How do we monitor the use of exploratory modelling to make sure these outcomes do not occur?

Since computational models do not sacrifice animal participants or take the time of humans, they are touted as more ethical. Some studies involving conflict are not ethical in human research, but we can create a computer model of hundreds or thousands of little warriors and let them battle for territory as a way of exploring ideas about social conflict (see Chapter 22 for one modelling platform that can be used for this type of research).

Can we generalize from such data though? How do we validate hypotheses gained in this way?

Coherence and Concreteness

Words are subtle, and may mean different things to different people at different times. They may even mean something different to the same person at different times. Have you ever read something you wrote and wondered, "What was I thinking?" Models typically involve translating our ideas from words into formulas or computer programs. A by-product of this reformulation is a concreteness and clarity that may be lacking from our most careful phrasings. Even if a model does not say anything "new" or make novel predictions, this clarity can aid communication and improve reproducibility.

Modularity and Simplification

One attraction to modelling cognitive phenomena is that one can pull out a piece of a larger process and focus on it alone. This is justified, in part, by asserting that cognition is modular. The same rationale can be applied to modelling the "basal ganglia" as an isolated, functionally defined construct. Is this justification persuasive? Is cognition simply the result of isolated processes summed up? If we defined each of the important cognitive modules could we study them in isolation and by "gluing" them together understand the brain?

Can you think of a school of psychology that concerned itself with emergent properties, a psychological school that emphasized that wholes were more than the sum of their parts? What do you think this school would have felt about computational modelling in psychology?

In complex environments it is often the embedding of elements in an environment that is necessary for observing a desired effect. A common example is the role of raindrops and rainbows. Water droplets are essential for the production of rainbows, but the study of rainbows cannot be reduced to the study of water droplets. It cannot even be reduced to collections of raindrops. One could have a complex modular model of water and its coalescence into drops, and still not have rainbows. If one wired a water droplet model to a sunlight model, would the models then have rainbows? Or would there need to be an observing visual apparatus (i.e., a person)? A name for phenomena that only appear in the large or from interactions is emergent; these are phenomena, like the sand dune, that cannot be understood from their individual pieces alone.

Models for Exploring the Implications of Ideas

One of the fathers of connectionism as an approach to modelling in psychology (Chapters 11 and 13 introduce two types of simple neural networks), James McClelland (2009), has emphasized two main purposes behind his own work. He states that he seeks to simplify complex phenomena, and that he wants to investigate the implications of ideas.

Implications

A justification for models as a route to implications rests on the assertion that models are more transparent than behavioral experiments. Computational models are suggested to be more transparent because they require greater specificity, and because they do exactly what you tell them to do (even if you did not realize what you were telling them at the time, a "logic bug").

As modellers, we specify the rules and the players. There is no ambiguity. This gives us an opportunity to demonstrate the sufficiency of our ideas. Models do not have to be biologically realistic to provide sufficiency proofs. If I assert that variation in light intensity across facial photographs contains information sufficient for identification, it is enough for me to build a program that can do it, even if I use methods that are inherently biologically implausible. My model represents an existence proof. While it does not show that people actually recognize faces from light intensity, it proves that they could. Note that this argument is one way. While a successful program shows that luminance information is sufficient for identification, we cannot draw a similarly strong conclusion from a failed program. We can only conclude that that program was inadequate, not that no program could ever be designed to do the same.

Typically, though, we have higher aspirations than simply stating our ideas clearly or providing existence proofs. We want to advance our understanding of the phenomena in question; we want to travel beyond where our ability to forecast can take us. When we specify a computational model we want to be able to ask, "What if?" In order for our models to be computationally tractable, and to permit us to still be able to follow what is going on, we can usually only implement simplified models. This brings us back to the questions considered above. Is our simplified model too simple? Can we make inferences about more complex systems from simpler ones? If the only circumstances in which we can take advantage of model concreteness for investigating model implications are those situations where we have had to simplify, reduce, or modularize the situation, do we ever really achieve this advantage? One criticism of studying cognition by computational simulation is that our simplifications are arbitrary. In the process of simplifying, paradoxically, we lose our transparency.

1.5 Do Models Need to Be Biologically Plausible?

When we review neural networks (Chapters 11 and 13), we will see that modellers often draw inspiration from biology, but how close do models need to be to biology in order to be useful? Back-propagation is a tool used in neural networks. This error correction method relies on propagating the error signal from the end of a computation

> "There are more things in heaven and earth, Horatio, than are dreamt of in your philosophy."

back to earlier nodes in the chain. It is not obvious that neurons in our brains have the requisite wiring or methods necessary to propagate errors backwards. Therefore, what can we conclude from a computational model that uses the backpropagation error correction algorithm?

One response is philosophical. This response claims that it is just too early in our research program to presume that our knowledge of biological mechanisms is sufficient to reject *any* possible account. Just because we do not know *now* of any way for real neurons to backpropagate an error signal does not mean that we will not know it next week, or the week after. This justification gives renewed vigor to the use of models as exploration and for examining the implications of ideas. If something turns out to be very useful in a computational model for solving a particular problem then maybe we should look harder for that mechanism in biology?

Another response is to simply answer no: models do not need to be biologically plausible. Models are abstractions. The scope of a model does not have to feature *neural* mechanisms to inform ideas about cognition. Further, goals from modelling can include coherence, concreteness, or sufficiency. None of those objectives require biological plausibility. Which answer prevails in a particular circumstance will depend on the questions being addressed with the model and the purposes behind the model's construction. Biological plausibility should not be used to abjure modelling, nor should it be required of all psychological and neuroscientific models.

1.6   Do Computational Models Require Computers?

Computation does not require a computer. It is true that presently we tend to associate computational models with computer programs, but this not a prescriptive relation, it is a descriptive one. Perhaps the best demonstration of this idea is that Alan Turing's ideas about computation came not from digital computers, but from human computers.

Before the word meant a machine, the term "computer" was used to describe a person. Turing thought about the stages in the process of doing a mathematical computation, the need for a temporary scratch pad to record interim results; it was from these ideas that he developed his thoughts on the limits of computation and ultimately the description of the Turing machine. One can assert a formal equivalence between people and machines, and Turing developed the idea of equivalence into a test to assess when machine intelligence rivaled a human's.

If human and machine computations are equivalent, then it is not *necessary* that computational models be implemented by machines. It may, however, be more convenient or efficient.

Many models that can be stated in simple formulas yield more insight when they are *not* converted to programs, because that makes it easier for humans to follow the cause and effect relationships. Simple probabilistic models (some of which appear in Chapter 15) often give a better glimpse into their overall behavior when they are stated as formulas instead of as computer programs. Models can be viewed as abstractions that emphasize some features and ignore others. The utility of a particular method of presentation depends on a model's purpose. Road maps and topological maps emphasize different features of a landscape and ignore others. Both are useful, but in different settings, and both are more helpful printed out than described as a computer program.

As further evidence that computational models do not have to be written as computer programs, there are the results of early computational investigations that preceded the invention of digital computers. For example, signal detection theory is a computational model commonly used in psychological experiments that was developed during World War II to characterize the challenges for radar operators in attempting to distinguish the blips that were planes from the blips that were not. In the early 1900s Lapicque came up with a model of neural activity that was a mathematical model in the pre-computer age. Psychophysics was elaborated by Fechner drawing on the data of Weber. It was developed from first principles. Fechner conceived of how to make physical and psychological measurement scales commensurate and his justification was logic and calculus. While rather exceptional, these examples demonstrate that computational models do not have to be computer programs. The modern digital computer is a technical convenience. For some types of models, the implications are clearer when they are stated as formulas rather than computer programs.

However, for other types of models, the term "convenience" may not go far enough. It is true that all the calculations specified in a digital computer program might, in principle, be equivalent to those carried out by hand, but it is also often the case that the labor and time to do so would be prohibitive. This fact is the major reason that the growth of computational approaches in psychology and neuroscience has so closely paralleled the growth of desktop computing power.

Discussion: Can a Model be Too Simple?

Watch and read the following items and then discuss the following questions.

- Blue Brain TED talk by Henry Markham[3]
- Cat Fight Over Simulations[4]

What do we learn by simulating the brain as a large collection of single elements? How simple can those elements be?

1.7   How Do You Evaluate a Model?

The prior sections highlighted issues about whether modelling can be justified, and for what purposes it can be used, but once you have decided to use a computational model how do you examine its quality? Specifically, are any of these the right way to evaluate a model:

- Goodness-of-fit
- Sufficiency
- Optimality
- Consistency with human performance?

It is probably fair to say that at this point in time it is premature to be prescriptive. Just as it may be premature for us to say that computational methods must comply with current biological knowledge, it may also be too early to require that our models fit data well. With our current knowledge limited, and with our current machines still not sufficiently powerful, requiring our model implementations to closely fit actual data might be a bar too high. Failure would lead us to throw away good ideas simply because we did not have the means to properly test them. Still, we cannot be too forgiving of ourselves or we would never discard one model in favor of another, and all models are always above average. In line with these ideas it seems we ought to expect that a model does what it claims to do. We cannot have a model of memory that never stores or recalls anything. If we are to be cautious in using models, we ought to expect new models to be in some way better than the models they seek to replace. Of course, better is a hard word to define in practice, and leaves us with the same sorts of options outlined above. One notion not included in the above list is the idea of simplicity or elegance. Are those adequate criteria for comparing models? Is it reasonable to think that a cognitive apparatus cobbled together over some tens of thousands of years, mostly in an effort to meet immediate environmental challenges, would be simple or elegant?

1.8 Do Models Need Assumptions?

Like almost any question of this type, the answer is, "It depends." Model assumptions can be conflated with model capabilities and model properties can be confused with claims about the process being modelled. Given that most current models will be much simpler than human cognition, it would be a mistake to look at what a model cannot do, and to infer that the model builders were making broad claims about underlying human cognition. Rather, models are built from certain points of view and with certain base claims. These claims provide properties for model operations and from these claims there emerge models that can do certain things. Such models can be used to argue whether certain properties are necessary for certain functions, but they cannot be used to claim that such demonstrations provide evidence for the mechanics of human cognition. Certain properties entail certain effects. It is the role of models, at this time, to point the way to properties that can be examined as possible assumptions about human cognitive processes.

1.9 Additional Questions

The preceding is meant to introduce some of the controversial and unresolved issues about the purpose and nature of computational modeling in psychology and neuroscience and to point out some of the remaining hard questions about what a model tells us and how we evaluate model success. Before rushing out to use a model, it is good to decide for yourself where you stand on these issues, and especially on how to evaluate model success. You might develop your own ideas by considering a few final questions:

1. Are neural network models better than other types of psychological models because they are built from biologically inspired elements?
2. What are the advantages and disadvantages of neural network models when compared to systems of if–then production rules?
3. What ultimately do you think it is reasonable to learn about human psychology from the use of computational models?
4. Is the current popularity of computational modelling deserved by new knowledge, or is it a fad for computers or taking the easy way out?
5. If behavior is a product of brain events, and our knowledge of the brain is very incomplete, is there any purpose at the present time to making computational models of neural or psychological phenomena?

1.10   Road Map

This chapter sets the broad agenda by asking each of us to examine what we think are the strengths and weaknesses of computational modelling and to decide what role we think it should have in psychology and neuroscience. The rest of the book is devoted to considering, in turn, a selection of mathematical topics and examples of how models are used. The organization for each section is similar. First, we consider a mathematical topic. To start simply, the mathematics is presented in isolation from much that has to do with psychology or neuroscience, although I do try to offer some motivation by giving glimpses of where we are heading. This may make things a bit dry, but it helps us to avoid distractions and it allows us to concentrate on terminology and notation. The early chapters of a section serve to highlight how a basic familiarity with mathematical topics, and a willingness to implement routines on a computer, can serve as the basis for some impressive simulations. The subsequent chapters develop the use of the mathematical ideas for a neuroscience or psychological model.

Part I

Modelling Neurons

Chapter 2

What Is a Differential Equation?

Objectives

After reading this chapter you should be able to:

- describe an area of computational neuroscience where differential equations are used;
- define what a differential equation is, in words;
- describe how a slope and a derivative are related; and
- use a differential equation and numerical integration to simulate a simple physical process in a spreadsheet.

2.1 Overview

We begin by looking at differential equations (also called DEs). DEs are used in many neural and psychological models. DEs are also one of the oldest approaches to neural modelling, and are one of the most current as well; they are used in the dynamical systems approach to cognition.

We also begin with DEs because they carry the stigma of being hard and abstruse. I want to eliminate at the outset any concern that mathematics is "too hard." By beginning with DEs we can see that their confusing qualities have been overrated and that for practical use we can ignore much of what makes them challenging for mathematics majors. They have to solve DEs analytically, but we can get away with simulations.

Our goal for this chapter is to motivate this focus on DEs by reviewing some of their uses in computational neuroscience. The goal for this section of the book is to introduce the terminology of DEs and some of the ideas behind them, work through some simple DEs, and then undertake to employ DEs in modelling single neurons as both integrate and fire elements and as Hodgkin–Huxley neurons. Along the way we introduce the idea of a programming loop and implement it in a spreadsheet program. Lastly, we will discover how to treat neurons as simple circuits.

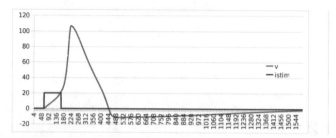

Figure 2.1 A graph of a simulated neuronal action potential produced with a spreadsheet program. In the 1950s generating the data for an image like this might have required a few weeks operating a hand-cranked calculator. The model behind it warranted the 1963 Nobel Prize. You will be able to do Nobel-level work by the end of Chapter 7.

2.2   Modelling Individual Neurons

One of the greatest successes of computational modelling is the Hodgkin and Huxley model of the action potential. From carefully collected experimental data Hodgkin and Huxley built a computational model that anticipated discoveries at the level of proteins and ion channels. The Hodgkin and Huxley model can be seen as a progenitor for the field of computational neuroscience. By the end of Chapter 7 you will be able to generate a figure similar to Figure 2.1.

2.3   Differential Equations: The Mathematical Method of the Hodgkin and Huxley Model

DEs are a core mathematical tool of computational neuroscience. Prior to the computer era, developing an analytically tractable solution was obligatory. However, for most practical purposes we no longer need to limit ourselves to DEs that have analytic solutions because we can approximate the answers we need numerically.

What is the difference between analytic and numerical solutions? Analytic solutions are ones that you get by manipulating symbols. Numerical solutions are ones you get by plugging in numbers.

If I asked you to solve $x^2 = 4$ you could take the square root of both sides and learn that $x = \pm\sqrt{4}$. That is an analytic solution, but not a particularly useful one. It is a solution discovered by the manipulation of symbols to isolate the variable of interest, x. But we might actually want a number, even if only approximate.

You could also solve this problem, numerically, using Newton's method and your computer. For Newton's method you start with a guess, say $x = 3$, and you revise your guess depending on the results.

Newton's Method

Newton's method uses the derivative to refine our guess. For the equation $x^2 = 4$ we want to find the value of x that makes $f(x) = x^2 - 4 = 0$. This is called finding the

	A	B	C	D	E
1	x	y	f(x)	f'(x)	
2	3	4	5	6	
3	2.16666667		0.69444444	4.33333333	
4	2.00641026		0.02568212	4.01282051	
5	2.00001024		4.096E-005	4.00002048	
6		2	1.049E-010	4	
7		2	0	4	
8					

Formula bar: A3   =A2 - C2/D2

Figure 2.2 The spreadsheet program for the numerical (as opposed to analytic) calculation of square roots.

roots or zeros. For this equation, the derivative is $f'(x) = 2x$. The derivative describes the line that just touches a curve at one point. We know that the slope of a line is rise over run. Using this relation we say that $f'(x) =$ change in y over change in x or $f'(x) = f(x_0) - 0/x_0 - x_1$ where x_1 is our new, revised, guess. This equation can be arranged, using the rules of algebra, to get x_1 on one side by itself: $x_1 = x_0 - f(x_0)/f'(x_0)$.

Exercise: Programming Newton's Method to Find Square Roots in a Spreadsheet

Open up a spreadsheet and create columns for x, y, $f(x)$, and $f'(x)$. We will use x to record our first guess, y to be the number we want to find the square root of, $f(x)$ our equation, and $f'(x)$ our derivative.

Enter your first guess, say 3, in cell A2, 4 in B2, and the equations for $f(x)$ and $f'(x)$ in C2 and D2. Then enter the formula to find the new guess in A3. Now you can copy the remaining columns down and you should see numbers like those in Figure 2.2. Note that the equation for cell A3 is displayed. You should be able to use this spreadsheet to calculate by *numerical* methods the square root for any number by changing the value of y in cell B2.

To approach this another way, imagine that I ask you to draw a graph of $x^2 + y^2 = 1$. This is the equation for a circle, but if you try to draw it, you might generate a series of points; select some of the xs and compute the ys. This is the spirit behind a numerical approximation. Numerical answers do not have the absolute certainty that you get with analytic solutions, but they are good enough for current computational methods in psychology and neuroscience.

One of the benefits in the advance of computing power is that in our laptops or on our desktops we have sufficient computational power to simulate DEs. We no longer have to be as mathematically knowledgeable about the analytic methods of solving DEs.

We only need to have a general understanding of the basics. Since we can now use brute force, we have a great deal more flexibility in the variety of problems we can pursue.

Since Newton's method (above) had a derivative in the equation, it is a sort of DE. Another example of using a derivative to help solve a problem numerically is numerical integration. This, too, is something we can do easily in a spreadsheet program. At this point, it may not be clear what it means to "solve" a differential equation. Do not fret. Have some patience. It is not possible to learn everything at once. It also is not possible to learn most mathematical ideas on a single pass. Concepts become clearer with examples. Most mathematicians will tell you that when learning about a new area or new approach

> Newton's method(s). Newton's name is used for more than one method. The above describes Newton's method for finding the roots of an equation. Newton's method for optimization is similar (it is also called Newton–Raphson). Instead of finding the point where an equation equals zero, it looks for the point where a derivatives is zero. If derivatives are rates of change, then finding the point where a derivative is zero means there is no change and this is a *stationary* point.

they work through problems and frequently re-read and re-study what it is they are trying to learn. We will often need to do the same.

To continue our development of DEs we will review some terminology and a little bit of mathematical subterfuge.

2.4   The D in DE

What Is a *Differential* Equation?

> What does "C" mean? "C" is the common symbol used by mathematicians to represent a constant value as opposed to a variable. You might think that constant means unchanging, but to a mathematician it just means uninteresting. You may see equations where the symbol "C" is used for several different numerical values. The variation is just ignored because it is "just a constant." Do not be put off by this, you may be doing it soon yourself.

$$\frac{dy}{dx} = C \qquad (2.1)$$

A DE is simply any equation that contains a derivative in its expression. Derivatives, you may recall, have dx or dy terms. These terms are meant to represent very small, essentially infinitesimal, differences in x and y. That is how the terms derivative and differential have come to be associated. Our Equation 2.1 is in fact a differential equation. To "solve" a differential equation requires us to find another equation that will make our DE true. Restated, if our DE involves dy/dx we have to find some function $y = \ldots$ that when we take its derivative will give us the right-hand side of the $dy/dx = \ldots$ equation we started with.

> ### Exercise: Are Solutions to DEs Unique?
>
> Can you find a solution for Equation 2.1 above?
>   Is there only one unique solution?[1]

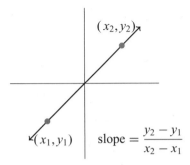

(x_2, y_2)

(x_1, y_1) slope $= \dfrac{y_2 - y_1}{x_2 - x_1}$

Figure 2.3   Derivatives are instantaneous slopes. For lines this is the familiar formula of "rise over run." For curves we have to be more careful.

Derivatives

DEs contain derivatives, but what more precisely is a derivative? A good rule of thumb when dealing with any mathematical concept you don't understand is to go back to the definitions. These are usually simpler and clearer than most applications since a lot of the non-essential details are eliminated. Further, the more complicated expressions we often see were often built from much simpler and more accessible beginnings. The definition of a derivative is

$$\frac{df(x)}{dx} = \lim_{\Delta x \to 0} \frac{f(x + \Delta x) - f(x)}{\Delta x} \tag{2.2}$$

Understanding what this definition is saying may take a bit of decoding. Remember the d in expressions like dx means a little difference, and that you can set $y = f(x)$. Now the difference between two values of y could be $y_2 - y_1$ and the $dx \approx x_2 - x_1$. Now make a fraction of those two and you have the "rise over run" slogan for the slope that was taught in high school. A derivative is a fancy slope. It is the extension of the idea of a slope from a line, which has the same slope everywhere, to a curve, where the slope may differ from place to place along the curve. If you know what a slope is, you know what a derivative is. To be more concrete, pick any two points on a line, call them $p1$ and $p2$, each having an x and y coordinate. Then the slope of the line is as shown in Figure 2.3.

Applying our intuition about lines to curves means that we can imagine gradually moving $p1$ and $p2$ closer together. At some point they are "close enough." The difference separating them is infinitesimal[2] and the slope does not change enough from one point to another for us to worry about and we can assert that we have the instantaneous slope, the slope at a particular point along a curve. See Figure 2.4 for some graphical intuition.

Differential Equation Jargon

What is a linear differential equation? The dependent variable, and all its derivatives, are never multiplied together nor are of a power greater than one.

What is an ordinary differential equation? The solution is a function of only a single *independent* variable.

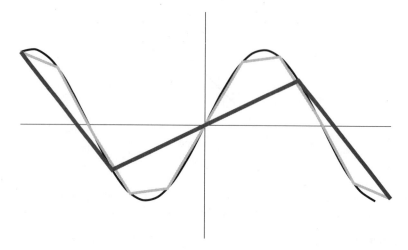

Figure 2.4   Derivatives are instantaneous slopes. We wish to be able to calculate the slope of the black curve at any point, but the curve's slopes change as we move along it. The intuition for how we calculate derivatives is to imagine that we approximate our curve with a sequence of straight lines. Each straight line has a slope that we know how to calculate. As we move our points closer together, the difference between our line segments and the curve decreases. Our line segments begin to more closely approximate the slope of the curve. When our line segments become infinitesimally small, we have approximated the slope of the curve at every point with teeny tiny lines, each of which gives us the slope at a point, the derivative.

What is a partial differential equation? Not ordinary; multiple independent variables.

What is a homogeneous differential equation? This is a bit trickier, because there is more than one definition, but it may mean that the solution is a function of both the dependent and independent variables.

Note: Many mathematical terms are used with slightly different meanings in different domains of mathematics, so generalize with caution. For example, "homogeneous" is used frequently and its meaning varies with the context.

More on Solving Differential Equations

A solution for a DE is any function that makes it true. Recall that a DE means that we have a derivative equal something: $dy/dx = f(x)$.[3] This equation has the derivative on the left-hand side, and tells us what it is equal to on the right-hand side, but we don't want to know what the derivative equals. We want to learn a formula, without a derivative, that if we took its derivative would give us the DE we are looking at. It's like a murder mystery. There is a body in the parlor, we are trying to find a solution that begins with no body in the parlor, but from which we can derive a body in the parlor.

As an aside, note that this equation could have also been written $dy(x)/dx = f(x)$. Since the value of y changes when we change x, y is a function of x. But often when you read mathematics, the writer will try to highlight the essential elements by leaving out things that the writer thinks the reader will understand. In this case, it is understood that y is a function of x, and so we simplify the notation. The problem with this approach is that one has to assume what is "understood" and this can vary a lot between the writer and the reader. If I have assumed too much regarding your knowledge of functions, you can look ahead to page 27 for another, informal, description.

When reading equations, it is useful to realize that a lot of what is abbreviated is not special, but habit. Functions do not have to be abbreviated with the letter f. They could be g or h and often are. The use of f, g, and h for functions is just a common convention, but those letters are not special.

> This is probably the most difficult part of this chapter. You should not be surprised if you have trouble grasping this right away. Understanding in mathematics often only follows repetition, practice, and time. This is as true of the experts as it is of amateurs. Do not quit if you do not understand something right away. Just push on and have some trust that it will all work out, and come back to re-read puzzling sections when you see how they are to be used. One of the pertinent differences between mathematicians and we lay people is that mathematicians expect to be confused. They ignore it and just push on.

The simplest way to solve a DE is to integrate. It is so simple that most mathematics books do not include this in their discussions of DEs, but it is still true. Usually, the discussion of how to solve DEs is limited to problems that cannot be solved by direct integration. How do we solve these? It may surprise you to learn that mathematicians often guess. There is no single method for solving differential equations. Which method is tried depends on the experience, expertise, and intuition of the solver. With practice, mathematicians come to recognize particular types of equations, and they can often guess the solution, and then they prove it is correct by differentiating their solution and showing they end up with the expression they set out to solve.

We too will usually be able to guess the general form of the solutions to the DEs we need to solve. In biology, neuroscience, and psychology, we deal almost entirely with a certain form of DE that has a particular form of solution. With practice you will be able to recognize it too.

Another Differential Equation

$$\frac{dy(x)}{dx} = x$$

This DE looks similar to Equation 2.1, but instead of the C term on the right we have the variable x. This type of DE is one that can be solved by direct integration. When all the *independent* variables are on the right, and only the differential is on the left, then you can usually solve the DE, if it can be solved, by integration. But saying that a solution can be achieved through integration, does not mean it will be easy. The integration can be very tricky. Generally, solutions requiring integration are *not* the type we will typically see.

A solution is

$$y(x) = 1/2 \; x^2 + C$$

Radioactive Decay

If you have a bar of uranium sitting around, you will observe that it slowly dissipates (and that you have cancer and there are a lot of governmental authorities interested in you). We know that how much uranium disappears is related to how much uranium you started with. That is an experimental observation. Many of the DEs we are interested in will come to us not from mathematical circumstances, but from empirical observations.

For radioactive materials, the equation for the rate of decay is: $\Delta N = -kN\,\Delta t$.* Look for words like "rate" and "change." These often indicate a DE lurking in plain English. Here we are talking about the difference in the number of particles per some small difference in time. Δs are often used to represent the idea of change, and are similar to the d we used before. This equation says in words that the *change* in our number of particles N is equal to the number of particles we have, multiplied by how long we are waiting, and some other numbers, which we lump together under the symbol k. These other numbers are constants, do not change, and are therefore uninteresting.

In psychological and neuroscience applications we do not usually need to solve the DE. We often just use the DE "as is" to approximate the behavior of something we are interested in, such as neuronal voltage or the rate of change of evidence before making a decision or the changing strength of a memory trace with time. But while we may never need to solve DEs analytically, it is useful to understand what this means and to see how it can be done. Knowing this will make our later use of DEs easier to follow.

Here are some steps to a solution to the DE for radioactive decay:

$$\Delta N = -kN\,\Delta t$$

$$\frac{\Delta N}{N} = -k\,\Delta t$$

$$\int \frac{\Delta N}{N} = \int -k\,\Delta t \quad \text{equality does not alter if we do the}$$
$$\text{same thing to both sides of the equation}$$

$$\ln N + C_1 = -kt + C_2$$

$$N = e^{-kt+C_3} \quad \text{where } C_3 = C_2 - C_1$$

$$= e^{-kt}e^{C_3}$$

$$= e^{-kt}e^{\log C_4} = C_4 e^{-kt} \quad \text{where } C_4 = e^{C_3}$$

> Describe what is happening to the constant. Note that it would be common to see a mathematician simply use the letter C in all the places where I have shown C with a numeral subscript. Does this matter?

Solutions relying on exponentials (represented usually by e, but sometimes by exp()) are almost all you will ever see in biological and psychological applications. Whether you are talking about predators and prey, birth rates, or chemical reactions, you will find that often an exponential equation gives you the solution you need. Further, there is a huge hint as to when a DE can be solved by some sort of exponential expression. If you observe that the *dependent* variable (left side) is also on the right side, that is, the rate of change of something is proportional to itself, then the answer will

---

*Note that I have used a different notation here for symbolizing the differential. Though it is confusing, there are several, often with different forms used by different specialists. I will try to show you several of these so you will not be confused later.

involve an exponential. For example, if we have a lot of people, the growth of our population will be greater; populations grow exponentially.

To give you some experience with exponential functions and their behavior, this chapter concludes with an exercise involving a practical example. It is often easier to develop our intuition of how equations behave if we work through examples that deal with concrete entities we are familiar with. Before worrying about neurons we can worry about coins.

Classroom Exercise – Principal and Interest

1. Open up your spreadsheet program and generate the numbers for an exponential function and plot this.

   - Generate a column of numbers from 0 to 3 in steps of 0.1 in column A.
   - In cell B1, enter the formula to compute the exponential value of the number in cell A1.
   - Copy that formula down column B.
   - Plot columns A and B.

2. Repeat for an interest-earning bank account where the amount of money you have at the next point in time is equal to how much you have now, plus the interest rate per unit time multiplied by time multiplied by the amount of money you have.

3. What do you observe about the shape of your plots for the exponential and the interest-earning account?

4. Write out an equation for the rate of change of your principal (amount of money in the bank) and see if you can find a reason for the resemblance you might see in the curves.

2.5   Summary

The goal of this chapter has been to introduce you to the ideas and terminology of DEs and their solutions. For psychological and neural applications our DEs will usually deal with the rate at which something is changing in time. For example, how the voltage of a neuron changes when you inject some current. To increase our experience and comfort with working with DEs the next chapter introduces us to the techniques of computer simulations using some simple numerical examples with the real-world objects of springs. In subsequent chapters we will apply our practical skills to simulating models of spiking neurons.

Chapter 3

Numerical Application of a Differential Equation

Objectives

After reading this chapter you should be able to:

- implement a spreadsheet model of the frictionless oscillator;
- use Euler's method of numerical integration for simulation; and
- understand what a *function* is informally.

3.1   Overview

In the previous chapter I talked about what a DE was and what it meant to solve one. To exploit DEs in our models of neurons or memory, we have to understand how to use them in simulations. For us, DEs will be principally used to express relationships between variables that allow us to use computers to simulate the evolution of a system over time. Neurons and cognitive models bring with them their own complications. Rather than trying to tackle those as well as computer simulation, I have decided to focus this chapter on a more concrete example: springs. Once we have learned the basics about how to use a DE for simulating a simple system, we can apply that knowledge to implementing the integrate and fire model of neurons in Chapter 5 and the Hodgkin–Huxley model in Chapter 7. Since the idea of computer programming can be just as daunting as mathematics, we will do everything in an environment we feel more comfortable with: computer spreadsheets.

3.2   First, We Assume a Spherical Chicken

Models in general tend to be greatly simplified versions of the target phenomenon. How much simplification is too much is one of the thorny problems introduced in Chapter 1. For our concrete introduction to numerical simulation we will use the example of a spring sliding back and forth. Real springs are messy: there will be surface friction and air resistance. Treating those variables would make things needlessly complicated, so we instead treat an abstract version of a spring where we model it as an idealized and simplified harmonic system.

> While it is common to begin modelling with simple abstract systems we must always remember that everything should be made as simple as possible, *but no simpler.*

To be in harmony means to be in sync. Harmonic motion is motion that is "in sync": it oscillates back and forth, like a pendulum, perhaps forever. An idealized spring attached to a weight also shows harmonic motion. It slides back and forth on a frictionless plane compressing and expanding.

> Try to choose variable names that are simple, but meaningful.

Is our model too simple? We can only determine that after implementing it. If we fail to get behavior that matches empirical observations we will have to increase the model's complexity, but until then we will simplify without mercy. This eases our work, and it makes our model understandable. This penchant for the wholesale adoption of simplifying assumptions is the basis for many jokes at the expense of the stereotypical theoretical physicist. A poultry farmer approaches his neighbor, the vacationing physicist, to help the farmer figure out the most efficient way to house his hens: "That's trivial," replies the physicist. "First, we assume a spherical chicken..."

Modelling—First Steps

Before writing any equations or any computer code, we should begin all modelling with a simple characterization of the problem. Often, simple line drawings can help to clarify the core features that the model needs to include. For our model of a weighted spring, we have the spring and the weight, and we can see how we will need variables to represent the distance the spring has moved (Figure 3.1).

Very few models are the result of theoretical considerations alone. When it comes to springs we are given an important empirical fact: the acceleration of our weight is equal to a constant (P) and our current location. Why should it be this way? That is an important question, but it is a different question from the question we are trying to answer. We want to find a formula that will tell us where the spring is at a given time, given that we know how long ago movement began, and its starting, or initial, position.

Again, the fact we are given from experimenting is: $a(t) = -Ps(t)$. How do we get from this to something that we can write a program for and that isolates the quantity we are interested in, namely, $s(t)$? Often some judicious guessing and a little practical knowledge will go a long way. Our given equation already has the term we want: $s(t)$. We just need to do away with the pesky $a(t)$ that represents acceleration.

Exercise: Describing What We Model

- Present in words a definition for velocity in terms of space (or distance) and time.
- Present in words a definition for acceleration in terms of velocity and time.
- Present in words a definition for acceleration that uses your prior two answers and gives a relation between acceleration and space and time.

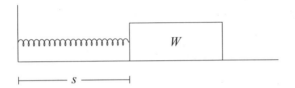

Figure 3.1   This is a depiction of our first model. We have a weight attached to a spring. I have labeled the weight W even though it is not clear if we need to take the weight's weight into account. On a truly frictionless surface the weight is not relevant, and maybe we can treat the property of the spring and the weight together? This is an effort to make things as simple as possible, and to only add in details when they are found to be necessary for accurately capturing the phenomena of interest. After we stretch our spring, we will let it go. The location of the weight is denoted by a variable s that I chose because it reminds me of space. After we have let the spring go, it will move, and so the value of s will change. This makes s variable, and the value of s will depend (as in dependent variable) on how long ago we let it go. This means that the value of s will be a function of time (t) and we will write $s(t)$ to show this.

What you stated in words, we need to do in symbols. Sometimes it helps to be concrete. Since the terms "velocity" and "acceleration" come up when talking about cars, let us use a car example for intuition. When we say that a car is accelerating, we mean that it is going faster as time goes by, that is, its velocity changes as a function of time. In symbols this is

$$\text{Acceleration} \approx \frac{V(t1) - V(t0)}{t1 - t0} \approx \frac{dV}{dt}$$

We take two velocity measurements and compute the difference. We divide this difference by the difference in the two time points. From these we compute the ratio and see that it has the form of a slope, and if we imagine the two points in time getting closer, it begins to look like the derivative we saw before (Equation 2.2).

If we continue in this way and ask what velocity is, we answer that it is our change in location (or position) between two points in time:

$$\text{Velocity} \approx \frac{s(t1) - s(t0)}{t1 - t0} \approx \frac{ds}{dt}$$

This formula again looks like a derivative. If we chain them together, like we did in words above, we can see that

$$\text{Acceleration} = \frac{d^2 s}{dt^2}$$

The notation with the superscript 2 means that we took a derivative twice, as indeed we did. We took it once to get velocity, and then again to get acceleration. Now that we have gained some understanding of the terms of our problem, we can return to thinking what it would mean to solve this problem. The problems we confront will not be stated with textbook clarity. Often, answering the question is a lot easier than figuring out what the question should be.

Recall the physical situation we are modelling. We have pulled on a weight attached to a spring and stretched the spring. At some point we release the weight, and the spring slides back and forth. We would like to know where our weight will be (which is equivalent to knowing the length of our spring) at any point in time we should choose. We would like an equation for $s(t)$. Then, we can plug in any value for t that we choose, and we will get back a number for location. We begin with the known equation $a(t) = -Ps(t)$.

Without knowing exactly what good it will do us, let's substitute for acceleration our equation involving $s(t)$. Then we will only have the terms in our equation that we want. Even if you do not know how it will help, trying to simplify an equation until it contains only meaningful terms is often a valuable strategy. Thus,

$$\frac{d^2s}{dt^2} = -Ps(t)$$

To solve this equation means finding some other equation for $s(t)$ that when we take its derivative twice, we will get back exactly what we started with (multiplied by some constant, here denoted P; constants do not have to always be called C).

If you look closely at this equation and remember some of the lessons above, you should be able to guess the form of the answer. Remember DEs are often solved by an educated guess.

One reason for why I like this problem is that it is something real and physical that we can literally get our hands on. Also, we can solve this question *analytically*. That allows us to compare the accuracy of our simulation to ground truth. For our models of neurons, analytic solutions are not always possible.

3.3   Numerical Simulations

Whether we know how to "solve" this DE or not, we can still make use of it to simulate a solution for $s(t)$. In this section we will use a spreadsheet to program our solution. Our basic method is to bootstrap from what we know. Imagine that you are driving somewhere at 50 km/h. If I ask you where you will be in five minutes, you could figure this out by knowing your current location and your velocity, which tells you how your position changes in time. Because your car does not travel at a perfectly constant velocity, there would be some inaccuracy, but your estimate would be close. If I made the time step smaller, one minute say, you would be more accurate, because there would be less opportunity for errors to accumulate.

We can do the same with our spring since we have an equation that tells us how our position changes in time. In order to have an accurate simulation, we will take teeny tiny steps. At each step, we will update our representation of where we are using our equation for how our location changes with time. That will give us a new location, and then we will repeat the same sequence of actions at this new step, ad infinitum. To program repetitive actions over and over again on a computer we use a loop. Some forms of loops exist in all programming languages (see page 33 for more details). They are often called *for* loops because they are written with the keyword "for", instructing the computer *for* how long it is to do the repetitive action. The exact formatting of the command varies between languages and we will see examples later on. For our spreadsheet simulation we will use individual rows to capture our individual steps.

If we ignore the limit sign in Equation 2.2 and rearrange the terms with a little algebra it reads something like

$$f(x + \Delta x) = f(x) + \frac{df(x)}{dx} \Delta x \qquad (3.1)$$

In our spring problem, $s(t)$ takes the place of $f(x)$. Notice that the letters are different, but the form is the same with some letter preceding another letter in parentheses. This is a "function." It is the form that is important. A function is like a mathematical meat grinder. Put steak in the top, and out comes hamburger. It processes the input to get a new output. The parentheses symbolize

> If it isn't immediately obvious how to get this equation from our original form it is a good idea to pause and work through the steps.

the input chute of our processor (here we feed it xs) and the leading letter, for example, f, is the type of machine we have. We might chop meat f or we might grind meat s. In each case, we have an input, and the result is a processed output. That is how you can try to see that at a higher level, ignoring whether it is an x, s, t, or f, the form of the equation is similar.

In the following exercise you will use a spreadsheet to write a simple numerical simulation of the trajectory of our frictionless spring using the equation for how location changes with time to repetitively update your model. Take it one step at a time. Confer with a friend or an instructor if you get stuck, and have some patience and persistence.

Exercise: New Value = Old Value + Change in Value × Time

1. Create the following column headings in the spreadsheet program of your choice: P, t, delta_t, s, a, v, delta_v, delta_s

2. Pick some small positive number for P and enter it in the spreadsheet under the "P"; you might want to try 1. Remember: we want to start simple. Later we can explore how our model changes for different values of P.

3. Pick a small time step, such as 0.05, and put that under "delta_t". Now copy it so that the time column (t) grows bigger row by row (see Figure 3.2).

4. *Initial values:* Every journey starts somewhere. The same is true of numerical simulations. You need to enter a starting value for your first position (I picked 1), velocity (it should be zero–why is that?), and time.

5. *First challenges:* Enter formulas for acceleration, change in velocity, and change in space (or position/location) in the cells immediately under the titles (and only in this cell). You will have to use the language of your spreadsheet program for this. We want to have the acceleration row use what we know the relation to be between current position, our constant, and acceleration, therefore we might write: = -1 * A2 * D2 in cell E2. The "$" sign means that those row and column references will not change if we copy this formula. You need to enter the formulas for delta_v and delta_s. Remember

	P	t	deltat	s	a	v	deltav	deltas
1	P	t	deltat	s	a	v	deltav	deltas
2	20	0	0.05	1	-20	0	-1	0
3		0.05	0.05	0.95	-19	-1	-0.95	-0.05
4		0.1	0.05	0.8525	-17.05	-1.95	-0.8525	-0.0975
5		0.15	0.05	0.712375	-14.2475	-2.8025	-0.712375	-0.140125
6		0.2	0.05	0.53663125	-10.732625	-3.514875	-0.53663125	-0.17574375
7		0.25	0.05	0.33405594	-6.68111875	-4.05150625	-0.33405594	-0.20257531
8		0.3	0.05	0.11477783	-2.29555656	-4.38556219	-0.11477783	-0.21927811
9		0.35	0.05	-0.11023917	2.20478345	-4.50034002	0.11023917	-0.225017
10		0.4	0.05	-0.32974421	6.5948843	-4.39010084	0.32974421	-0.21950504
11		0.45	0.05	-0.53276205	10.6552409	-4.06035663	0.53276205	-0.20301783
12		0.5	0.05	-0.70914178	14.1828355	-3.52759458	0.70914178	-0.17637973

Figure 3.2   A segment of a spreadsheet set up for the spring and weight exercise.

that our change in velocity is a function of our acceleration and how much time has elapsed. The same is true of velocity and time for computing our position.

6. To observe our spring we need to *iterate* or loop our model simulation. That means we want new values to be a function of the old values stepped forward. For example, our new velocity in row 3 will be equal to our old velocity plus the change (see Equation 2.2 again).

7. After you have done that for a couple of hundred rows (once you have the spreadsheet set up you should be able to drag and copy entire rows of your spreadsheet) you can generate a plot of location versus time. What do you see?

Challenge Questions

- What happens when P is made negative? Why is that? What does P mean?
- What happens if you modify the size of your time step variable?
- Modify your model to consider the damped oscillator (details are given in the Notes).[1]

3.4   Numerical Integration and Differential Equations: Euler's Method

The numerical method we used to simulate our spring is one of the simplest and most straightforward. The basic logic is quite simple: we figure by how much the value we are interested in is changing and multiply that quantity by how much time has passed. We add this to our old value and get the new value. The new value then becomes the old value and we repeat. Where does this idea come from? From the definition of the derivative. That is,

$$\frac{df(x)}{dx} = \lim_{\Delta x \to 0} \frac{f(x + \Delta x) - f(x)}{(x + \Delta x) - x}$$

$$\frac{df(x)}{dx} \approx \frac{f(x + \Delta x) - f(x)}{\Delta x}$$

$$\dot{f}(x) \approx \frac{f(x + \Delta x) - f(x)}{\Delta x}$$

$$f'(x)\,\Delta x + f(x) \approx f(x + \Delta x)$$

The first equation is the definition of the derivative with the denominator rewritten to emphasize its "rise over run" character. The next line makes it clear that we are now *approximating* the derivative by using a small change in the value of x. In the third line, I use another of the many notations for a derivative, a dot over the letter representing the function. The "dot" notation is used a lot by physicists when the independent variable, the one on the bottom, is time. The last line repeats our use of algebra to rearrange things. This time the derivative is denoted with a "prime." The prime notation is convenient for multiple derivatives. Just keep on adding primes.

Most importantly, just know that these are all different ways of saying the same thing. Each different area in science that uses mathematics seems to develop its own jargon, just as we do in neuroscience and psychology. Part of our challenge is to learn to recognize these different, but equivalent, ways of writing. Yet another form of writing derivatives it to use Oliver Heaviside's* operator notation: $d^2s/dt^2 = \mathcal{DD}s = \mathcal{D}^2s$. The curly Ds are conceived as operators that operate (like a surgeon operates) on the functions that are presented to them. They are sort of like functions that take other functions as inputs. If you look clearly at this last equation, you will see that the t representing time vanished. It is still there, just not written. After having written $s(t)$ so many times, I decided it was "obvious" that s was a function of t and I dropped it from the equation. You will find these assumptions are often made in published articles using equational relations.

All these variations on writing the derivative are not meaningless to mathematicians, but for our purposes they are not essential. We can use whichever among them is most convenient and clear. We might prefer that everyone wrote a derivative the same way (world peace would be nice too), but they don't; we just have to learn to recognize them and live with the variety.

The last line of the derivation states the relationship we are using when updating our location. The old value of the function ($f(x)$) plus the rate of change of f for one unit of x (the derivative) times the amount that x has changed gives us the new value of f when x is now just a tiny bit bigger.

This method of estimating the new value from the old value is simple, but error prone. For the functions we will be using it is almost always good enough if a small step size is chosen. It is good enough for us because the functions we will be modelling are relatively gradual in their changes. In general, for more precise calculations or when applying this approach to complex and rapidly changing functions, we might want to use a more accurate updating method. We would still be using old values and derivatives to compute a new value and then "looping," but the formula for the loop would be more complex. A standard method is called the Runge–Kutta method. Most spreadsheet programs have this method built in, and you can try it to see how much of a difference it makes. Virtually all common programming languages will also have a built-in version of this function in their standard libraries.

---

*A brilliant and bizarre mathematical innovator who painted his fingernails pink and died a recluse in a house with granite furniture.

3.5   Solving the Spring Differential Equation

Although we will not be solving DEs analytically, we can get a better grasp of how accurate our simulation is by comparing it to the analytic solution since, in this case, we can get both. If you do not follow what is happening here, don't worry. It is not necessary, and you can always come back to it again later.[†]

In Chapter 2 we learned that when DEs have the dependent variable in the derivative and on the right-hand side, the answer usually involves an exponential. We also learned that DEs are often solved by guessing. Let's guess that we have an answer that involves an exponential. We will be vague to start with and fill in the details as we go.

First guess: $s = e^{rt}$ for some r. What I mean by "for some r" is that I will specify exactly what r is later. For now, I am just using it as a placeholder while I test out my idea (aka guess) that the answer is going to involve an exponential:

> If you do not know what the derivative of e^x is, now would be a good time to look it up.

$$\frac{ds}{dt} = re^{rt} \text{ follows from my guess}$$

$$\frac{d^2s}{dt} = r^2e^{rt} \quad \text{taking the derivative of both sides and substituting in our prior equation}$$

$r^2e^{rt} = -Pe^{rt}$ substituting my guess into what we know, this implies $\Rightarrow$

$r^2e^{rt} + Pe^{rt} = 0$

$e^{rt}(r^2 + P) = 0$ by factoring out the common term

> What value of r or t could make $e^{rt} = 0$?

I only need to worry about the $(r^2 + P)$ term (see marginal note). It should be easy to figure out what will make this zero. And since anything times zero is zero, it will make my equation true. We see that $r^2 = -P$. Unfortunately, we have to take the square root of a negative number, and that gives us imaginary solutions (truer words were never spoken some of you will be saying). Remember that P also has to be positive (we saw that when doing our simulation); that leaves us with $r = \pm i\sqrt{P}$.

Since the sum of any possible pair of solutions to a DE is itself a solution, this means that if our guess is correct then

$$e^{i\sqrt{P}t} + e^{-i\sqrt{P}t}$$

is a solution. You can verify how accurate our numerical simulation is by adding another column to your spreadsheet that computes these values using the same t column, and then plotting the analytic solution next to your numerical estimate for $s(t)$.

Now for a Visit to the Mathematical Zoo

Why does our answer oscillate when we saw earlier that exponential functions climb off the charts? To answer this we use a fact discovered by Euler, the same Euler our

---

[†]This section should be viewed as optional, especially on a first reading.

numerical integration method is named for. He proved that $e^{i\theta} = \cos\theta + i\sin\theta$. If we use this with our formula we get,

$$e^{it} + e^{-it} = \cos t + i\sin t + \cos t - i\sin t$$
$$= 2\cos t$$

And if you look at your graph again, you will see it looks an awful lot like a cosine and if you change the value of P you will see that it affects the frequency of the cosine wave and that is why changing P in your spreadsheet changes how fast things go up and down.

3.6   Summary

This chapter has been difficult, but it was a necessary hurdle. We have to learn the rudiments of simulation and some of the nomenclature and notation to use DEs in neural settings. By focusing on a classic example we have been able to focus on the mathematics without the additional complications of applying it to a neural setting. Now that this has been done, we can move on to the next chapter where we will see how to use the same method to produce a spiking neuron.

The major lessons to have been learned are that when asked to solve a DE, guess! And for our applications, guess an exponential. Generally, the applications of DEs in neural and psychological modelling will be as helpers in numerical simulations, where we don't have to solve them, but can just use them.

Chapter 4

Intermezzo: Computing with Loops

In the previous chapter, we learned to iterate the same equation with incrementally changed values. We did this by copying and pasting rows of our spreadsheet. I described this as a loop. In this intermezzo, I will introduce you to the notion of an imperative programming language, discuss a few examples of loops, and show you an example program of the harmonic exercise so that you can see the similarity to your spreadsheet implementation.

4.1 There Is More Than One Type of Computer Programming Language

All computer languages are not the same. In addition to the differences between individual languages, there are differences in types of languages. Think about these like the differences in alphabets. English and Arabic have very different alphabets visually, but for both languages the characters of the alphabets represent letters that are strung together to create words; the alphabets are of the same type. This is different from Egyptian hieroglyphics or Chinese characters where each pictograph represents a word or concept. The types of English and Chinese alphabets are different. Similarly, computer languages can differ in details or in their types.

Two major types of computer languages are imperative and functional. I will discuss imperative languages here.

4.2 Imperative Programming

Imperative programming is like a cooking recipe. I tell you exactly what steps I want you to take and the order I want you to take them in. Any programming language that is designed around this concept of a serial set of instructions is imperative. An imperative is an order: Do this now.

There are many different examples of imperative languages. The one I will introduce here is Python. Other examples will be listed later. Python is a popular language with many examples to be found online. It is free, and there are a number of convenient tools that will ease your introduction to the language. In addition there are a number of very useful libraries for the Python language.

Language Libraries

A programming language is usually defined by a set of keywords that have special meanings and are protected. Programs are written by stringing these elements of the language together. Many programming tasks are common and the procedures for performing them will be used by many people. Rather than expand the core definitions of the language to try and incorporate all these different potential applications, language designers usually keep the core language simple, but facilitate some method for allowing individual users to pick and choose other functions to import and use in their programs without having to write everything from scratch. These add-ons are often called *libraries*, *packages*, or *modules*. They are often written in the same programming language, but they do not have to be.

One of the oldest computer languages is Fortran (for formula translation). Some excellent mathematics routines are written in the Fortran language. Many newer languages wrap the Fortran commands in their own language so that it is possible, for example, to call a Fortran function by using a Python command.

Since Python is a popular language there are many libraries. Most of the standard ones are used widely and they have become robust, efficient, and of a high quality. As two examples, scipy is a library that has functions for a number of common scientific routines such as Fourier transforms, and PsychoPy is a toolbox for performing psychophysical experiments. You can create random dot displays with a single line of Python code. When selecting a language for your personal work, it is a good idea to choose a language that has well-developed libraries for your particular area of interest. Different languages tend to be adopted by different communities, and so the breadth of libraries will differ.

Looping

A frequent requirement of computer programs is to implement a set of instructions repeatedly (as we did in updating the position of our spring). When we want to go through the same set of instructions over and over, we call it a loop.

Two of the most common terms used for loops are `for` and `while`. These exact words are used in many programming languages, although the exact syntax usually varies slightly.

`for` loops are used for iterating a set of instructions a particular number of times. For example, if I have a list of numbers and I want to compute the square of each, I might have code that looked like the following.

Listing 4.1   Pseudocode for loop

```
# A simple {for} loop example

myListNum = [1,2,3,4]
myNewListNum = []

for i in myListNum:
    myNewListNum.append(i*i)
end
```

Pseudocode is a term used in programming books and articles to present an example of the steps that a program needs to do. It looks like a computer program, but may not be "legal" in any actual programming language. It is supposed to offer specificity, without requiring familiarity with any particular language.

The first line of this pseudocode is a *comment*. Comments in computer code are not there for the machine to read, but are for the human users of the computer program. Comments can serve several functions. They may document a function's purpose or intended use. Comments can document the program's author, and when the program was written. Comments are not required, but are simply available as a convenience to help programmers remember what they did, and to help users figure out how to use the code. Different computer languages will use different symbols to indicate that the text that follows is to be treated as a comment and not as a programming instruction. In this example, the hash ("#") symbol is used. Other symbols may be used, for example, "%", "–", and each is specific to a particular computer programming language. To help you understand the function of comments in computer code you can think of the column titles in a spreadsheet program. Those titles, and cells of text, help you communicate what the spreadsheet is doing, but they are not essential to the spreadsheet's computations.

Next, we create a list of numbers. I am using square brackets to represent the list and I have assigned that list to a variable with the name myListNum (note the camel case). I also create an empty list ([]) to hold the output I generate in my for loop. Then I enter the loop. I create a new, temporary, variable called i. For each spin through the loop i changes to the new value. It begins with the first element of the list and goes through the loop. When it reaches the end, it returns to the top, resets the value of i, and repeats the loop. It continues until it reaches the end of the loop.

Inside the loop I am using a *method* of lists to append a value to the end. Many modern programming languages use objects. A car is an object. It has attributes (e.g., color) and methods (go forward). Computer objects similarly may be given attributes and methods. Here our particular example of a list item is an object. The attribute of this list includes the value of the numbers that we have stored in the list. The function append is a method of lists in this Python-like pseudocode. If you think of an appendix as the chapters that come at the end of a book, you understand what append does. It takes its input and appends it to the end of itself. This works here to create a gradually increasing sequence of numbers. However, to save space we have taken the extra step of processing the number first, before we use it. The value in this case is $i * i$; this equation computes the square of the element of the list I am working on, and after this is completed the value is appended.

But How Does it Know?

We do not have to worry about how the program knows that it is at the end of the list or when to reset i. All this is handled for us by the authors of the language. They worry about the low-level actions that have to happen in terms of registers and bits flipping. We get to concentrate on a higher level of abstraction that is more relevant to our particular problem. In the early days of computer science, the need to program closer to the level of hardware was necessary to extract maximum efficiencies. With time, computers have become faster and this is less of a factor. Now, modern languages handle the low-level details for us.

---

while loops are a variation of this theme. In a while loop we tell our program to do something until a particular condition is met. These conditions are sometimes called predicates. The convention is that a while loop continues as long as its predicate is true. When the predicate is false, the loop is broken and you exit.

Listing 4.2   Pseudocode while loop

```
myListNum = [1,2,3,4]
myNewListNum = []

i = 0
while i < length(myListNum):
    myNewListNum.append(myListNum[i]*myListNum[i])
    i = i + 1
end
```

The while loop may look stranger, but the logic should be clear even if the details are perplexing. We create the same two variables to start. Then we *initialize* our variable i with the number 0. In many computer languages counts start with zero. The first element of a list is thus in the zeroth position. Seeing if a person starts counting from zero is a good test to see if someone is a computer programmer.

The predicate for our while loop tests to see if our value of i is less than the length of our list. Our list has length 4, and it has positions 0, 1, 2, and 3. So the last true value of i will be 3 since 3 is less than 4, but 4 is not less than 4. Inside this loop, I use the value of i as an *index* to access a particular element of the list. Those get multiplied by themselves and appended to the output. Next, I increment the value of our *counter*. In most languages you can use the variable name like this, on both sides of the equation, to update. Essentially, this line says to add 1 to the current value of i and store that output back into the variable i. Now, pause for a moment to ask yourself what would happen if I did not do this?

I would never exit the loop; i would remain at 0. I would always get the first element of my list, square it, and append it, and I would repeat it forever, never exiting. This is called an *infinite loop*. And it is a big headache for new programmers when using loops. Your program works, it just never quits, and you have to use some special command to "kill" it.

4.3 The Harmonic Exercise in Python with Loops

Listing 4.3 Python and our spring

```
import pylab as pyl

dt = 0.05
p = -5.0
sp = 5.0

acc = [p*sp]
vel = [0.0]
s = [sp]
t = [0.0]


for i in range(1,100):
    acc.append(s[-1]*p)
    vel.append(vel[-1] + acc[-1]*dt)
    s.append(s[-1] + vel[-1]*dt)
    t.append(dt*i)


dp = pyl.plot(t,s)
pyl.show()
```

This code snippet is actual Python code that will run. Later on, I will give some instructions on putting a working installation of Python on to your computer, but if you want to try now, look at the instructions on page 137. Type the text into a file and save it with a name, for example, de.py. Then open up a command line on your computer and navigate to the directory where you saved the file. Then you should be able to type python2 de.py and after a suspenseful delay you will see a figure like Figure 4.1 pop up on your computer screen.

This code is only slightly more complicated than our pseudocode examples of loops. In the first line I import the library that I am going to use to make the figure. I do not have to worry about creating the window to display the figure because someone else has already done that for me. I import the library and give it a name that I will use later in my program. Next, I initialize values for my constants and create the lists that I will be using, giving them their first values. Then I enter my for loop and run it for 100 steps. I create this list of 1 to 100 using the Python built-in function range. Next, I append new values to my lists using the equations that we programmed into our spreadsheets. I use a Python trick to get the last values from my lists. I use the number −1. This is like counting in reverse. If 0 is the first position in my list, then −1 is the value right before it, or the last value of the list, if you think of it as a circle. After I am done with the loop, I create the plot with its "x" and "y" values, two of my lists for time and location. Then I show it.

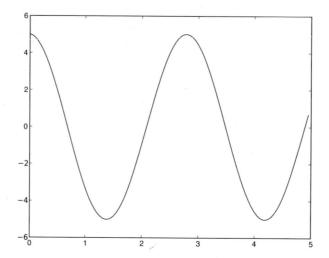

Figure 4.1   The example Python program shown will produce this figure of an oscillating spring position.

Compare this to your spreadsheet. First, it seems simpler and more compact. Second, all the challenges of keeping track of rows are eliminated. But more importantly, since your spreadsheet does exactly what this code does, you were programming when you wrote your spreadsheet. You were using the computer language of a spreadsheet program. You can program!

Chapter 5

From Action Potentials to Programming Neurons: Integrate and Fire

Objectives

After reading this chapter you should be able to:

- have a general understanding of the nature of the action potential;
- understand how the integrate and fire model can be derived from treating the neuronal membrane as a capacitor; and
- generate a spreadsheet version of the integrate and fire model of the spiking neuron.

5.1 Overview

In this chapter we will use our ability to program numerical simulations to create a spreadsheet version of the integrate and fire model of a spiking neuron. This model builds on the basics of the neuron action potential.

Although historically the integrate and fire model followed its more famous cousin, the Hodgkin and Huxley model, it is simpler to begin with. In developing this model we will introduce some very basic ideas of electrical circuits. This excursion will give us more of the jargon and notation that we need in order to use computational techniques.

In summary, this chapter will:

- introduce the action potential;
- describe the integrate and fire model of the action potential;
- show how this model comes from considering the neuron as a simple electrical circuit;
- implement a spreadsheet version of the simple integrate and fire neuron model.

5.2   Action Potentials

With our spring example of the previous chapter, we began our model with an empirically determined relationship between the acceleration and the location. Our model of the action potential will also originate in empirical data. Therefore, before we can model a spiking neuron, we must make ourselves conversant with the relevant empirical observations on the action potential.

The action potential is introduced in physiological psychology and biological psychology courses. Here I provide a schematic glimpse only, just enough to inform our computational models. If you feel rusty on this material and do not have a textbook to hand, you could check out Wikipedia's detailed entry[1] or *Brain & Behavior: An introduction to biological psychology* (Garrett, 2011).

Neurons and Ions

Neurons are cells and their internal fluids are enclosed by a cell membrane. That cell membrane is leaky in two ways. First, there are specific channels, essentially tunnels, that allow certain ions and not others to cross the membrane. Second, there is a general leakiness that allows everything through to varying degrees. The important distinction for us is that the channels are selective. They allow ions to pass as a function of concentration and electrical potential.

An ion is a charged particle.

Normally, a neuron has more negatively charged ions inside than positively charged ones. It achieves this by pumping out sodium (Na^+) and pumping in potassium (K^+). However, since potassium and sodium are each piled up on opposite sides of the membranes, their concentration gradients exert forces for them to move back in the other direction. Unfortunately for sodium, it cannot get back in, but the potassium can leak out. When it does so, it leaves behind an unmatched negative charge. Enough of these and potassium begins to be pulled back by electrical attraction. At some point the concentration gradient pushing it out and the electrical attraction pulling it back balance, and it attains its *resting* potential.

A *potential* refers to the electrical charge stored on the two sides of the membrane. This has the *potential* to do work. It is like a battery.

When one neuron talks to another neuron across their synapse, certain ion channels on the post-synaptic cell open up and allow ions to move into the cell. This causes a small change in the post-synaptic neuron's electrical potential. If enough channels open, the charge inside the cell will increase sufficiently that it hits a point of no return. Sodium channels open up and the interior of the neuron becomes rapidly more positive. This is the *action* potential. In a sense it is automated. Ion channels open and subsequently close and everything resets to the baseline.

5.3   Computational Models of the Action Potential in Action

A good preparation for building our own model is to see another version in action. This also provides a demonstration of what models are good for. They let us easily simulate experiments that might be complicated, expensive, or impossible to explore in the laboratory.

An excellent tutorial model is available at afodor. net: http://www.afodor.net/HHModel.htm. This model requires that you have a computer connected to the internet and that you are able to run Java applets.

> What ions are responsible for the *repolarization* of the neuron back to its resting potential?

Exercise: Online Exploration of a Computational Model of a Neuron

To prepare for building our own model of a spiking neuron, let's review some of the features of the action potential in simulation. Initiate the applet from the website referenced above and run it by doing the following:

- Push the **Start** button.
- You will see a line began to scroll across the screen.
- Push the **Stimulate** button.
- Before the line scrolls off the right edge, push the **Stop** button.

Now explore the following questions (see Figure 5.1):

- What is the value being plotted on the "y" axis? Look at the checkboxes on the right. What else can you plot?
- What do you call the up and down waveform?
- Use this applet to answer the question, "Which ion is responsible for returning the electrical potential back to baseline after a neuron spikes?"
- If you start the applet scrolling again and deliver two stimuli very close together do you get two action potentials? Why not, and what do you call this phenomenon?

Additional Reading for Modeling Action Potentials

If you wish to learn more about the mathematics than what I present here, consider consulting Gerstner and Kistler (2002): *Spiking Neuron Models*. This is an excellent textbook that has an online version http://lcn.epfl.ch/ gerstner/BUCH.html.

5.4   The Integrate and Fire Neuron Equation

The above demonstration shows the full Hodgkin and Huxley neuron model. We will tackle this model in Chapter 7. First, we will ask if all that complexity, all those ion channels, are necessary? Could we not achieve all we need with a much simpler version of this model? If instead of worrying about sodium, potassium, and other ions, what if

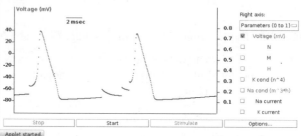

Back to my home page

The Hodgkin-Huxley model of the action potential

In a classic series of papers from the early 1950's, A.L. Hodgkin and A.F. Huxley performed a painstaking series of experiments on the giant axon of the squid. Based on their observations, Hodgkin and Huxley constructed a mathematical model to explain the electrical excitability of neurons in terms of discrete Na^+ and K^+ currents. A Java version of their Nobel prize winning model (as described in J. Physiol., 1952, 117: 500-544) is presented below:

Figure 5.1   A screen grab of the Hodgkin–Huxley Java Applet. http://www.afodor.net/ HH-Model.htm. You will need JAVA installed on your computer for this web demo to work properly. Note that there are two action potentials displayed, but that before the second one there are several false starts. What is the period of time called when the neuron cannot fire again after having recently discharged an action potential? What explains this phenomenon?

we amalgamated them into a single term? If we did this, if we pared the Hodgkin and Huxley model back to its bare essentials, we would get the integrate and fire model. The equation for this model of the spiking neuron is

> "Our life is frittered away by detail. Simplify, simplify, simplify!" Henry David Thoreau

$$\tau \frac{dV(t)}{dt} = R I(t) - V(t) \qquad (5.1)$$

In addition to the formula above, the integrate and fire model includes another assumption that is an essential feature of the model: the *reset*. Unlike the Hodgkin and Huxley model, the integrate and fire equation will not automatically generate an action potential. For the integrate and fire model we fix a threshold. Whenever our voltage exceeds this threshold we assert that an action potential has happened, and we reset the voltage to the baseline.

Exploring the Equation

We cannot model what we do not understand. This equation is very similar to what we saw before in our spring example. However, it does use more and different variables. One of the best ways to think about how you will build a model is to patiently work your way through a simple conceptual understanding of the core assumptions. For the integrate and fire model those assumptions are represented in Equation 5.1. Let's consider in turn some of the key components. I will print a list of questions to guide you. I will provide the list without answers first, and then again with my interpretations; try to answer them first on your own. And do not be afraid to take issue with my interpretations.

- What does dV/dt mean?
- What does τ represent?
- Why does the voltage on the right have a negative sign?
- What is $I(t)$?
- Put it all together and explain what it means.
- Why, if we don't reach a threshold to fire an action potential, do we see an exponential decay?

Some possible answers:

- **What does dV/dt mean?** It is a derivative. It is a slope. It is the rise (voltage) over the run (time). Putting all this together, it represents the rate of change of voltage as a function of time.

- **What does τ represent?** τ is the conventional abbreviation for the membrane time constant. You will almost always see this particular Greek letter used with this meaning. For our particular equation it is a combination of resistance and capacitance – more on these shortly. If you were to solve this differential equation you should be able to see why the label "time constant" applies.

- **Why does the voltage on the right have a negative sign?** Equations can give you insight into qualitative behavior even when you do not solve them for the details. Do not overdo calculation. Mathematicians talk about how an equation "behaves." By focusing on the general, instead of the specific, you can gain greater insight into phenomena that are describable mathematically. And like everything we are discussing, this gets easier with practice. Let's break this question down into two sub-questions. What would it mean if dV/dt were positive? It would mean that the voltage was growing with time; the rate of change is positive. And if the $V(t)$ on the right side were similarly positive? It would mean that a positive voltage was associated with a positive increase in voltage which would lead to a bigger, more positive voltage, which would lead to an increasing positive rate, and so on until our equation would "blow up." With a negative sign, it means the bigger the voltage, the bigger the change is to shrink the voltage in the opposite direction (big positive voltage, big negative rate of change and vice versa). This leads to self-correction. You may not know why this equation was developed, but you will know this is a feature it should have. Neurons do not have infinitely large voltages; a self-correcting mechanism like this is required by empirical data. This is something the equation must have had. What is dV/dt at equilibrium and what does that mean in words?

- **What is $I(t)$?** It is the current term. I is the common abbreviation for current and is used for historical reasons. In the early days of electricity and telegraphy, current was referred to as the intensity and the abbreviation of "I" stuck.

- **Put it all together and explain what Equation 5.1 means.** The equation tells us how the voltage evolves over time, just like our spring equation told us how the location of the weight evolved over time. We can see from this function that the voltage in the future will be a sum of whatever current is being injected into our cell (e.g., if an investigator stuck in an electrode) minus some portion of the current voltage.

- **Why, if we don't reach a threshold to fire an action potential, do we see an exponential decay?** This is the same lesson we learned before. Note that the dependent variable in the derivative is also on the right-hand side. Rate of change is proportional to itself. What function when you take its derivative looks the same? The exponential. But note the sign of the right-hand voltage term; it is negative. That is why it is an exponential decay instead of an exponential growth.

Origin of the Leaky Integrate and Fire Model

Jargon moment: Why is it the *leaky* integrate and fire model? Because of the negative V term. Without this term, each new increment in current would accumulate, but since the change in voltage is inversely proportional to itself, we tend to gradually decrease our voltage towards the resting potential. Voltage leaks out like a bathtub with a faulty plug.

Historically, the integrate and fire model of the neuron came about as a simplification of the Hodgkin and Huxley model, but it can be justified on its own by considering a simple electrical circuit model of a neuron. This digression allows us to introduce some simple electrical terminology. Since reference to concepts like resistance and capacitance show up frequently in computational neuroscience discussions, it is useful to understand some basics of the terminology.

How to Be an Electrical Engineer in Two Simple Steps

The two simple steps are to learn the formula for Ohm's and Kirchhoff's Laws. The majority of what you need to know for understanding simple electrical circuits is contained in these two principles.

$$V = I R \qquad (5.2)$$

Ohm's Law: although it is called a "law," it developed as a description of empirical data.

$$\sum_{k=1}^{n} I_k = 0 \qquad (5.3)$$

Kirchhoff's Law: all the currents coming into a junction must sum to zero.

Using Ohm's and Kirchhoff's rules we can take a simple schematic view of the neuron, and its membrane, as a simple electrical circuit (Figure 5.2) and derive the relationship used for the integrate and fire model.

To derive the integrate and fire model from this circuit we will benefit from a few additional relationships:

1. Charges are represented by the letter Q.
2. Current is the movement of charges as a function of time.
3. From 1 and 2 above, we derive $I = dQ/dt$.
4. Capacitance can be thought of as a source of current. If we apply positive charge to one side of a capacitor, the charges build up as if they were piled up behind a

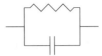

Figure 5.2 Simple circuit representation of the neuron. The jagged line represents the resistance: how hard it is for ions to travel across the membrane from left to right. The symbol that looks like a vertical equals sign is the capacitor. Charge builds up on one side. From this simple conception of a neuron's membrane, we can derive the integrate and fire model of a neuron.

    dam. They cannot get across the gap. Since opposites attract, the positive charges on one side will attract negative charges to the other side.

5. Capacitance is a property of materials and is *defined* by $C = Q/V$. This is the amount of charge that a certain voltage can build up.

    With these relations, and a little algebra, we can get our integrate and fire model. Rearrange the symbols to get $CV = Q$. Then, remember that whatever you do to one side of an equality, if you also do it to the other side then the equality will still hold. Let's differentiate both sides with respect to time. This yields

$$C \frac{dV}{dt} = \frac{dQ}{dt} = I(t)$$

Since capacitance is a function of the material, and our material, the neuronal membrane, is not changing, it is a constant. This lets us move it outside the derivative.

    Kirchhoff's Law states that all the currents going into a node must equal zero. On the left side of Figure 5.2 the current going in (I_{in}) must equal the currents going out due to resistance (I_R) and capacitance (I_C). Thus,

$$I_{in} = I_R + I_C \qquad \text{by Kirchhoff's Law}$$

$$I_{in} = I_R + C \frac{dV}{dt} \qquad \text{replace capacitive current with the above alternative}$$

$$I_{in} = \frac{V}{R} + C \frac{dV}{dt} \qquad \text{replace resistive current using Ohm's Law alternative}$$

$$I_{in} - \frac{V}{R} = C \frac{dV}{dt} \qquad \text{subtract term from both sides}$$

$$R I_{in} - V = R C \frac{dV}{dt} \qquad \text{multiply both sides by } R$$

$$R I_{in} - V = \tau \frac{dV}{dt} \qquad \text{substitute } \tau \text{ for RC}$$

$$\tau \frac{dV}{dt} = R I_{in} - V \qquad \text{reverse order to make it look like 5.1.}$$

5.5 Coding the Integrate and Fire Model of the Neuron

In Chapter 3 we began with a formula relating something we were interested in, location, to its change in position as a function of time. From that we were able to generate a simulation that used this formula for a rate of change to generate an updated position and so on. This gave us our graphical trace of position over time.

We want to apply the same logic here to making a simulation of a neuron in response to different amounts of injected current. To do that, we have to identify our independent and dependent variables. What is the value for our neuron that serves the same role as location did for the spring? Examine again Equation 5.1 to try and identify the key variables. It may help to look back at what it is that electrophysiologists record with their microelectrodes, or what it is that electroencephalography (EEG) measures.

> In this exercise, we treat a derivative as if it were a fraction. This is no accident. It is why Leibniz invented this notation and why it won out over Newton's.

We are interested in the voltage. This is the quantity that varies over time and reflects the imbalances of the ions on the two sides of the neuronal membrane. Our formula above (Equation 5.1) gives us a formula for voltage and for how voltage changes over time. In fact, it is even simpler than our spring example, because there is no second derivative that requires us to update an intermediate value. In addition, there are constants that we need to specify, namely, τ and R, and the value of I. With these facts we are prepared to do what we did before: use our old value and add to it our rate of change per unit time multiplied by the time step. Then we use this as our "new" old value.

The integrate and fire model requires one more step or assumption. If you code the model just as written you will see that the neuron never spikes. Its voltage will rise in response to current input and decay when the current is taken away. To make this model a spiking neuron model we introduce a "hack," sometimes obfuscated by the name "non-linearity." We establish a hard threshold and a hard reset. When the voltage of our model reaches some value that we choose to call the threshold, we "manually" say that a spike has occurred and reset the voltage back to baseline. Of course, we do not actually do this manually, but we have to write special rules in our program to handle this particular special case. Below, we work through the programming of this model and I try to lead you through the steps necessary for implementing all these features.

Exercise: Spreadsheet Program for the Leaky Integrate and Fire Model

For this exercise, you will write a version of the spiking form of the leaky integrate and fire model. To do so, work your way through the following steps:

1. Open up a spreadsheet program and create the following columns: time step, time, tau, threshold, voltage, resistance, spike, current.

2. Go to the next row and enter the following starting values: 0.1, 0.0, 10, 4, 0.0, 5, 0, 0.

3. Go to the following row and enter formulas that will allow this row to update its values using only the constants and values from the row immediately above. Figuring out these formulas is left up to you. As an example to get you started, note that the time step should always stay the same. Therefore, in cell A3 you could enter "= A2" and since time is the old time plus the time step, you could enter "B3 = B2 + A2".

voltage

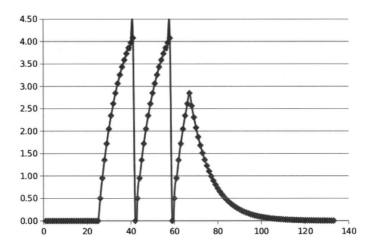

Figure 5.3 A screen grab from a spreadsheet program implementing the integrate and fire model. Note the straight lines. These come from resetting the voltage every time it goes above threshold. Look at the last discharge. Here I gave an input current insufficient to cause a spike. Note the shape of the curve as it relaxes back to zero. That curve should remind you of a function. Which one and why?

4. Make your equations that refer to constants refer to a single spreadsheet cell. Many spreadsheet programs use the dollar sign for this purpose. The equation above says that when you copy and paste, keep the column and the row unchanged.

5. Make the spike column report 0 if the voltage is less than the threshold and 1 if it is greater. Use the help in your spreadsheet program to figure out how to do this using an `if` function.

6. Compute the new voltage from the old voltage. The new voltage is the old voltage plus the change in voltage. Change in voltage is simply dV/dt; the equation we derived above multiplied by the change in time. Think of the derivative as a fraction – you want to cancel time.

7. Use an `if` rule in the voltage column to check if a spike has occurred. If it has, reset the voltage to zero. If not, use your update equation.

8. Repeat entering things by hand for a few rows, then copy and paste the last row a few hundred times.

9. Plot the voltage column. If you have done everything correctly it will show a straight line. Pause for a moment and ask yourself why.

10. Pick a few consecutive cells in the current column and replace those zeros with a series of ones and re-plot. You should see something like Figure 5.3.

This basic spreadsheet program is already adequate for performing some interesting computational investigations.* For example, does injecting a constant current result in irregular or regular spiking patterns? Compare your answer to the spiking seen by Mainen and Sejnowski (1995). What are the implications for integrate and fire modelling?

You might also be interested in examining how the regularity of spiking output is affected by changes in the regularity of the input. You could input a sinusoidally varying current or even a smoothed version of random noise. What happens to the consistency of the spiking response in this setting?

5.6   Summary

The integrate and fire model is an actively used current research tool in computational neuroscience. Each year hundreds of new research articles are published using this tool, and you just programmed it in a spreadsheet. This shows that computational techniques are within your abilities. You can follow the mathematics well enough, and apparently using a spreadsheet program is more like programming than you may have realized.

The integrate and fire model is appealing as a research tool because of simplicity and robustness. It can be viewed as a simplification of the Hodgkin–Huxley model or justified in its own right as the consequences of a simple circuit view of the neuron.

Your integrate and fire model uses a forward estimation approach in which the last value and the DE are used to generate the estimate at the next point in time. For this simple model and assuming a constant current you can analytically solve the DE for future voltage values and compare the discrete time step version of the model to the analytic solution. However, in most settings an analytic solution for the integrate and fire model is not practical or possible. For that reason, researchers do exactly what you have done. They use an iterative approach.

It is easy to see how one could make a complex network of a population of these elements. One could for example string together a series of computers all running the program you wrote and using the output of each to create an input for other "neurons." More practical is to rewrite the spreadsheet version of the model in a more flexible language and string a population of those computational units together. Either way, it is essentially a cut and paste operation once the first version is written.

Whether or not the hard-coded discontinuity for the representation of a neuron's spike is or is not a disadvantage depends on whether the specifics of the spike generation process are critical for the scientific question that you are interested in. For many applications it is enough to know that a spike occurred and when it occurred. It is not necessary to know the shape or height or duration of the spike itself. For other applications, this detail may be critical, and we can use variations of the Hodgkin and Huxley model to get it. Ultimately the answer as to whether any given model (all of which will include some simplifications) is good enough is, "It depends." It depends on the questions that you are asking.

---

*See the intermezzo after this chapter (page 49) for more about `if` functions in programs. Also, `if` rules are a core feature of "productions." Productions are at the heart of many agent-based modelling approaches such as ACT-R, which is discussed in Chapter 21.

Chapter 6

Intermezzo: Computing with `if` Statements

The prior chapter introduced an `if` statement into the spreadsheet implementation of the integrate and fire model. `if` statements are a kind of programming construct called a *conditional* and they are common in imperative and functional programming languages. As the name implies, a conditional establishes a condition for testing whether or not some particular instruction, an imperative command, should be executed. Usually `if` statements come paired with `else` statements. The typical use would be something like the following:

Listing 6.1   Pseudocode `if`−`else` statement

```
myListNum = [1,2,3,4]
myNewListNum = []

for i in myListNum:
    if (isEven(i)):
        myNewListNum.append(i*i)
    else:
        myNewListNum.append(i)
end
```

This is pseudocode again. I have expanded one of our earlier `for` loop examples to include a conditional inside. I imagine that we have written a function that tests whether or not a number is even.* If our number is even, `ifEven` returns a TRUE value and if not a FALSE value. When the expression inside the parentheses evaluates to TRUE we do what is underneath the `if`. Otherwise, we do what is underneath the `else`. Here we square the even numbers and leave the odd numbers unchanged.

---

*Such functions may already exist in your favorite programming language. If not, they are not too hard to write. Just test if the remainder after dividing by 2 is or is not zero.

6.1   Code for a Simple Version of the Integrate and Fire Model

Listing 6.2   Simple integrate and fire model in Python

```python
import matplotlib.pyplot as plt

r = 1
c = 1
tau = r*c
dt = 0.05
t = 0
v = 0
threshold = 5
i = []
tdata = []
vdata = []

#This will be our current pulse
for z in range (0, 40):
        num = 10
        i.append(num)

#Now return input current to zero
for z in range(40, 75):
        num = 0
        i.append(num)

#This loop calculates our voltage
for j in range(0, 75):
        dvdt = (1/tau) * (r*i[j] - v)
        v = v + dvdt*dt
        if v > threshold:
                v = 0
        t = t + dt
        tdata.append(t)
        vdata.append(v)

plt.plot(tdata, vdata)
plt.axis([0, t, -1, 7])
plt.xlabel('Time')
plt.ylabel('Voltage (arbitrary units)')
plt.show()
```

This code should look very similar to our spring example. After importing the plotting functions, it begins by initializing the constants and variables that we will need, including several empty lists. To demonstrate the use of comments, three are inserted here as comments for the for loops. The comments record a summary statement of what

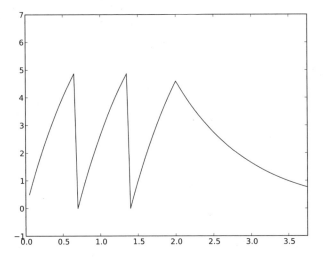

Figure 6.1   The output of the simple Python program listed above.

each for loop is doing. The first two are for creating our current input; how much and for how long. The last is for updating our voltage. It uses an if statement to test if the voltage is over threshold. If so, it uses 0. Python does not require an else statement; some languages do. Here the if statement overwrites our prior calculation of voltage. After the loop is done, we print the results. Note that there is not an explicit word that says that a loop or if statement is concluded. Python uses the indentation to tell it whether or not lines of code go together in a block.

The result of our code is two spikes and an exponential decay to the baseline. I have used some additional methods of the plotting object to label the x and y axes (Figure 6.1).

Chapter 7

Hodgkin and Huxley: The Men and Their Model*

Objectives

After reading this chapter you should be able to:

- appreciate the examples of Hodgkin and Huxley for interdisciplinary training;
- understand that the Hodgkin and Huxley model is conceptually similar to the integrate and fire model; and
- implement the Hodgkin and Huxley model in a spreadsheet program.

7.1   Overview

Our work so far has been building to this model: a complex, partial differential equation. The Hodgkin and Huxley model demonstrates many important themes of computational modeling. Models grow out of data. Hodgkin and Huxley used neuronal recordings from axons as the empirical basis for their computational version. Models force one to be specific. The Hodgkin and Huxley model led to predictions about the character of ion channels that were later tested through further experiment.

In this chapter we take a brief look at the men behind the model to learn the lesson that an interdisciplinary education fosters innovative research. We will then look at the specific model developed by Hodgkin and Huxley and implement it as a program running in a computer spreadsheet.

7.2   Who Were Hodgkin and Huxley?

Alan Lloyd Hodgkin (1914−1998)

Hodgkin entered Cambridge at age 18. He came from a family of broad talents and he pursued a career in biology, but he was advised early on to train broadly and acquire

---

*Some readers and instructors may wish to regard this chapter as optional. The material does not cover new ground conceptually, but it does increase greatly the complexity of the implementation. To get the Hodgkin and Huxley model working correctly requires patience and persistence, but I find the rewards in terms of satisfaction and confidence worth the time and effort.

quantitative skills. It was the advice of a zoology tutor, Carl Pantin, that Hodgkin make the study of mathematics a lifelong activity. Pantin also advised Hodgkin to purse extra-mural training activities. Hodgkin spent time at biological research stations in England. It was through these diverse educational and practical experiences, in combination with his natural ability and energy for work, that Hodgkin was intellectually and technically capable of undertaking his work on the squid giant axon.[1]

More biographical information on both men can be found through the Nobel Prize website.

Andrew F. Huxley (1917−2012)

Huxley seemed to take the complementary path to Hodgkin. He, too, was a Cambridge undergraduate, but elected to concentrate on the physical sciences. However, Cambridge had a requirement that all its physicists still had to take at least one natural science course; Huxley selected physiology. Later, he too would also spend time at marine laboratories where there was research on the squid. The collaboration of Hodgkin and Huxley (and of course others) required physiological knowledge and intuition. It required technical skills to manufacture their research instruments and to learn how to use them. Their research also required the mathematical know-how to conceive of and computationally implement their mathematical model of the neuron's action potential.

In addition, Hodgkin and Huxley owed some of their success to selecting the right experimental model. Their recording equipment was crude by modern standards, and by selecting the squid as the experimental animal, an animal that contains axons that are large enough to be viewed with the naked eye, the researchers were able to conduct many physiological experiments that would not have been technically possible otherwise. It was these novel experiments that were the necessary foundation for their mathematical model.

What Can We Learn from the Lives and Careers of Hodgkin and Huxley?

1. Train broadly. Both Hodgkin and Huxley were educated in computational *and* experimental methods.
2. Seek broad training experiences. Both scientists learned of tools and met future collaborators because they left their home institutions to seek extramural experiences.
3. Collaborate. The Hodgkin and Huxley model is a product of the synergy of two bright minds focusing and cooperating on the same difficult problem. In fact, many other scientists made important contributions to the nature of the action potential, both before and after Hodgkin and Huxley's work.
4. Do not limit yourself to techniques and models already in use. It often seems that important new discoveries are the direct consequences of technological and methodological innovations; be willing to expand beyond established protocols.

Observe the Masters at Work

A series of short video clips of the methods of Hodgkin and Huxley are preserved.[2] Take a moment to watch them and then discuss what role you believe methodological innovations played in the development of the Hodgkin and Huxley model.

7.3   The Hodgkin and Huxley Model

For our purposes, think of the Hodgkin and Huxley model as an elaboration on the integrate and fire model of the preceding chapter. Instead of a single current term, we will have current terms for each of three different ion channels. Each of these channels will also change their *conductance* in response to voltage and time.

Recall that when we wanted to develop our integrate and fire model from the circuit model of a neuron we used Kirchhoff's point rule stating that the currents entering to a point must sum to zero ($I_{total} = I_{Resistance} + I_{Capacitance}$). For the Hodgkin and Huxley model we replace the single resistance term with three separate resistance terms, each relating to different ions: sodium, potassium, and a catch-all for all the negatively charged ions. Resistances in parallel sum up and we now have

> Conductance is the inverse of resistance. If you put your finger over the end of a hose you increase its resistance and decrease its conductance. If you remove your finger you decrease the resistance and increase the conductance. By convention, conductance is symbolized by g and resistance by R and mathematically $g = 1/R$.

$$I_{total}(t) = I_c(t) + \sum_i I_i(t)$$

where the i refers to an index that scrolls over our three ions Na^+, K^+, and all anions collectively (denoted L for "leak current").

To get to the full equation for the Hodgkin and Huxley model, we need to expand the terms for each of the individual ions, and also utilize the relation we learned before for current and capacitance. In addition, we need to include several additional variables that were determined by Hodgkin and Huxley to be necessary if the computations were to fit the data they recorded in their experiments on the squid axon. The result was

> Question: What is the alternative way of expressing the capacitive current that we have learned? See Page 45.

$$C\frac{dV(t)}{dt} = I_{injected}(t) - [(\bar{g}_{Na}m^3h(V(t) - E_{Na}) + \bar{g}_K n^4(V(t) - E_K) + \bar{g}_L(V(t) - E_L)]$$

$$(7.1)$$

What are the *m*s, *n*s, and *h*s?

One answer is to say that they are necessary parameters to enable the model to fit the data; however, they do have a physical interpretation. We can imagine each channel as having a series of gates. For an ion to move through the channel, all the gates need to be opened at the same time.

> Lions and tigers and bears. Oh my! – Dorothy (*Wizard of Oz*)

Therefore, one interpretation of these terms is as representing the odds for a gate to open. It is like flipping a series of biased coins (biased means that the odds of a head and tail are not equal). When all of the coins come up heads at the same time the gates are all open, and an ion can pass through. The different ion channels have different biases and therefore have different parameters. The powers of these terms were determined to fit the data, but when the sodium and potassium channels were finally sequenced it turned out that the number of protein sub-units coincided exactly (e.g., the sodium channel has four sub-units and the model has m to the fourth power) (Catterall et al., 2012).

Discussion: What Do the $E_{(\cdot)}$s Represent?

This is another example of looking at an equation to try and understand qualitatively (as opposed to quantitatively) what it is saying and how it behaves. To develop an understanding of the $E(\cdot)$s consider what happens when $V(t)$ is greater or less than them. What would that mean for the flow of ions?

A further complexity in the Hodgkin and Huxley model is that not only are there more terms for currents, but also each of the parameters modifying the current terms also varies with voltage. This makes sense of course. The probability of a channel opening must depend on the voltage or we would not get an action potential, but this also means that our equation becomes substantially more complex.

Each one of m, n, and h also has its own differential equation. The general form is: $\dot{m} = \alpha_m(V)(1-m) - \beta_m(V)m$. Each of the m, n, and h has an identical formula except that the αs and βs are different for each.

Question: What does the dot over the m mean? Answer: Derivative with respect to time. It means the same thing as dm/dt or $m'(t)$.

In order to get the full set of equations for each m, n, and h substitute the appropriate subscript. The presence of the α and β terms is also necessitated to get the model to conform to empirical results. This is yet another demonstration of how the best models are tightly linked to empirical observations.

What Are the Parentheses for?

Parentheses can serve a couple of different purposes in an equation. They can delimit operations, for example, $2(3+4)$ means you multiply the two by the value inside the parentheses. But when you see parentheses in an equation with variables they probably mean something different. $V(t)$ does *not* mean $V \times t$. It means that V is a function of t. You put in a value for t and you get out a number.

Note that the equations for the αs and βs contain a (V). This means that the values are functions of the value of V.

At this point we can appreciate the intellectual accomplishment of Hodgkin and Huxley in deriving and testing this model in the days before digital computers. Equation 7.1 is a complicated partial differential equation. It is not possible to analytically solve this equation. The only way to make use of it, to conduct a simulated experiment, is to run a numerical simulation. Fortunately for us computing power has grown and made this a desktop problem. We can, with patience, use the same basic approach we used for our spring and integrate and fire models to simulate this system also. As we did with our prior projects, we can also implement this in a spreadsheet and use the plotting functions of the spreadsheet program to visualize our results. One of the things to note about this exercise is that the concept you are using, getting a new value from an old value by computing its change from a DE, is the same as you have already used. What makes this algorithm harder is the number of terms and potential for typos and circular references. Keep this in mind when collaborating in the future. The devil is in the detail. What makes for a successful computational experiment may have less to do with intelligence than with patience and a tolerance for grunt work.

The remainder of the chapter is devoted to helping you get started on your own version.

> Ever wonder why we refer to mistakes in computers as "bugs?" One version holds that in tracing down a problem with one of the early computers, the kind that used mechanical relays, the problem was found to be a moth trapped in one of the relays. Hence tracking down bugs.

7.4   Simulating the Hodgkin and Huxley Model with a Spreadsheet

Warning: Here Be Dragons

Because of the complexity of this model, you should be prepared to have some hiccoughs. You almost certainly will make mistakes on building this model the first time you try. If things are not working well, check the following:

- Check your numbers carefully. Are all the constants exactly correct? Our earlier projects were forgiving of slight variations in the choice of constants. Not so the Hodgkin and Huxley model. Every number and equation must be exactly correct.
- Check your cell references carefully. There are a lot of ms and ns and αs and βs; it is easy to refer to the wrong column.
- Is your time step small enough?
- Are you iterating enough? You may need a lot of rows.
- Try it first with no injected current. Everything should stay relatively stable if you have all the values correct. There may be some small changes due to the finite precision of the program, but large drifts in your value of voltage mean problems. If this happens try to find which column of numbers is changing first. This may give you a hint as to where your bug is.

> Care about the units. One way to make sure that an equation is written correctly is to make sure that the units going in and coming out make sense.

Exercise: The Hodgkin and Huxley Model in a Spreadsheet

For this exercise you will implement a spreadsheet version of the model. After "injecting" a supplementary current pulse, you will observe the action potential.

First, you will need to create a column in the spreadsheet that will hold the constants you will need for this simulation (Table 7.1). Type carefully.

Because this is a more detailed and complex simulation it helps to pause before you start typing and think about your overall goals:

- What is the value that you ultimately want to plot? Voltage versus time. You might also want to overlay the current trace, just like the Java applet you viewed on page 41.
- How do we compute new voltages? By using our same old rule: new value is equal to old value plus the change in value. We figure out the change in value by using the DE that gives us a rate of change per unit of time and multiplying that by the time step.
- Now what else do we need to know to estimate these quantities? If you review Equation 7.1 you will see that it depends on values for n, m, and h. Each of those has its own DE. For each of those we will need to follow the same rubric: old value + rate of change × time step. The basic formula for the derivatives m, n, or h is $d*/dt = \alpha_*(v)(1 - *) - \beta_*(v)*$. Replace the * with the appropriate variable.
- Each n, m, and h depends on its own α and β. Each of these has its own formula (see Table 7.2; I know, "Ugh!"). These too need to be updated each round as the voltage (v) changes.

One last tricky point: How do we get started? What are the initial values? For this we assume that our system begins from a state of rest where the voltage is not changing. If everything is at rest then what should all the derivatives be?

If the system is at rest then nothing should be changing. That is, dV/dt should be zero and the voltage should be at its resting potential. For the set of constants that we have chosen, this value is 0 (in biological neurons the resting potential is closer to –65 mV, but this represents only a shift in the baseline and is not important for observing the qualitative behavior of our model, the shape, and the automaticity of the action potential).

What are the values of n, m, and h at time zero? It works out to be: $m_{atrest} = \alpha_m/(\alpha_m + \beta_m)$. And similarly for n and h. You can figure this out by using the basic formula for the derivative of m, recognize that dm/dt is zero, and rearrange the terms. The formula is similar for each of n and h.

With this list of formulas you will have all you need to implement your program.

Still Confused?

Remember that Hodgkin and Huxley won a Nobel Prize. Therefore this is not a trivial exercise. As I said in the Preface, what separates those who can from those who cannot use mathematical methods is less ability than it is persistence. The fact that you cannot sit down and write the model in the same way you write a paper is normal. Just start slowly, be prepared to make mistakes, and keep at it. If you get completely blocked, talk to someone, and then come back and try it again. You can solve this.

Hodgkin and Huxley: The Men and Their Model 59

Table 7.1 Constants for the Hodgkin and Huxley model values from Gerstner and Kistler (2002). Using these values gives us a resting potential of zero and makes the capacitance one so that we can essentially ignore it.

Sodium reversal voltage	115 mV
Sodium conductance	120 mS/cm^2
Potassium reversal voltage	−12 mV
Potassium conductance	36 mS/cm^2
Leak reversal voltage	10.6 mV
Leak conductance	0.3 mS/cm^2

Table 7.2 Equations for computing the α and β values

α_n	$\frac{0.1-0.01v}{e^{1-0.1v}-1}$
β_n	$0.125e^{-v/80}$
α_m	$\frac{2.5-0.1v}{e^{2.5-0.1v}-1}$
β_m	$4e^{-v/18}$
α_h	$0.07e^{-v/20}$
β_h	$\frac{1}{e^{3-0.1v}+1}$

	A	B	C	D	E	H	I	J	K	L	M	N	O	P	Q	R	S	T	U	V	W	X
1	Constants		v	dvdt	dt	an	bn	am	bm	ah	bh	n	m	h	dndt	dmdt	dhdt	ik	ina	il	istim	itot
2	ena	115	This row figures out the starting values for m,n,h when t = infinity and all is at steady state																			
3	gna	120																				
4	ek	-12																				
5	gk	36																				
6	el	10.6																				
7	gl	0.3																				
8																						

Figure 7.1 A screenshot of a spreadsheet with one possible collection of column headings. Note that the first row of data will be different from those that follow because it will include your initial values. After that most of the values will be some form of "new value = old value + change in value."

If you cannot even figure out where to begin look at Figure 7.1 for some example column headings you could use to get started, and Figure 7.2 shows you sample outputs for a correctly programmed spreadsheet that will help you determine if you are on the right track.

Explorations

If you are successful in implementing your model then you can investigate how accurate the model is as a model of neuronal function. Does your model, for example, show an absolute or relative refractory period?

In addition, you can repeat the same experiment you did with the integrate and fire model and inject a prolonged constant current. Do you see constant or irregular spiking?

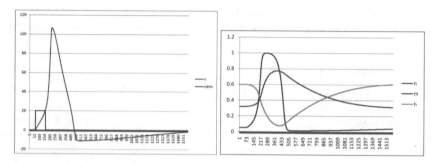

Figure 7.2   Plots generated from a spreadsheet program of the Hodgkin and Huxley model. The left panel shows a superposition of the voltage and current traces. An action potential is shown. The right panel shows the corresponding changes in the *m*, *n*, and *h* values as a function of time.

How sensitive is your model to manipulations of the time step? How sensitive is the model to slight variations in the parameters? Can you utilize this method to determine which ion is most critical for the repolarization of the voltage after an action potential? Is it possible to cause a spike by injecting negative current?

These few examples give you some slight idea of the range of experiments you can perform once you have built a functioning computational version. Experiments become trivial and investigations, like changing the conductance of a channel, that would be difficult or expensive to do *in vivo* become a few minutes' work. This is the power of computational modeling. And if you have made it this far, you know you have the ability to pursue this direction if you desire.

7.5   A Final Word about Differential Equations

In the preceding chapters I have introduced elemental aspects of the nomenclature, notation, and use of DEs. I have focused on their application to neuronal modelling because that represents one of their great successes. However, you should not be left thinking that DEs are only relevant for modelling individual neurons. Any time you find yourself thinking about a neural or psychological process in which you are interested in some rate of change, or how one continuous variable changes with respect to another continuous variable, you have a setting where modelling and simulating by the use of DEs may be informative.

Chapter 8

Intermezzo: Computing with Functions

The previous chapter guided you through a spreadsheet version of the Hodgkin and Huxley model of the neuron. This is a challenging exercise because the model is complicated, but it is also challenging because the traditional use of a spreadsheet is not well adapted to this sort of programming. It is difficult to keep track of which row and cells are referring to each other. It is easy to end up with a circular reference that is hard to fix. Even dragging and copying can be complex. If you fail to freeze the reference for a particular cell reference, numbers may increment that you want constant and you cannot see this by looking only at the numerical entries on the spreadsheet. Something as simple as a slip of your finger on the mouse leads to an error.

As a result you can appreciate that developing a complex algorithm can be easier if you can work in small, self-contained pieces. More complex structures can be built out of these smaller pieces.

To facilitate this approach, programming languages have a mechanism for defining functions. The actual keywords and syntax used for the definition vary slightly, but the overall result is the same. You create a new, special term that expects inputs and gives you new, processed outputs.

For example, what if we wanted to write a function that would add together two numbers and then square the result? The input to our function would be two numbers. The output would be the mathematical result. The basic idea would look like the following pseudocode:

Listing 8.1   Pseudocode function definition

```
addNSq = functionDefinition (x,y):
         output = (x + y)^2
```

In this snippet, we define two temporary, local variables x and y that are placeholders for whatever input we will later use. The body of the function follows the line that defines the function's name and inputs. There is some keyword that tells the function to output a value (often this is called "return"). We would use our function above like addNSq(2,3) and we would get back the number 25.

The benefit of this approach is that we can make our own virtual Legos that we slot together to make bigger constructions. While our final product may be large, we can work our way through the details because each piece is simple and tractable. If we are trying to find a mistake, we can test each piece individually.

The following code example is a Python script for the Hodgkin and Huxley model. It demonstrates many of the concepts that we have learned up to now including `for` loops and `if` statements. In addition, it introduces the Python procedure for defining a function that we can then use inside our program.

Listing 8.2   Python code for Hodgkin and Huxley model

```
import pylab as pyl
import math as m


vinit = 0.0
dt = 0.01
ena = 115
gna = 120
ek = -12
gk = 36
el = 10.6
gl = 0.3


def upd (x, dlta_x):
    return (x + dlta_x * dt)

def mnh0 (a,b):
    return (a / (a +b))


def am   (v) : return ((2.5 - 0.1*v) / (m.exp (2.5 - 0.1*v) - 1))
def bm   (v) : return (4 * m.exp((-1)* v / 18))
def an   (v) : return ((0.1 -0.01 * v) / (m.exp(1 - (0.1 * v)) - 1) )
def bn   (v) : return ( 0.125 / m.exp((-1) * v/80))
def ah   (v) : return ( 0.07 * m.exp ((-1)* v/20))
def bh   (v) : return ( 1/(m.exp(3 - (0.1)* v) +1))


am0 = am (0)
bm0 = bm (0)
an0 = an (0)
bn0 = bn (0)
ah0 = ah (0)
bh0 = bh (0)

m0 = mnh0(am0,bm0)
n0 = mnh0(an0,bn0)
h0 = mnh0(ah0,bh0)


def ina (m, h, v):
    return(gna * (m ** 3) * h * (v - ena))
def ik (n,v):
    return(gk * (n ** 4) * (v - ek))
```

```
def il (v):
    return(gl * (v − el))


def newS (v, m, n, h, t):
    if (t < 5.0) or (t > 6.0):
        istim = 0.0
    else:
        istim = 20.0
    dv = (istim − (ina (m, h, v) + ik( n, v) + il (v)))
    dm = am (v) * (1 − m) − bm (v) * m
    dn = an (v) * (1 − n) − bn (v) * n
    dh = ah (v) * (1 − h) − bh (v) * h
    vp =   upd(v,  dv)
    tp = t + dt
    mp = upd (m, dm)
    np = upd (n, dn)
    hp = upd (h, dh)
    return (vp ,mp, np ,hp , tp )


vs = []
ms = []
ns = []
hs = []
ts = []
a ,b ,c ,d ,e = newS( vinit ,m0, n0 ,h0 ,0.0)
vs . append (a )
ms . append (b )
ns . append (c )
hs . append (d )
ts . append (e )
for i in (range (2 ,3000)):
    a ,b ,c ,d ,e = newS(vs[−1],ms[−1],ns [−1],hs [−1], ts [−1])
    vs . append (a )
    ms . append (b )
    ns . append (c )
    hs . append (d )
    ts . append (e )

pyl . plot (ts , vs )
pyl . show ()
```

If you save this script on your computer, say with the name handh.py, you will be able to run it from a command line with python2 handh.py. If you have the two libraries that are imported, then you will see a voltage trace of an action potential on your screen. Let's walk through what is happening in this code.

In the beginning we import the plotting library and a mathematics library that we need in order to be able to take an exponential. After this we set the variables we will be using to represent the constants.

Following this there are a series of statements that begin with the word def. This is the Python keyword for defining a function. When Python sees this it knows that the next word will be the name of a new function and that the parentheses after this word will enclose local variables to be used inside this function. The colon then starts the actual operations of the function.

Our first function defines our updating rule: upd. We can use this function any time we have something to update. It makes it clear that we are using the same formula for every update, and it means that we can reuse code. We don't have to reinvent the wheel each time we need a new value. If we write this correctly once, it will be correct every time.

Many of the functions that follow are one-liners. We could have simply substituted the operations wherever the name of the function appears. But the way we have done it makes our code more readable. We do not have long strings of mathematics, but a sequence of simple statements. If we selected our names well, a person could tell what our code was doing even if they did not understand all the details of the operations.

Python requires that we first declare a variable or a function before we can use it. The order matters. This explains the gradual way that we go about developing our code.

Our big function is the newS function which gets the new values from the old values and incorporates all our updates. It is sort of like one big long row of the spreadsheet, but the organization makes it easier to follow what is happening. Note that we begin this function with an if statement to select the value for our current so that we have a transient pulse early on. This is not the only way to do this, just one particular way. Almost always there are many ways to program the same basic routine, and what you choose will depend on your style and the purpose of the program.

At the end of our program we loop through a series of rows using the last prior values and appending these to lists we have created for this purpose. From there it is a simple matter to generate and view a plot.

8.1   Conclusion

You have now seen the principal features of imperative programming. There are methods to declare variables that can be constant or changing. There are *control* structures, like if statements, that make our program do one thing or another as a result of certain conditions. There are also loops that automate the performance of repetitive tasks, what computers are best at. On top of these there are our own defined functions that let us encapsulate particular procedures we would like our program to do, and that do so in a way that makes them portable and reusable. Lastly, we access libraries that give us easy access to additional functionality without us having to write our own routines.

If you have succeeded in programming these early exercises in a spreadsheet you have an understanding of the algorithm. If you find the structure of the Python programs to offer advantages over a spreadsheet, pick a computer language of your choice and try to rewrite the exercise in that language.

Part II

Neural Networks

Chapter 9

Neural Network Mathematics: Vectors and Matrices

Objectives

After reading this chapter you will be able to:

- understand the topics that fall under the heading of linear algebra;
- know what a vector is;
- know what a matrix is; and
- perform simple operations, such as addition and multiplication, with vectors and matrices.

9.1 Overview

The preceding chapters began our study of computational methods by introducing DEs and their application to models of the cellular level, models that drew their inspiration from biophysical considerations. One step up from biologically realistic models of single neurons is to consider simplified versions that obey simple rules to determine if they are "on" or "off." We can assemble these simple units into collections. Commonly, collections of simple on–off neurodes are called *neural networks*.

The relatively simple structure of these units and the rules for their combination make large networks computationally tractable, and an attractive setting to assess for properties that emerge with scale. Neural networks are used widely in computational modelling by both neuroscience and psychology. Some of the advances in this area are the result of a productive collaboration with computer science and physics. These disciplines have an expertise for mathematically analyzing large collections of simple elements. We use their tools when we assemble our collections of on–off units. The primary area of mathematics important for neural networks is *linear algebra*. Linear algebra is the mathematics of vectors and matrices. In this chapter I provide a brief fly-over of linear algebra. Then we examine how we can use these tools to develop our own versions of two types of simple neural networks: perceptrons and the Hopfield network.

9.2   Linear Algebra

Linear algebra is the branch of mathematics that deals with vectors and matrices. Like DEs, linear algebra is a broad domain of mathematics with many subdivisions and deep results. However, our needs are modest. A little familiarity with matrices will take our modelling a long way. Further, in many ways matrices are simpler than DEs, because the relevant operations are things like multiplication and addition, things we are already familiar with. We will have to learn new versions of these operations so that we can apply them to our new mathematical objects, but the concepts will be the same.

What Is a Vector?

We can think of vectors in several different ways, and these different ways may help us understand how to use vectors in different situations. A very direct way to think of a vector is as a list of numbers [1,2,3] (the resemblance to a Python list is intentional). However, it is better if we can think more generally. A richer conception of a vector is that it is a geometrical object, an arrow pointing into space. Think of the list of numbers as specifying the coordinates of the arrow's head in some coordinate space. The length of the numbers determines the *dimension* of the space. With this conception, our regular numbers can be seen as a special case of a vector with dimension 1. The points from the Cartesian plane (x, y) that we learned in secondary school are also vectors in a 2-D space.

The dimension of a vector can be arbitrarily large, even infinite, though in applications we stay finite. While it might seem complex to think of a vector as an arrow in a large, say 100-dimensional space, in another sense all vectors are just functions of two things: a direction and a magnitude. It does not matter how high the dimension of the space–a vector is just an arrow of a particular length pointing in a particular direction.

This geometric way to think of vectors as object in space with direction and magnitude helps us look for the qualitative behavior of equations involving matrices and vectors. From this point of view we can see that there are really only two things that we can do to a vector, geometrically speaking: change how long it is or change the direction it is pointing. All our mathematical operations on vectors, which make up the computations of neural networks, can be reconceived from this geometrical perspective.

Because vectors and matrices are the substrate of many neural network applications, we have to learn some basic notation and operations if we are to be able to make sense of the literature in this area. When a variable refers to a vector, instead of a single number (also called a *scalar*), it may be depicted as a lower case letter in a bold font, for example, **v**, or less commonly, with a little arrow on top, like $\vec{v}$.

Row or Column

When vectors are written out as a list of numbers it is conventional to place them between square brackets. It is also the convention that the orientation of this list is columnar (up and down). Row vectors exist, but they arise from *transposing* a column vector. You denote a transposed vector with a little "T" or apostrophe. To transpose means to to exchange rows with columns, and we will see this again with matrices.

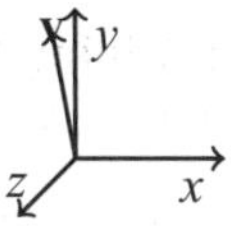

Figure 9.1 This is a visualization of a vector.

For example,

$$\mathbf{v} = \begin{bmatrix} 1 \\ 2 \\ 3 \end{bmatrix}$$

and

$$\mathbf{v}^T = \begin{bmatrix} 1 & 2 & 3 \end{bmatrix}$$

Matrices

If we think of vectors as collections of numbers that specify a point in space, we can think of matrices as collections of vectors. With the convention that vectors are aligned in columns, a matrix can be thought of as having several vectors aligned side by side. Just as we could transpose a single vector (converting a column vector into a row vector) we can also transpose a matrix converting every column into a row. When a variable specifies a matrix it is usually represented as a bold font capital letter, e.g. $\mathbf{M}$, with the transpose being written with a superscript "T" ($\mathbf{M}^T$).

If vectors live in a space, what defines the space? Other vectors. If you look at Figure 9.1 you will see that the coordinate axes could be thought of as vectors too. The x, y, and z vectors are orthogonal and we can construct any other vector in this space by adding up a little from each of them. Any collection of vectors that is sufficient to define any other vector in the space is called a *basis*. The x, y, and z axes are a basis for 3-D Cartesian space, but there are other bases, and although we usually think of the elements of a basis as being orthogonal (a higher dimensional version of perpendicular) they do not have to be.

9.3 Elementary Vector and Matrix Operations

There are a few fundamental operations that can be done on vectors and matrices. Since we will be using our spreadsheet programs to implement simple neural networks, the following exercises take us through the basics of how to do this with a spreadsheet as well as their general definition. I present the operations you should try to work through on your own. I present the answer immediately afterwards.

Exercise: Adding Matrices

Open up your spreadsheet program and write the addition of,

$$\begin{bmatrix} 1 & 2 \\ 3 & 4 \\ -4 & 6 \end{bmatrix} + \begin{bmatrix} 1 & 3 \\ 2 & 4 \\ -4 & 4 \end{bmatrix}$$

Adding vectors or matrices is just glorified addition. We add each term of one vector/matrix to the number in the same position of the other vector/matrix. This means that not every vector can be added to every other. They have to be the same size, otherwise they will not have numbers in exactly the same position for all possible positions:

$$\begin{bmatrix} 1 & 2 \\ 3 & 4 \\ -4 & 6 \end{bmatrix} + \begin{bmatrix} 1 & 3 \\ 2 & 4 \\ -4 & 4 \end{bmatrix} = \begin{bmatrix} 2 & 5 \\ 5 & 8 \\ -8 & 10 \end{bmatrix}$$

Multiplication by a Scalar

Use your spreadsheet to calculate the scaled vector

$$4 \times \begin{bmatrix} 1 \\ 2 \\ 3 \end{bmatrix}$$

When multiplying a matrix by a scalar, that is, a single number, you multiply each element of the matrix (or vector) by that same number:*

$$4 \times \begin{bmatrix} 1 \\ 2 \\ 3 \end{bmatrix} = \begin{bmatrix} 4 \\ 8 \\ 12 \end{bmatrix}$$

There is a spreadsheet shortcut for implementing this. You can use the formula "MMULT." Most spreadsheet programs have some version of this function. It will let you specify one collection of cells in the spreadsheet for a matrix and then another number as the scalar for multiplication.

9.4   Think Geometric

As alluded to above, a geometrical conception of vectors and matrices can help you acquire a great deal of insight into neural networks. Geometrically, vectors have direction and magnitude. To use those quantities we need to be able to calculate them. Another

---

*This is how you get subtraction. First, multiply by -1 then perform addition.

way of thinking of the term "magnitude" is as a vector's length. But before we can talk about how to compute a vector's length, we need to say what we mean by "length."

Something that refers to the size of mathematical objects is a *metric*. Metrics can be thought of as functions. They take a mathematical object as input and spit out a size. For a function to qualify as a metric it must obey a set of rules.

Metric Rules

- $d(x,y) \geq 0$
- $d(x,y) = 0, \Rightarrow x = y$
- $d(x,y) = d(y,x)$
- $d(z,x) \leq d(x,y) + d(y,z)$

Metrics cannot only tell us how big something is, but they can be used as a measure of distance. Therefore, I chose to use the letter d instead of f to emphasize that a metric function is related to distance.

We can repeat these rules in words:

- The function must give a size of at least zero when comparing two items; distance cannot be less than zero.
- If the distance between two things is zero, then they must be the same thing. Only one item per location.
- Whichever direction we go, the distance is the same. Running a lap on the track is the same distance whether I run clockwise or counterclockwise.
- Known as the triangle inequality, it is basically the same ideas as the old saying, "The shortest distance between two points is a straight line."

It is important to see that these rules do not tell you how to calculate the distance of something. The rules just tell you whether a function qualifies as a measure of distance. This abstractness is how higher mathematics gets its power, but it is also one of the reasons that non-mathematicians can feel at sea when dealing with mathematical ideas. The abstractness of the definition of a metric should suggest that there is more than one function that could qualify as a metric, but the lack of a specific example may leave you feeling uncertain about your understanding. When faced with abstract definitions, try to think of a concrete example in order to firm up your understanding. Just do not fall into the trap of thinking your concrete example is the sole example, or even the most important one.

A common distance metric is *Euclidean distance*. We used this in geometry to figure out the length of the hypotenuse of a right triangle. We squared each leg of the triangle, summed them together, and took the square root. We can do this for higher dimensions too:

$$\text{Length of vector } \mathbf{v} = \sqrt{\sum_{i=1}^{N} v_i^2} \qquad (9.1)$$

$$\begin{bmatrix} 1 \\ 2 \\ 3 \end{bmatrix} = \sqrt{1^2 + 2^2 + 3^2} = \sqrt{14}$$

If Euclidean distance is not the only metric, what other metrics are there? Try to think of how you would calculate distance on a sphere, like our globe. Does it make sense to use Euclidean distance on a curved surface? And what if you were in Manhattan? Would the distance between your favorite coffee shop and delicatessen be most accurately described by the Euclidean distance (as the crow flies) or by some other metric?

Inner Products

If you have taken any physics, you may have learned of the dot product operation for vectors. This is an example of a more general class of operations called an *inner product*. Like metrics, inner products are a sort of function that takes in objects, like vectors, and produces outputs like a scalar. Also, like metrics, "inner product" is a class where membership means obeying rules. We will not review the rules here, but it is worth knowing that the vector dot product is not the only example of an inner product, just like Euclidean distance is not the only example of a metric.

Vector Dot Product

The vector dot product is

$$\vec{x}^T \vec{y} = \sum_{i=1}^{\text{length of } \vec{x}} x_i y_i$$

In words this means that you match up the elements of the two vectors, same position, each with the other, and multiply them together. After this you add up the total. Note that the dot product takes in two vectors and spits out one number. It converts vectors to a scalar.

It should remind you of the formula for the length of a vector (Equation 9.1). Taking the square root of the dot product of a vector with itself gives you the length of the vector.

Matrix Multiplication

As a mnemonic you can think of matrix multiplication as taking a repeated sequence of vector dot products, but with more bookkeeping. Remember that vectors can be columns or rows. When we multiply a vector against a matrix or a matrix against another matrix, the rows of the first one match up against the columns of the second one.

In the example below we take the first row [1,2] from the left matrix and match it up to the first column of the second [1,2]. We then multiply the pairs of numbers ($1 \times 1, 2 \times 2$), and sum up to get the new number that goes into spot (1,1) of the matrix. That is, we compute the dot product. The answer then goes in spot (1,1) because we used row 1 of the first matrix and column 1 of the second matrix. When you see an index to a matrix, like (2,3), remember that rows always come first.

> If you are looking for a simple project for trying your hand at coding in a conventional computer language, see if you can write a function for computing the dot product between two lists of numbers.

Exercise: Matrix Multiplication in a Spreadsheet

Program your spreadsheet to multiply these two matrices:

$$\begin{bmatrix} 1 & 2 \\ 3 & 4 \\ -4 & 6 \\ -2 & 3 \end{bmatrix} \begin{bmatrix} 1 & 3 & 2 & 3 \\ 2 & 4 & 4 & -2 \end{bmatrix}$$

Did you use the "MMULT" function to make your life easier?

$$\begin{bmatrix} 1 & 2 \\ 3 & 4 \\ -4 & 6 \\ -2 & 3 \end{bmatrix} \begin{bmatrix} 1 & 3 & 2 & 3 \\ 2 & 4 & 4 & -2 \end{bmatrix} = \begin{bmatrix} 5 & 11 & 10 & -1 \\ 11 & 25 & 22 & 1 \\ 8 & 12 & 16 & -24 \\ 4 & 6 & 8 & -12 \end{bmatrix}$$

Based on this experience try to figure out why it is that you cannot multiply these two matrices together?

$$\begin{pmatrix} 1 & 2 \\ 3 & 4 \\ -4 & 6 \end{pmatrix} \begin{pmatrix} 1 & 3 \\ 2 & 4 \\ -4 & 4 \end{pmatrix}$$

If you are not sure, try it.

It is because the matrices are not of compatible sizes. There are not enough columns of the left matrix to match up with the number of rows in the second matrix. This is a repeat of what we saw with addition. Unlike scalars where any one number can be added or multiplied against any other number, for vectors and matrices only some of them can be added or multiplied to some of the others.

Another difference from conventional multiplication is that order matters. That is, you will not necessarily get the same answer if you change the order of matrices in a multiplication. A quick question to test your understanding is to try and guess what shape two matrices must have for the question of the order of multiplication to even be an issue. To prove that the order of multiplication does matter for matrices try, either with pencil and paper or with a spreadsheet, to multiply the following two matrices in both directions **AB** and **BA** where

$$\mathbf{A} = \begin{pmatrix} 1 & 2 \\ 3 & 4 \end{pmatrix}$$

$$\mathbf{B} = \begin{pmatrix} -1 & 2 \\ -3 & 4 \end{pmatrix}$$

Situation Normal

In many applications, the length of the vectors which are elements of the space is not pertinent to the questions being asked, and having vectors of different magnitudes may obscure important relations. To eliminate the problem you can make all the vectors the same size. Take a moment to pause and see if you can figure out how you might do this. The name given to this process is *normalization*.

Here I named the vector **u** just so you don't start thinking there is any reason that a vector has to be called **v**.

The formula is

$$\hat{u} = \frac{\vec{\mathbf{u}}}{||\vec{\mathbf{u}}||} = \frac{\vec{\mathbf{u}}}{\sqrt{\sum_{i=1}^{N} u_i^2}}$$

What is the length of a vector after this procedure?

If we follow this procedure for a collection of vectors, they will all be the same size. How do we then measure the distance between them? This is another example of a distance metric. If all the vectors have their feet anchored at the origin of the coordinate system, and if they are all the same length, the only thing that can be different between them is the direction in which they are pointing. How can we calculate the angles they make one to another? If the angle is zero, they are pointing in the same direction. If it is 90 degrees they are perpendicular. We do not need to get out our protractors for this problem, because there is a formula relating the dot product to trigonometry:

$$\vec{\mathbf{x}} \cdot \vec{\mathbf{y}} = ||\vec{\mathbf{x}}|| \, ||\vec{\mathbf{y}}|| \, \cos\theta \tag{9.2}$$

θ is the angle between the two vectors. Knowing this relation, can you determine what the angle between two vectors must be if $\vec{\mathbf{x}} \cdot \vec{\mathbf{y}} = 0$?

9.5   Functions for Matrices and Vectors

Just like there are functions for numbers, there are things that are like functions for vectors. Remember that our image of a function is as a machine that takes in a number and spits out another. This same metaphor can apply to a vector. A function for a vector would take in one vector and spit out another vector. Functions like this have the name *transformation*. Transformations are also special matrices. If you take a matrix of the proper size and multiply it against a vector you will get back a new vector. Thinking of a matrix as a function can be confusing at first, but it is powerful if you can absorb it. This is because it lets you think about matrices more generally, in terms of what they do, rather than some long, anonymous list of concatenated numbers. To help you develop this insight, figure out what the matrix

$$\begin{bmatrix} 4 & 0 \\ 0 & 4 \end{bmatrix}$$

does when multiplied against any vector of dimension 2.

And what kind of transformation does this matrix produce?

$$\begin{bmatrix} \cos\theta & \sin\theta \\ -\sin\theta & \cos\theta \end{bmatrix}$$

As another hint, try setting θ equal to 90 degrees and then sketch the answer.

Remember when considering your answers that a vector has both magnitude and direction.

9.6 Test Your Knowledge

To help you internalize some of these ideas about matrices, and to develop some knowledge of a few additional facts that will prove useful shortly, I have written a scavenger hunt of sorts. Using any old textbook, or even Wikipedia, try to find answers to the following questions:

1. What does it mean for a matrix to be invertible?

2. What is the transpose of a matrix?

3. What is an outer product? Compile a spreadsheet (or computer program) that performs this operation.

4. What does $[\mathbf{AB}]^\mathsf{T} =$ equal? Express your answer in terms of matrices $\mathbf{A}$ and $\mathbf{B}$.

9.7 Summary

This chapter has given you a quick glimpse of some essential facts about vectors and matrices that are commonly used in the field of neural networks. In addition, I presented some of the common notation and concepts. In the following chapters, I will develop the powerful idea behind neural networks, that complexity can emerge from collections of simple elements, and then we will develop our own simple neural network models.

Chapter 10

Intermezzo: Interactive Computing

When beginning to work on a computational program it is often useful to try out ideas by programming in an *interactive* mode. Interactive programming is not a type of language like imperative or functional, rather it is a style of programming where individual commands and statements can be entered one at a time and results immediately displayed. It is a useful method for exploring ideas or testing lines of code. It is also useful for *debugging*, the process where you check your code for accuracy.

Many modern programming languages can be used in an interactive mode. Sometimes it can be invoked directly at the command line, but many programming languages will also have an *integrated development environment* (IDE) that includes this capacity as one of its many aspects. The types of programming languages that cannot be run interactively, or at least not as directly, are those languages where programs must be *compiled* as opposed to those that are *interpreted*.

10.1   Compiling

Compiled languages take the entire program and send it to another computer program called a compiler. This compiler reads through the program, sometimes several times, and translates it into the language used by the particular type of machine that the program is to be used on. C and C++ are two examples of compiled languages. This means that if you write a program in C, you will have to compile it for the system on which it will be running. A C program compiled for Windows will not, generally, run on a computer running Linux or Mac OS X. In addition, if you compile a program to run on a computer with an Intel processor and the Linux operating system it will not typically work on your phone also running Linux, but using a different type of computer processor (e.g., ARM).

The advantage of compiling is that the code can be optimized for the operating system and computer hardware that will be executing the program. This can make programs that perform a lot of numerical processing much faster. However, it can lead to a slower development cycle since the procedure of revising your code, compiling your code, and then executing your code can be much slower.

10.2   Interpreting

On the other hand, interpreted languages read your code line by line and translate it into something executable by your machine as they go along. Because interpreted languages allow you to write and run code in this way, on a line-by-line basis, interpreted languages are also called *scripting* languages.

Because of the line-by-line translation, a computer program (i.e., code) written in an interpreted language does not typically execute as quickly as code written in a compiled language. However, this is often not relevant with today's computers. First, computers have become much more powerful, so that interpreted code is still fast enough to provide almost seamless execution for the human user. In addition, the development process can often be much faster for interpreted languages, making up for any slight decrease in execution speed. This advantage is especially true for small programs like the kinds we are writing here. Further, the ability to process your code and then test it in an interactive fashion often helps you develop insights about your computational project. This insight comes from being able to inspect and plot variables as you develop. Lastly, if execution speed ever does become an issue, a program written in an interpreted language can be rewritten in a compiled language. This rewriting often goes fairly quickly since the logic of the routines has been established.

Note, that the above statements are *generally* true, but many exceptions exist. For instance, many IDEs for compiled languages provide facilities for inspecting variables and stepping through the compilation process. In general, making use of such facilities requires an advanced understanding of computer programming.

10.3   Interpreted Languages for Linear Algebra

A popular interpreted language for matrix mathematics is MATLAB. The name MATLAB is a combination of the words Matrix Laboratory. MATLAB began as an educational tool to aid students learning linear algebra. It allowed them to use a computer to explore matrix operations without worrying about how to code a triple loop in the C programming language (a triple loop is needed to write a looped version of matrix multiplication).

Since that time The MathWorks, Inc. has developed the MATLAB language and its companion products (Simulink) into a widely used, industrial-grade programming environment for scientific and technical computing. While it is an excellent platform for this purpose, it can be costly. In an enterprise environment the quality and standardization may offer substantial advantages, but for smaller projects it may be just as efficient and far cheaper to use an open source alternative.

One of the options is Octave.[1] Octave is free to use and supports an interactive mode for exploring matrix operations. Octave and MATLAB are not the only options. Most programming languages have support for linear algebra. Many of these libraries reference the same set of optimized Fortran functions.

```
                                    britt@britt-fr07
octave:5> a = [1,2,3;3,4,5]
a =

   1   2   3
   3   4   5

octave:6> b = [[1;2],[3;4],[5;6]]
b =

   1   3   5
   2   4   6

octave:7> a'
ans =

   1   3
   2   4
   3   5

octave:8> a'*b
ans =

    7   15   23
   10   22   34
   13   29   45

octave:9> █
```

Figure 10.1 An interactive Octave session. The prompt is the text on the left of the screen with the ">" sign. The text to the right of the prompt is a record of what I typed in. Below is the result of Octave evaluating these statements. Two different ways of entering a matrix are shown. First, a comma is used to separate elements in a row, and a semi-colon to start a new row. The matrix b is created by gluing together a series of three column vectors. The apostrophe sign is the instruction for a transposition. Since Octave is designed for matrix operations, two matrices can be multiplied, if they are of compatible sizes, just by using the "*" sign.

10.4 An Introduction to Interacting at the Command Line

Windows, Mac OS X, and Linux all have command line or terminal programs that will support interactive programming. Usually you invoke the interactive mode of a language by typing its name (e.g., python2 or octave) at the terminal *prompt*. If you have Octave installed on your computer, you can try this for yourself and follow along with some of the examples. After you type octave you will see the prompt change. A prompt is the character or symbol that is along the left edge of your terminal window (Figure 10.1).

Figure 10.1 demonstrates a few basic commands for entering Octave commands and declaring variables. You can see how defining two square matrices would allow you to easily test for yourself whether $\mathbf{A} \times \mathbf{B}$ is equal to $\mathbf{B} \times \mathbf{A}$. Only a single counterexample is necessary to falsify the proposition.

One of the opportunities when using an interactive programming language is to write your own functions and then import them into the interactive space. Then you can run your own simulations in an interactive fashion. This procedure will be explored further in the next intermezzo (see page 97).

Chapter 11

An Introduction to Neural Networks

Objectives

After reading this chapter you should be able to:

- describe what neural networks are and how they are used;
- compute with simple cellular automata;
- solve a simple classification problem with a perceptron;
- understand the delta learning rule; and
- appreciate the limits of simple neural networks.

11.1   Overview

We have learned some of the procedures and notation important for working with vectors and matrices. We did this to be able to program a neural network. Before we do that, we should review what we mean by the term "neural network." What is a neural network? More importantly, what are the key ideas, at a non-mathematical level, which motivate this type of work? We will examine these two questions in this chapter and work towards a simple spreadsheet-based implementation.

11.2   What Are Neural Networks?

The answer to this question depends on context and scientific specialty. In biology, a neural network might well refer to a collection of real, physical neurons. For example, one could grow a collection of nerve cells on a microscope slide and see if they established synapses. If so, then they would have formed a network, and you could study its properties. In the computational literature a neural network usually refers to a collection of simple processing elements that are "wired" together in some way. Here the term "neural" is used to emphasize the neurobiological inspiration, but the connection to neurobiology may be quite remote. The term *connectionism* or *connectionist network* may be used to label a neural network that is only compared against behavioral, and not biological, data; an example of this is the interactive activation model of single word reading (McClelland & Rumelhart, 1981). The term *artificial neural network* is sometimes limited to refer to models that measure themselves against neuroscientific or neuropsychological data, and not behavior alone.

Neural networks can loosely be thought of as functions. Neural networks take in a vector or matrix of "inputs" and output a transformed version. We learned in the previous chapter that transformations of vectors may be matrices. A neural network can sometimes be thought of as a matrix, a matrix of weights. We will clarify this statement shortly. At their heart neural networks are mathematical methods for input:output mappings. In practice they usually share some subset of the following features:

1. They are inspired by biology, but are not expected to slavishly emulate biology.
2. They are implemented as computer programs.
3. They have "nodes" that play the role of neurons, collections of neurons, brain structures, or cognitive modules. Their role depends on the modeller's intent and the problem being modeled.
4. Nodes are interconnected: they have functional equivalents of "dendrites" and "axons."
5. The individual nodes produce outputs from inputs. The network's output is the collection of all these local operations.

There is not one canonical kind of neural network. Rather, there are many varieties of neural networks, all having some family resemblance according to the above criteria.

While most neural networks are inspired by some aspect of biology, many applications of neural networks are not intended to be models of biological or cognitive systems. Such neural network applications are simply meant to be practical solutions to practical questions. Their success is judged by performance and not biological verisimilitude. You might retrieve such articles when doing a literature search. It is important to remember this when determining if a particular approach is relevant for pursuing a neuroscientific or psychological question. We are usually interested in neural network approaches that emphasize neurological or cognitive phenomena and that are not simply used for a generic engineering purpose.

It may be natural at a first reading to think of the single node in a neural network as the network's representation for a neuron, but this should be reconsidered. It may be possible to regard a node in a neural network as depicting an individual neuron, and the inputs as analogues of individual dendritic subtrees, but it may be just as "correct" to think of the node as representing a population of neurons or even that it represents a cognitive module. For examples of this last sort it may not matter much if the neural network's procedures violate biology at the level of the local unit since we are not trying to match the network's node with our brain's neurons, but with some more abstract idea of neural or cognitive functioning.

II.3   Some Neural Network History

Treating neurons as computational abstractions has a history that precedes the computing age. One of the first advances was made by a collaboration between the neurophysiologist

Warren McCullough and Walter Pitts (McCulloch & Pitts, 1943). In 1943 they provided a mathematical demonstration that things like neurons, formally conceived, could compute, in principle, any computable function (see also Section 17.2 and the entry about Turing on page 164). While these results preceded the rise of the digital computer, it was with the digital computer that neural networks began to receive a wider hearing and broad application. The father of digital computing, John Von Neumann, was aware of the resemblance between digital computers and brains and of the work of McCullough and Pitts and their bipolar, on or off, formal neurons. Von Neumann discussed these relations in a series of lectures he was working on at the time of his early death from a brain tumor (Von Neumann, 1958). This work, written by one of the greatest minds in the history of humankind, is still worth reading for its ideas and insights. A brief biography of von Neumann is in the box below.

Von Neumann was explicit in discussing the connection between collections of simple off–on elements and the brain. It was Frank Rosenblatt who brought them into the heart of psychology (read Rosenblatt, 1960, for an introduction, and consult Rosenblatt, 1958, for a complete treatment). He emphasized the connection between computation and learning. Learning could be automatic and rule-based and still lead to interesting varieties of behavior. The dependence of this research on computing can be seen by looking at Rosenblatt's institutional affiliation: the Cornell Aeronautical Laboratory.

John von Neumann (1903–1957)

John von Neumann was a unique combination of intellect and *joie de vivre*, and one of a generation of great Hungarian mathematicians born in the early 1900s. He was a child prodigy who learned calculus by the age of 8 and mastered the German and Greek taught to him by a governess. He was taught in public schools and privately tutored, and published mathematical papers before he was 20. He acquired a PhD in mathematics and simultaneously, to please his father, a degree in chemical engineering. The fact that the universities from which he earned these two degrees were in two separate countries seems not to have been too much of a problem, since he obtained his PhD by age 22.

In 1930, he came to the Institute for Advanced Studies in Princeton, NJ (where Albert Einstein and Kurt Gödel were also appointed), and later became a US citizen. He continued his seminal work in pure mathematics, but also contributed to a wide range of other areas. Together with Oskar Morgenstern, he largely invented the field of game theory and made explicit game theory's relations to economics and other practical domains. He contributed to the US efforts to construct a nuclear weapon, and had time to play the *bon vivant* at frequent cocktail parties where he was a wit and good host. In addition to all this, he can be said to have invented computer science. He understood the possibility of self-reproducing machines, a simple example of which are cellular automata.

He died from brain cancer. Von Neumann was not religious, and his uncertainty in the face of death was extreme and a source of great anxiety and discomfort. Even on his death bed, his eidetic memory remained intact, and he is said to have entertained himself and his brother by reciting from memory the lines on specified pages of Göethe's *Faust*.

11.4   Global Structure from Local Interactions

Neural networks have global and local aspects. Just as the entire network produces an output for an input, so does each of the constituent nodes. The individual nodes typically have no access to the global state of the network or even information regarding what problem the network is programmed to solve. The component neurodes have only their local inputs and their individual rules as to how to process that input. The input comes into each node from other nodes within the system. The nodes send their output locally to other nodes through specified connections. In summary, a network can be thought of as a collection of little elements that each have a local rule for processing inputs to produce outputs. In addition, there is a matrix that encodes the connections between nodes in the network. The "meaning" of a network comes from outside the network. It comes from us, the users or programmers. Barring a bug in the programming, networks always give the "right" answer. We just may not like the answer. Whether the answer is *useful* is determined by us and the requirements of our application.

To rephrase, neural networks are collections of individual elements following local rules that give rise to global behavior of an interesting sort. How interesting depends on the person outside the network. An analogy is seeing the "wave" when it goes through the crowd at a football stadium. In this case, each gentleman spectator is following a local rule. He stands up when the people on one side of him stand up, and he sits down when they sit down. From his perspective the rule is local: "if these three people stand, I stand; if they sit down, I sit." The spectator receives an input, that is, they are standing or they are sitting, and he produces an output, that is, he stands or he sits. But viewed from outside this local perspective we can see a wave undulating around the perimeter of the stadium. This is the global behavior produced by the application of local rules in an interconnected network. We, looking from outside (or on the stadium's big screen), can see the global result, but it is emergent from our local actions and interactions.

11.5   Cellular Automata

My intention in this section is to give you a practical hands-on experience with the procedures of neural networks. We will observe interesting global structure produced by the labor of local, ignorant elements. We will do this by using pencil and paper to implement a simple rule-based system. The action of each cell in our network will be determined by the actions of nearby neighbors. None of these local elements will know what they are trying to produce. We can be sure of this, because you will be doing all the calculations for them and you will have no idea what the goal is, so how could a square on a sheet of graph paper?

This exercise uses cellular automata. Cellular automata have a lot in common with neural networks: local elements, local rules, connections, and global behavior. Cellular automata have been suggested as a general framework for computation and were featured in von Neumann's book on the brain.

For this exercise you will need a sheet of graph paper and a *rule*. Begin with the top row of the graph paper. Your rule will specify how the color of a square of the graph paper depends on the color of neighboring cells in the row immediately above

1	2	3
	?	

Figure 11.1   For the cellular automata classroom exercise, you decide whether a particular cell in the grid on your graph paper should be colored or not based on the three squares immediately above it and to the left and right.

(Figure 11.1). Our rule depends on three cells only and is like the gentleman at the football match deciding whether to stand or sit when making the wave. Each square in the grid of your graph paper decides whether to be blank or colored-in based on the three squares above it.

Exercise: Cellular Automata

1. Pick one of the rules from the choices in Figure 11.2.
2. Color in the very center square of the very top row of the graph paper.
3. Proceeding from left to right, color every square in the second row based on the rule you selected. In this row every cell will be left uncolored except for those near the center, because these rules all specify that a cell with three uncolored grids above remains uncolored. But how you treat the ones near the center will depend on the rule. For example, for rule 60, the cell immediately beneath the center, colored, square of row 1 will be colored, as will the one immediately to its right.
4. Repeat this process working down until you can clearly see the pattern, or give up in despair.
5. Compare your results from using different rules.

What this exercise illustrates is that remarkable global structure can emerge from the consistent application of simple rules. By analogy think of a neuron computing whether or not to spike based on the input it receives from a small set of neighbors. A spike becomes a decision, like whether or not to color a grid of the graph paper. The neuron does not need to know the global objective in order to do its job properly. The global structure takes care of itself.

How many rules are there? This is an exercise in combinatorics, the field of mathematics for computing combinations. You know how many inputs there can be: there are three cells and each can be white or gray, $2 \times 2 \times 2 = 8$. But how many output patterns are there that each rule can be matched with?

This example also emphasizes the components of many neural networks. Each grid square is a node. It took inputs, the colors of the three squares above it, and it (or rather you) computed its output: its color. The connectivity was implicit in the structure we used. Each node (grid cell) was wired to the three nodes, and only those three nodes, above it (for its input) and wired for output to the node directly beneath it and one to either

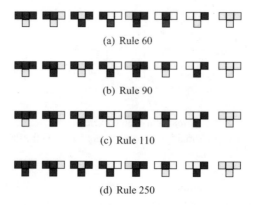

(a) Rule 60

(b) Rule 90

(c) Rule 110

(d) Rule 250

Figure 11.2   For the cellular automata classroom exercise, you decide whether a particular cell in the grid of your graph paper should be colored or not based on the three squares immediately above it and to the left and right. Take rule 90 as an example. If all three squares on one line are colored, then the square on the next line below that falls directly underneath is uncolored. For each line, and working left to right, look at the three cells directly above, one to the left, and one to the right. Then, based on the patterns in this figure, color in, or leave white, the cell you are working on. Then move one cell to the right, and repeat. At the end of each line, move over to the far left, drop down one line, and repeat.

side. If we change the connections, we change the network. If we change the rule for coloring, we change the network. There is nothing special or necessary about choosing to use three cells. In fact, von Neumann used a different, more complex architecture. Some mathematicians argue that such simple programs can give rise to all of our complex world (Wolfram, 2002).

11.6   The Perceptron

Although the cellular automata example captures many of the features of a neural network, it is not typically what people mean when they refer to a neural network. To begin our programming of a neural network, we will start with one of the oldest and simplest examples: Rosenblatt's *perceptron*.*

Rosenblatt took the rules that we have already seen, and added an important amendment. He provided a way for the elements to change or learn. He expanded the purview of the automatic local rules to include instructions for altering the output of a node based on experience. This idea was extended for many other types of networks. Often the focus is on the connection strengths between nodes. This is true of Rosenblatt's network too, but we must see the connections as existing between a layer of nodes that communicate the inputs from the outside world into our perceptron

Neural network learning mechanisms divide neural networks into two classes: supervised and unsupervised. In *supervised* learning there is a right answer. After each run of the network, the performance of the network is assessed by comparing the output of the

---

*Named, as you might guess, to suggest a combination of automaton and perception.

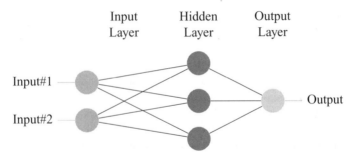

Figure 11.3 A simple neural network architecture. Two input units pass the data along to each of the three intermediate, "Hidden", nodes. In turn, after processing their input, each of the three hidden nodes sends its output to the output unit. This unit computes the final output of the network. For a supervised network this output is compared to the desired output and used to update the connection strengths between nodes.

network to the correct output. This comparison results in some feedback to the network that adjusts its future output to the same input so that it more closely approximates the correct answer. This adjustment procedure may be automated, but the idea of supervision invokes something external to the network that "knows" what the network is supposed to output and teaches it, as a teacher supervises and instructs a classroom. *Unsupervised* learning algorithms adjust future network outputs via an automated method that does not require the network to be given access to the true, correct answers. How this might work will be seen in the next chapter, which covers Hopfield networks (Chapter 13).

The Connection Between Neural Networks and Vectors and Matrices

It is common to conceptualize a neural network as a graphical-like structure or even as a physical "thing," some collage of balls and strings (Figure 11.3). While this can be useful for planning purposes, the actual programming of a network benefits from thinking of the actual computations. Neural networks are ultimately just numbers and equations. And those numbers and equations live in the world of linear algebra.

For the graphical structure in Figure 11.3 the input would be two numbers. We can represent these two numbers as a 2-D vector, for example,

$$\begin{bmatrix} 1 \\ 0 \end{bmatrix}$$

where each of the input nodes connects to each of the hidden nodes. We imagine a sort of gate that filters the input to the hidden node. This is called a weight. How do we represent the weights that regulate the strength of each input node's connection to each hidden unit? Remember that we described a neural network as transforming input vectors to new outputs. The output of the hidden layer will be, in this case, a 3-D vector. What transforms vectors? Matrices. The weights are represented as a weight matrix. For example,

$$\begin{bmatrix} 0.5 & 0.2 \\ -0.3 & 0.7 \\ 0.01 & -1.1 \end{bmatrix}$$

These numbers are not special. I just made them up to make the example concrete. Since we are dealing with vectors and matrices, we have to think about whether a vector is a row or a column of the matrix. Since we learned that the order of multiplication is important, we also have to decide if the weight matrix will be to the left of the vector or to its right. These are conventions we decide at the outset when programming our network in the language of linear algebra.

In this example, I have set each row of the weight matrix so that each hidden unit is a row, and the two numbers in each row represent the weight of its connection to the top and bottom input units. Each of the input units connects to each of the hidden units. For example, the element in the second row, first column represents the weight connecting our first input to the second hidden unit. To find the input activation for a hidden node we multiply the matrix (on the left) against the column vector (on the right). (Can you figure out the answer? It is in the note in the margin.) This column vector has one element for each of the three hidden nodes. By chaining operations like these together, we can have a compact representation that would take a lot of space to present graphically. Also, this gives us clear guidance on how to program a neural network.

Neural Networks and Geometry

The answer to the question about the activity of the hidden units is: 0.5, –0.3, 0.01?

In the prior chapter, I emphasized the value of thinking of a vector as a geometric object, an arrow with direction and length, and to think of matrices as transformations. This geometric orientation becomes useful for understanding the qualitative behavior of neural networks. This type of thinking, though, is easier said than done, and it is a challenge in the beginning. If we succeed, however, it means we will visualize our inputs as little arrows pointing in some direction in a space. Similarly, we will see the weight matrix as a way to move our vector around in space. The repeated application of weights to inputs will create a trajectory: a path of migration for our vector in space. We can visualize the learning process as moving one or another of the components of our network through this space. Before we get too high level, though, it is always good to make sure we understand how to perform the basic operations. We begin our work with the perceptron using a pencil and paper example:

Perceptron Learning Rule

$$I = \sum_{i=1}^{n} w_i x_i$$

$$y = \begin{cases} +1, & \text{if } I \geq T \\ -1, & \text{if } I < T \end{cases}$$

$$\mathbf{w}_{\text{new}} = \mathbf{w}_{\text{old}} + \beta y \mathbf{x}$$

$$\beta = \begin{cases} +1, & \text{if answer correct} \\ -1, & \text{if answer incorrect} \end{cases}$$

Table 11.1   Data for perceptron classroom exercise (adapted from Caudill & Butler, 1992).

Class	Input 1	Input 2	Correct output
A	0.3	0.7	1
B	−0.6	0.3	−1
A	0.7	0.3	1
B	−0.2	−0.8	−1

I will try to explain the rule in words. Between the equations and the description you should be able to puzzle it out. The "sigma" is the sign to add up things. The things to be added up are specified by the sub- and superscripts of the $\sum$ sign. The rule is for a single perceptron. The weight connecting it to the input is multiplied against the value of the input and all are summed up. This is like a dot product. Then this total is compared to a threshold, T, and the output of the perceptron is determined by whether it is above the threshold. We could make the output binary (1 or 0), but it is more convenient here to use the bipolar system of 1 or −1. The threshold is ours to choose, but we will often use zero. Next, we compare the output of our perceptron to what it should have been. This makes the learning rule a supervised learning rule. The value of the weight of the perceptron gets adjusted up or down depending on what we wanted, what we got, and what weight we were using before. From a repetitive application of this rule we will home in on the correct answer.

This rule highlights another characteristic of many neural network procedures. The processing of the nodes is typically a two-stage process. First, each node computes the net input it receives. This is the matrix operation of multiplying its weight vector against the input vector to get a weighted sum of the inputs. This calculation of the input activation is then followed by a *non-linearity*. This is a function that takes the net input and converts it to an activation that becomes the nodes' output. It is called a non-linearity because the plot of how inputs becomes activations would not generate the graph of a line. In this case all the values less than zero on the x axis would be −1 and then there would be a straight line up to +1 at T. Such a function is called a "step function."

Our example problem will use a single perceptron. Admittedly, a network of one unit is a very small neural network, but when tackling a new computational topic it is often advisable to start with the simplest example one can think of, and scale up as the problem requires and as one's understanding improves. If it helps our pride, we can think of this example as a two-layer network in which the first layer is the layer of units that translate from the outside world into the language of our perceptron. These are the input units.

Exercise: Manual Calculation of a Perceptron

Using the following inputs (Table 11.1) and the matching answers, train a single perceptron to solve this classification problem starting with weights = $(-0.6, 0.8)$.

This exercise can be a bit of challenge to get started with. Here is the first step worked through:

$$\vec{w} \cdot \mathbf{A}_1^T = -0.6 \times 0.3 + 0.8 \times 0.7 = -0.18 + 0.56 = 0.38$$

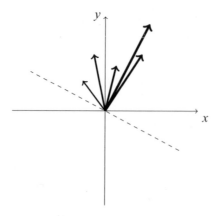

Figure 11.4   Interpreting the perceptron's weight vector. This plot uses the two elements of the weight vector as the (x, y) pair for points on a Cartesian plane. At each iteration of the perceptron learning process, the line gets thicker, and you can see how its direction changes. This allows you to exercise your geometric interpretation of vectors as arrows pointing in a space. The dashed line shows the perpendicular to the final weight vector. This is the decision plane. Every point on the same side as the weight vector will yield a positive number when multiplied against the weights, and every point on the other side will yield a negative number. The basis for this fact lies in trigonometry. There is a relation between the dot product of two vectors and the cosine of the angle between them (see Equation 9.2; page 74).

Since $I = 0.38$ is greater than or equal to zero, $y = +1$ and $\beta = +1$ the answer is correct, that is, we observed the desired output listed in our table. To update the weights we apply the perceptron rule:

$$[-0.6, 0.8] + (+1)(+1)[0.3, 0.7] = [-0.3, 1.5]$$

After doing the same for each of the three remaining patterns, test to see if the final weights correctly classify the four test patterns into their two respective groups (they should). You perform this by deriving y and comparing it to the desired output without further changes to the weight vector (Figure 11.4).

11.7   Another Learning Rule: The Delta Rule

The different types of neural networks can vary along a number of different dimensions. One way in which different flavors of neural networks come about is to change the learning rule the units use. The delta rule is an example of this. It makes a more elaborate use of Perceptron-like nodes. The delta rule is an example of using an *error signal*. An error signal is the amount that we are in error when generating the output. We compute the output our neural network unit gives us and subtract this from the output we wanted, and this difference is our error. We update our weights based on this value. To some degree, the use of the delta rule is similar to a linear regression model. In linear regression we weight the independent variables and sum them together to get an estimate of our dependent variable. With the delta rule we are finding the right weight for our inputs so as to produce the proper output. This analogy is not simply conceptual.

Because we are using the data to train the network, we risk the problem of over-fitting. We might train our neural network to solve a problem using a particular set of training data, and it might be perfect, but all we might have done is succeed in training it to detect some random variation in the particular examples we have selected for training. What we want to do is to use our neural network to extract some general characteristics of the data that distinguish two classes of inputs, for all examples of those input classes, not just the particular examples we trained on.

To control for this risk, it is common practice to have both a training set and a validation set. If data are not abundant, one can take the available data and arbitrarily divide these into two portions: one for testing and one for validation.

We will explore the use of both the validation samples and the delta rule in this next example.

Exercise: Delta Rule, Testing, and Validation

This exercise has several steps and will require patience on your part. It may be easier to follow the steps if you first have an overall view of the exercise's goals. I want you to develop the idea of *surrogate* data: data created by a procedure that matches the process of interest. I want you to develop test and validation samples. I want you to use random numbers to generate your data rather than hand-coding a particular example. This allows you to run the same process over and over, to test for consistency. And I want you to train a simple neural network classifier.

For these goals we will calculate a line of random slope and intercept. This line will be the "true" division between our two classes of points. We will shift some points of the line up and others down to create our two stimulus classes. We will use ten of this set (five examples from each class: the ups and the downs) to train and another ten (again five of each) to validate.

1. Use the random function in your spreadsheet program to generate a random slope and intercept for a line (e.g., =rand()). After doing this, you will need to copy and paste *values* to keep the spreadsheet from changing the random values every time you update the spreadsheet.

2. Use the random function to generate 20 random x values. You might wish to scale these numbers to be from –20 to 20 (or something similar, e.g., =rand() * 40 – 20).

3. Use the equation of a line ($y = mx + b$, substituting your random slope and intercept from above) to calculate the location on the line for each of your randomly selected x positions.

4. Again, use the random function, and remembering to cut and paste *values* shift half the y values above the line by a random amount, and the other half below by a random amount.

(Continued)

(Continued)

5. Create a column that will code the classes of your points: +1 for above the line, and −1 for below the line.

6. Use the first five examples of each set as the training set, holding the other ten in reserve for validation.

7. The neurode you will be building will have weights for both inputs and *a bias term*. Therefore, in addition to your two inputs x and y you will have a third input called the bias that also will have a weight. You can set the bias to 1 for each pattern.

8. To compute the activation of your unit multiply the three inputs for a pattern (x, y, and bias) against three, initially random, weights (w1,w2,w3), and sum the results. Set a threshold of 0 and code the outputs as greater than or equal to the threshold or less than the threshold.

9. Use the delta rule (Equation 11.1) for updating the weight vector after each pattern.

10. You use only a single, 3-D weight vector for your classifier. Those three weights change after it has seen each training pattern.

11. Continue to loop through all the training patterns until the neurode classifies all the training patterns correctly.

12. Then "freeze" the weights. This means they no longer change. Test how well your network did on classifying each of the validation patterns that you kept in reserve.

$$\Delta w_i = x_i \eta(\text{ desired} - \text{observed}) \qquad (11.1)$$

How do we know that the delta rule guarantees that the weights will stop changing if the perceptron matches all the inputs to their correct answers?

What the delta rule says in words is that we take the value we should have gotten (assume we are training on a class +1 pattern), and subtract what we got, say 0, from it. Then we multiply this error signal by a learning rate called η. η (pronounced "eta" not "nu") that is usually a small number, say 0.1. We multiply the result against the input. Since our input has multiple elements we need to keep track of which one we are using, hence the subscript i. We multiply all this together to get the amount that we change the weight for that input. All of this can be done in a spreadsheet. If you know how to use macros, you can make repeating the steps easier. In an intermezzo (Chapter 12), I show you how this can be programmed using Octave.

Additional Explorations

Once you have the basic method implemented, examine how the accuracy of your classification of the validation patterns improves if you put the training points close to the decision line, or far away. How does this interact with the number of training patterns? Plot the line that is at a 90 degree angle to the final weight vector and see how closely

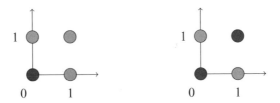

Figure 11.5 Linear separability. On the left we have a schematic illustration of the OR function. For each of two items, think apples and oranges, we have two possibilities: we have them or we do not. If not, we enter a zero; if so, a one. Each point corresponds to one of the situations. If a point is gray it means that the statement that we have apples OR oranges is true. On the right we illustrate the XOR Boolean operation. It is only true if we have apples or oranges, but not both (this makes it eXclusively OR). On this side it is impossible to draw a single line that separates the black and gray dots.

it tracks the true answer (which we know to be the random line you used to generate the division between the two classes of data). Why isn't the fit perfect? An additional exploration would be to look at the similarity between perceptrons and *support vector machines* (Collobert & Bengio, 2004). Support vector machines (SVMs) are a popular method for classifying and clustering data that relies on finding the right vectors to properly partition a space with a large number of vectors from more than one class. SVMs are widely used in machine learning applications, and would make an excellent topic for extending the ideas learned in our perceptron section.

11.8   Why Aren't Perceptrons the Only Type of Neural Networks?

To get the answer to this question, it helps to first consider a simpler one: Why did we use a line as the basis for creating our two populations in the last exercise? When we use a line to create the border between two classes, the classes become *linearly separable*. Linear separability is very important in the field of neural networks. Figure 11.5 demonstrates linearly separability.

When we use a perceptron-like neural network unit, the weight vector of that unit creates a virtual decision plane at a 90 degree angle to itself. All points on one side are above a zero threshold, and all values on the other side are below a zero threshold. Because of this, a perceptron can only correctly classify data that are able to be separated by some plane running in some direction. Perceptrons are limited to solving linearly separable problems.

In a famous book, *Perceptrons*, Minsky and Papert (1969) demonstrated that perceptrons were limited to this class of linearly separable problems. What is more, they showed that many apparently easy problems were not linearly separable. The *XOR* problem, illustrated on the right of Figure 11.5, is one example of a non-linearly separable problem. Because it was felt that interesting problems were likely to be non-linearly separable, a cold wind blew over the field of neural networks and limited the amount of research and the interest in neural networks for nearly 20 years.

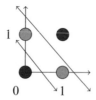

Figure 11.6   Multi-layer perceptron. This is the XOR again. Note that these two lines isolate the gray points between them. If we had an OR perceptron to classify all points above the lower line, and another perceptron (what would it represent in Boolean terminology (see Chapter 17 for more on Boolean functions)?) to classify the points that fell below it, we could feed the output of each to another perceptron that would classify points that were above line 1 AND below line 2, and we would have solved the XOR problem.

   The way to overcome this limitation of single layer perceptron networks is to develop multi-layer perceptron networks. While a single perceptron layer is limited to a single decision plane, multiple layers can use multiple planes, and the combinations of these planes can effectively carve the space into the compartments needed to solve many non-linearly separable problems.

   Figure 11.6 illustrates how this works. We use multiple perceptrons to create multiple subsets of our data. Then we test for combinations of those divisions with yet other perceptrons to find the appropriate set of conjunctions. The construction of multi-layered perceptrons makes the problem-solving capabilities of perceptrons more powerful and more general. However, their practical utility is limited by the fact that we have to know how to train each of the subsets. We need to know the correct mappings in order to build the correct separations.

   To test your understanding, you can try your hand at solving the XOR problem manually. If you have a good understanding of the decision planes needed, then with a little trial and error you could manually discover sets of weights sufficient for a three-perceptron network (two in layer 1, and one in layer 2) to be able to solve all the inputs of the XOR problem.

11.9   Summary

Neural networks are a fascinating addition to the computational toolkit of neuroscientists and psychologists. They can be used for very practical problems, such as discovering clusters in data or sub-categorizing complex data sets, and as we will see in the next chapter, they can probe in highly original ways basic cognitive functions. They may point the way for discovering, at a functional level, principles of cognitive and neural operations.

   However, we have only scratched the surface by beginning with one of the earliest and most basic examples of neural networks. Still, it is sufficient to demonstrate some of the advantages and disadvantages of this approach. The advantages include that fact that it provides a concrete demonstration that simple rules alone, when appropriately connected and trained, can produce complex behavior. A proof of concept, if you will, that maybe all we are is neurons. Practical disadvantages include the fact that actual simulations on interesting problems can take a *long* time. Further, although a particular network may solve a problem, the "reasons" why a network works may be opaque since it is, in a sense, contained in the pattern of weights (connection strengths) between units. An additional disadvantage is that if we are not careful we can make networks that are too good. They succeed because we have over-fit and are trained on the noise in our data. Such networks will not generalize.

In the next chapter we develop the Hopfield network. This is a network that works through its interconnections. It has the ability to remember and to correct errors, and it is an example of how interdisciplinary research expands understanding. The Hopfield network shows how the tools of mathematical physics can be brought to psychology, and the result is an ability to prove things with a definiteness that had eluded all workers since Fechner.

Chapter 12

Intermezzo: Interactive Exploration of the Delta Rule with Octave

Many of the instructions for the delta rule exercise can be challenging to implement in a basic spreadsheet. In order to provide a concrete example of how to approach this exercise, and to demonstrate the use of an interactive programming environment, I will complete this exercise using the Octave programming language.

12.1 Writing Functions

On page 61 I introduced you to writing functions in a computing language. Here we will extend this idea by writing several functions to help us with the delta rule exercise, and then we will run these from the command line in an interactive session to actually solve the exercise.

Listing 12.1 A simple function in Octave

```
function [m,b] = mkLine()
  m = rand();
  b = rand();
endfunction
```

This first function shows the basic syntax for an Octave function. It begins with the keyword `function` and concludes the block with `endfunction`. In addition, we have to name the output arguments (on the left of the equals sign) and the name of the function and input arguments on the right-hand side. Here there are no input arguments and that is why the parentheses are empty. We generate two random numbers using a built-in Octave function `rand`. Notice that the variables are the same as the two names to the left of the equals sign. This is how Octave knows what variables from the function to return to the calling interpreted session. We will see that at work in a moment. One last thing to notice is the use of the semi-colons. This suppresses an "echo." Without the semi-colons, Octave would print the result of each line to our command terminal. To see what this means, type in the above function without the semi-colons. Then open a terminal and *source* your file.

Computer programming languages with interpreters will give you a method for getting your code loaded into the interpreted session. The keywords are usually something
like "load" or "source" or "read". Octave uses source. If you called the file myOct.m
(".m" is the extension used for Octave files), and you stored the file in your home directory, you would then open a terminal and type Octave to start an Octave session, and
then source("/home/britt/myOct.m") to read in your function. Then you should
be able to type [slope,intercept] = mkLine() and you will have two variables
in your workspace for the slope and intercept of a randomly chosen line. I will now
present the rest of the functions we will use in a single listing and then explain their use
afterwards.

12.2   Octave Functions for the Delta Rule Exercise

Listing 12.2   All the Octave functions for the delta rule exercise

```
function  [m,b]  =  mkLine ()
   m  =  rand ();
   b  =  rand ();
endfunction

function  x  =  mkXs (n)
   x  =  rand(n,1)*  40  −  20;
endfunction


function  ymat  =  mkYs(m,b,xs)
   ys  =  m*xs  +  b;
   cl  =  repmat([1;−1],length(xs)/2,1);
   yp  =  ys  +  5*rand(length(xs),1).*  cl;
ymat  =  [cl,ys,xs,yp,repmat([1],size(xs))];
endfunction

function  o  =  compOut(t,wv,iv)
   a  =  wv*iv ';
   if  (a  >=  t)
      o  =  1;
   else
      o  =  (−1);
   endif
endfunction

function  nwv  =  dR  (eta,obs,des,iv,wv)
   nwv  =  eta  *  (des  −  obs)*  iv  +  wv;
endfunction
```

```
function nwv = oneLoop (t,eta,cls,iv,wv)
   obs = compOut(t,wv,iv);
   nwv = dR (eta,obs,cls,iv,wv);
endfunction

function nwv = onePass (dataMat,wv,eta,t)
   for i = (1:length(dataMat(:,1)))
      wv =oneLoop(t,eta,dataMat(i,1), \
         [dataMat(i,3),dataMat(i,4),dataMat(i,5)],wv);
   endfor
   nwv = wv;
endfunction

function nwv = train(dataMat,wv,eta,t)
   epsilon = 0.001
   owv = [0,0,0];
   nwv = wv;
   loopCnt = 1
   while (sum(abs(nwv - owv))> epsilon)
      loopCnt
      owv = nwv
      nwv = onePass(dataMat,nwv,eta,t);
   endwhile
endfunction
```

12.3   Using Octave to Solve the Delta Rule Exercise

First, create a file with the above functions. Give it a name ending in ".m" and then open a terminal and source your file. Now, if there were no typos, you should have all these functions available to you in your Octave session. Octave offers a diary function that allows you to save a transcript of your session. You invoke this by typing `diary on`. The following lines came from the diary of my interactive session.

First, I sourced my file. Then I used the functions above to create a random line, generate a series of 20 random x locations, and with those outputs create all the other columns of a data matrix. It has the "true" y points, the adjusted y points, and the class of each point (you can think of each point as a row in the data matrix):

```
octave:2> source("/home/britt/books/ICNPsych/code/octave/deltaRule.m")
octave:3> [s,i] = mkLine();
octave:4> xs = mkXs(20);
octave:5> dm = mkYs(s,i,xs);
```

Octave has a syntax that is convenient for letting us select subsets of the data in terms of either columns or rows of our matrix. In the next two lines I tell Octave that I want the first 10 rows, and all the columns (":" is a shortcut for "everything" and the numbers before the comma refer to rows and after the comma to columns) for the training set and the remainder for the test set:

```
octave:6> trainSet = dm(1:10,:);
octave:7> testSet = dm(11:20,:);
octave:8> saveWt = train(trainSet,rand(1,3),0.1,0);
```

My output weights from this operation are: -1.06406 2.71347 0.76049. We can test if they are correctly solving the problems by multiplying them against their inputs, thresholding, and using the fact that Octave uses 0 for FALSE and 1 for TRUE to recreate the class assignments. This is a tricky line of code, but it shows how I was able to cobble together something to let me check if things were working, and test it right away. In the section on page 49 we discussed the use of if statements in computer code. The line that follows uses a form of this if statement, but it is somewhat hidden. Inside the trainSet function I am comparing each element to the value of 0. *If* it is greater than zero, I get a value of 1. If it is less than zero, I get a value of 0. Then I do a little mathematics to convert the numbers to be either +1 or −1. This operation, where I check each entry and get two different values depending on whether a condition is, or is not, met, is called an *element-wise* if *statement.*

```
octave:9> (saveWt * trainSet(:,[3,4,5])' > 0) * 2 - 1
ans = 1 -1 1 -1 1 -1 1 -1 1 -1
```

We are perfect on the training set, but what about the test set?

```
octave:10> (saveWt * testSet(:,[3,4,5])' > 0) * 2 - 1
ans = 1 -1 1 1 1 1 -1 1 -1
```

As you can see, we do not do a very good job here. It shows the limits of trying to develop a general classifier from such a small set of examples.

Octave also offers plotting functions (Figure 12.1). Here is a simple one to visualize our data:

```
octave:13> h = plot(dm(:,3),dm(:,2),
dm(1:2:20,3),dm(1:2:20,4),'*',dm(2:2:20,3),dm(2:2:20,4),'d')
```

This intermezzo may seem a bit overwhelming on a first pass. Let's recap. We created a plain text file of functions that we want to be able to use. We wrote these in Octave, and then we imported them into an interactive session with the source command. Once in the interactive session we could use these to create our simulation by generating our random data and running the delta rule. We could use Octave facilities for plotting and keeping a transcript to have access to our data and explore these.

Is it realistic to think you will write something like this? I think so. The logic of the functions seems clearer than it does in a spreadsheet. You can break the exercise into its logical components one at a time. That is how I wrote these. I wrote the first function, sourced and tested. Only when that was working did I write the second function. Gradually, I built up the whole collection. One way to practice this would be to create

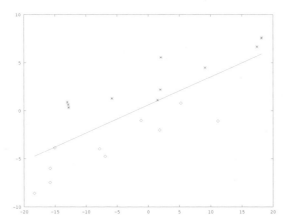

Figure 12.1 Plot of the sample data points. The line used for generating the data divides the two classes (shown with asterisks and diamonds). The plot was generated from Octave, but requires the GnuPlot program also to be installed.

a text file with all the same function names and arguments preserved, but all the details deleted. Then, working on one function at a time, recreate all the procedures.

Chapter 13

Auto-associative Memory and the Hopfield Net

Objectives

After reading this chapter you should be able to:

- compare the perceptron and Hopfield networks;
- understand how the Hopfield network can be considered a model of memory;
- understand the concept of a dynamical system;
- use different distance metrics; and
- create a simple implementation of the Hopfield net.

13.1   Overview

In this chapter we compare the Hopfield network to the perceptron and consider what it means for something to be a dynamical system. We then examine the Hopfield network in operation and look at how one can adapt the physicist's concept of energy to prove something about the capabilities of a neural network.

13.2   The Many Paths to Enlightenment

The multi-layered perceptron of Chapter 11 contains the core features of a neural network: there are elements (aka nodes, neurodes, or neurons), and these elements receive inputs that undergo a local summation and thresholding. The connections between the units are weighted. Although these features are common, they leave abundant room for variation. There can be variation in how connections are selected, maintained, and adjusted. There can be variation in the rules that individual nodes use for computing their activation and outputs. And there can be variation in how the network uses feedback from its activities to adjust future responses.

This approach is quite general and powerful. The perceptron, when wired together wisely and in multiple levels, can solve complex classification problems. But simply solving problems is the domain of the engineer rather than that of the computational psychologist. The goal of computational approaches in psychology or neuroscience is to use models to answer questions in such a way that we explore the implications of a particular theoretical approach. Our goal is not to learn whether some specific implementation of a network solves some specific example of a particular class of problems, but rather whether any network designed in accordance with a specific set of constraints could solve all examples of a particular class of problems. If not, what is the nature of its limits? It is in this way that we can we gain insights into cognitive operations through computational experimentation. But how does one do this in practice? How can one make statements about whether *any* network designed in a particular way can solve *any* example of a particular class of problems?

These are the questions and motivations that bring us to the simple version of the Hopfield network that is the focus for this chapter. Hopfield networks demonstrate memory and error correction. They show how our choices in network architecture can contribute to a better understanding of topics of psychological interest. An additional achievement of the Hopfield network is historical. John Hopfield demonstrated how the careful formulation of a problem allowed for the importation of tools from mathematics and physics. It allowed him to "prove" things about his networks with the definiteness of mathematics. No finite number of simulations could ever have achieved such certainty. This was a lesson for psychologists: these tools are powerful and we ought to learn more about them; but it was also useful for showing physicists and mathematicians the opportunities that were available to apply their computational techniques to problems in psychology and neuroscience.

13.3 Hopfield Networks: Similarities and Differences to the Perceptron

A Hopfield network is a *recurrent* network (Figure 13.1). By contrast, the multi-layer perceptron network before was *feed forward*. A recurrent network permits feedback from units that receive the input to the units that sent them this input. This is indicated in the Figure 13.1 by the bi-directional arrows. A recurrent structure has greater biological and psychological relevance because we know that most areas of the brain send feedback, or recurrent, projections to the areas that project to them. There is connection reciprocity: for example, the lateral geniculate nucleus of the thalamus sends projections to the primary visual cortex, and the primary visual cortex sends recurrent projections back to the lateral geniculate nucleus. In psychology, this idea is included in the concepts of bottom-up and top-down processing. The implication is that information flows in both directions.

When Hopfield (1982) published his network structure and analysis it was immediately recognized as a relevant model for memory. Hopfield also showed how physicists could use their mathematical tools to improve our ability to construct and analyze complex, computational characterizations of neural and cognitive systems.*

---

*Hopfield, a physicist, attended Swarthmore College as an undergraduate. There he took psychology from Wolfgang Köhler, the great Gestalt psychologist.

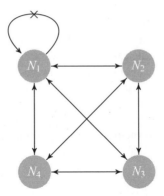

Figure 13.1   This is an elementary Hopfield network. All units connect reciprocally to every other neuron, *except* there are no self-connections. The Hopfield network is a single layer network.

A remarkable feature of the Hopfield network is its capacity for error correction and the ability to generate a complete output from an incomplete input. This also struck contemporary readers as psychologically relevant. For example, when a name is on the tip of your tongue, you might suddenly recall it when someone gives you only the first syllable. Or you might recall the face of a friend when a picture shows only their eyes. The kind of memory that allows you to use information to access other information, that is, where the content is used as the query to the system, is called content-addressable memory. This is in contrast to location-specific memory. In a computer, the latter is implemented by providing the address (i.e., the location) of the memory register you want the computer to look up. Content-addressable memory can be much faster. More importantly, it seems more human, and Hopfield's implementation of a content-addressable memory had obvious appeal for psychology. In addition to these appealing functional aspects of Hopfield networks, Hopfield also demonstrated how one could apply the mathematical tools from *dynamical systems theory* to the analysis of a neural network.

Dynamical Systems

Dynamical systems are a familiar concept even if the name is not. Things that change over time are *dynamic*. When we plot the location of an object as a function of time, we are generating the *trajectory* of a dynamical system. On airline flights it is now common to see a small map of the plane outlining the flight path and recording how much of the route has been covered. This is a plot of position as a function of time and it is quite literally the trajectory of your flight. The same kind of plot can be done for a computational system. For example, when we plotted the voltage of our Hodgkin–Huxley neuron as a function of time and current input, we were tracing out the trajectory of a dynamical system. It is not having an activation that makes a dynamical system. It is having something that changes over time that makes for a dynamical system.

If instead of considering a single trajectory, we plotted a representation of the many trajectories that would result from slight variations in our system, for example, as a result of altering the η or learning rate of the delta rule, we would generate a *phase plot*. This high-level view allows us to see particular points of interest in the *parameter space*, the points where interesting things happen. What is interesting depends on the system and our goals. Dynamical systems emphasize that understanding a system's behavior depends on knowing not only the input and eventual output, but also the path the system follows in between them. Learning rules can be viewed as dynamical systems.

13.4 Basic Structure of a Hopfield Network

A *parameter space* is a fancy way of discussing combinations of parameters. The parameter space is a "plot," like an (x, y) Cartesian plane, that depicts all combinations of the parameters as its points, with each parameter aligned along its own axis.

At its most basic, the Hopfield network is essentially a one-layer network. Inputs and outputs are read from the same units. They cascade their inputs to the other elements in the network, and receive feedback. The only exception to this full recurrence is that units never receive direct feedback of their own activity.

Although not depicted in Figure 13.1, each of the connections is filtered by a weight. For our purposes, these weights will always be symmetric. What this means is that if the output from unit A to B is weighted by 0.5, then the connection from unit B to A is also weighted by 0.5.

Mathematical Representation

All the words that I have been using to describe Hopfield networks can be replaced with a more concise equational representation. The activity of a unit called U_1 is

$$U_1 \times 0 + U_2 \times W_{1,2} + U_3 \times W_{1,3} + U_4 \times W_{1,4}$$

Exercise: Writing the Basic Equations

To verify your understanding of the equational representation of the activation of a Hopfield node, write the equation that expresses the activation of each of the other units in our simple four-unit network shown in Figure 13.1. And describe in words why there needs to be at least one zero in each of the equations.

Then, after having written it as four separate equations, rewrite all the equations as a single equation using matrices and vectors. What values will fall along the diagonal of the matrix (if you do not know what the diagonal of a matrix is, look that up first), and why does the **W** come first or does it even matter?

The matrix formulation for our network can be written as: $\mathbf{W}\vec{\mathbf{I}}$. This formulation comes with several advantages. One advantage is that we can say the same thing in a way that is much shorter. Do not underestimate the value of brevity for either a mathematical representation or a computer program. Shorter is good. The shorter the expression (or code), the less chance for confusion or a mistake. This makes it easier, usually, for human readers to understand what is going on. Those human readers may likely include you when you come back to a project or a program after a break of a few weeks or longer. This brevity does require a familiarity with the pertinent formalism.

One imprecision in this notation is that it implies that the updating of this network happens simultaneously. This is not typically the case for Hopfield networks, but for the time being this simplification works for our examples. Shortly, we will adopt asynchronous updating.

Do you agree that this association of vectors with vectors captures the spirit of the memory process as viewed by psychologists?

13.5   A Hopfield Network in Action

To make our points concretely, let's assume a specific input structure and inputs. Assume two input patterns $A = \{1, 0, 1, 0\}^T$ and $B = \{0, 1, 0, 1\}^T$, and a four-node network with a weight matrix of $\mathbf{W}$:

$$\begin{bmatrix} 0 & -3 & 3 & -3 \\ -3 & 0 & -3 & 3 \\ 3 & -3 & 0 & -3 \\ -3 & 3 & -3 & 0 \end{bmatrix}$$

Updating a Hopfield Network

Similar to our perceptron network (and many other networks) the Hopfield network uses a threshold non-linearity to convert activations into outputs. We will use the rule

$$output(\mathbf{W}\vec{\mathbf{I}}) = \begin{cases} 1 & \text{if } t \geq \Theta \\ 0 & \text{if } t < \Theta \end{cases}$$

Let $\Theta = 0$.

Exercise: Computing the Output of a Hopfield Network

Compute the output of our simple example network for each of the two inputs (A and B) shown above, and using the threshold updating rule. Then try to explain in words why you found what you did. What psychological term would you use to describe the ability for a single weight matrix to reliably produce these types of outputs for these types of inputs?

What would you predict the output of this Hopfield network to be for the input pattern $C = \{1, 0, 0, 0\}^T$ and why? Test your intuition.

The answer to the question in the prior exercise is that Hopfield networks are an example of *auto-association*. The ability of Hopfield networks to reliably and consistently produce a specific output for a specific input is one reason that the Hopfield network is taken as a computational model of memory. And why not? What is memory but the production of a particular output for a particular input.

Another Distance Metric

Recall the idea of a distance metric (see page 71). As we said at that time, a distance metric includes the Euclidean metric, but it is not limited to Euclidean distance measures. To see this, ask yourself whether the pattern *C* above is "closer" to the pattern *A* or *B* and say why.

For pairs of binary strings, how do the Hamming distance and Euclidean distance compare? Are they the same? Are they related? Do they preserve ordering?

To compare the Euclidean distance between a pair of vectors we could treat each as a point and then use the Euclidean rule for each component of the vector. We would calculate the differences between each pair of elements, square, total, and finally take the square root. But there are other distance metrics. One of these is the *Hamming distance*. The Hamming distance counts the number of locations where binary patterns differ. That is, we look to see how many ones should be zeros and vice versa. The number of these *flipped bits* is the Hamming distance. The Hamming distance is a popular distance metric in computer science for the obvious reason that computer science works with strings of binary digits. In our specific example, we can see that *A* and *C* differ by only a single bit, but that *B* and *C* differ by three bits. By the Hamming distance metric, *A* and *C* are closer, and it is no longer surprising that inputting pattern *C* would give back pattern *A* as output rather than pattern *B*. This result can be thought of as a method of *error correction* or pattern completion. The ability to correct or complete partial inputs seems to be an aspect of human memory. When we are trying to aid someone to remember a fact, we may prompt that person with a place or a name. In the case of vector *C* we gave the "first name" and the Hopfield network was able to recall the entire name.

An Angular Distance Metric

There are even more measures of distance than the Euclidean and the Hamming. One that is often used with vectors is the angle between them (remember, we can think of vectors as geometric objects). Using the relation between the inner product and the cosine of the angle they make together (see Equation 9.2), we can compute the distance between two vectors as the angle they make with one another, and we can compute this using the dot product. If two vectors are orthogonal then their dot product will be zero. If they are each pointing in exactly the same direction, the result will be the product of their individual lengths. If the vectors have been normalized, the product will be one. If we take the inverse cosine of these numbers (sometimes the inverse cosine function is called the arccosine or acos; it may also be represented as $\cos^{-1}$), we will have the angle. To test your understanding of this idea, try finding the angle between the vectors *A* and *B* above.

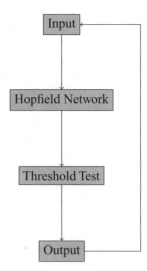

Figure 13.2   This is the flowchart for the asynchronous updating procedure usually used with Hopfield networks.

13.6   Asynchronous Updating

The matrix representation of the Hopfield network was introduced for the purpose of emphasizing certain structural aspects of the updating operation, but in general the typical way to update a Hopfield network is asynchronously. This means that one node, often picked at random, calculates its output from its input and updates its value. This new vector of activities is then used in the next round of updating with a new randomly selected node computing its output. For simplicity, in the following example, we pick our units sequentially. We repeat the process until none of the nodes changes its value.

Exercise: Asynchronous Updating

Using as input $\{1, 0, 0, 1\}$ and the weight matrix **W** above, perform the following steps (Figure 13.2):

1. Compute the first element of the input. You do this by taking the first row of the weight matrix and multiplying it against the input vector.

2. Compare to the threshold.

3. Update the value of unit 1.

4. Repeat for the second, third, and fourth units (shifting to the appropriate row of the weight matrix).

5. Repeat until there are no more changes.

13.7   Hopfield Insights

Hopfield networks have proved useful in fields far beyond psychology and neuroscience. For example, they have been employed in integrated circuit design (Kumar et al., 1995). Whatever your interest, computing science, physics, or engineering, you are sure to find some connection to Hopfield.

In Chapter 11 we talked about imagining a unit's weight vector as an arrow pointing in a direction in space, and to view the learning process as an adjustment of the direction in which the weight vector points. We can use a similar geometric intuition for the Hopfield network and imagine that the activity of the units of our networks as specifying the coordinates of a point in a four-dimensional space. As we update our network, this point moves around. If we connect the dots, we have a path through space. This perspective views our Hopfield network as a dynamical system, and the evolution of the network traces a trajectory.

Viewing a network as a dynamical system allowed Hopfield to emphasize new approaches to network analysis. His experience as a physicist allowed him to adapt classical methods to this new application.

Note that the algorithm in the exercise above says that the updating process should continue until the outputs of the individual units no longer change. How do we know that this will ever occur? In addition, I have, so far, provided the matrix that performs auto-association, but where did that weight matrix come from? Was it learned by trial and error or can we compute the weight matrix we need to represent certain patterns? Hopfield's introduction of techniques from physics allows definite answers to these questions.

Hebb and the Outer Product Rule

In his very famous book, *The Organization of Behavior*, Hebb (1949) described the idea that one method for establishing memories in a neural-like environment would be if neurons that fired closely together in time became more tightly tied or coupled. This idea can be remembered by the phrase that "neurons that fire together, wire together." To capture this idea mathematically we want to have a system where elements in our network can reinforce each other. This principle has given rise to the outer product rule of weight modification. The outer product of two vectors was mentioned at the end of Chapter 9. In neural networks, the outer product rule says that the change in weight between two elements should be a function of their joint activity. It can be represented as

$$\Delta W_{i,j} = \eta g[i] f[j] \tag{13.1}$$

We are imagining that f and g represent two vectors that are an input pattern and an output pattern that we would like to be associated by our network. Since in a Hopfield network each input location connects to every other one, we have to consider all the possible pairs of connections: activity of the first position of the input with the first position of the output, second position of the output, and so forth. The i and j in the above represent numbers that are going to go from 1 to the length of each input. In our example of A above, this would mean that i would take on values of 1, 2, 3, and 4. In words, the equation above says that the change in our weight (Δ is a common symbol for representing a change or difference) is one slot of f multiplied against one slot of g

with this product weighted by some small positive value, η, which we can again think of as a learning constant.

Remember that if we want to find the value of our output for a unit we do this by taking all the inputs to that unit and multiplying them by the connection weights. This means

$$g[j] = \sum_i W[j, i] f[i]$$

We can summarize this for the whole vector g with vector notation: $\mathbf{g} = \mathbf{W}\vec{\mathbf{f}}$.

Exercise: Writing the Whole Matrix

To demonstrate your understanding of this concept, and to demonstrate how this rule guarantees the input:output associations we want, do the following:

1. Take Equation 13.1 (page 110) as the learning rule for changing weights.

2. Assume you have two vectors each three elements in length.

3. Represent things abstractly (i.e., with letters rather than concrete numbers).

4. Assume that all weights start at zero.

5. Write the weight matrix after one update for each input position.

6. After filling in each of the locations of the weight matrix individually, determine the matrix representation for this relationship.

The result should be something equivalent to $\mathbf{W} = \eta \vec{\mathbf{g}} \vec{\mathbf{f}}^T$. If you compare this to the definition of an outer product for two vectors, you will see that they are the same. The idea that co-active units strengthen their connections gives rise to a matrix representation that is the outer product (scaled by a learning rate) and it explains why we call it the outer product rule. Many computer languages (including MATLAB and Octave) will have a special function for computing outer products for two vectors (many spreadsheet programs will as well, or you can easily program it yourself).

This exercise was adapted from the chapter on Hopfield networks in J.A. Anderson and J. Davis (1995).

Exercise: Proving the Updating Process Halts (i.e., Convergence)

This is a more substantial exercise. I would encourage you to take it slow and work in groups. What I will be trying to do is to outline for you the logic and methods of Hopfield. These will allow you to prove, in the sense of mathematics, that for a

(Continued)

(Continued)

given input pattern and the updating rule described above, the network's dynamic trajectory will eventually converge to a fixed point and it will do so in a finite amount of time. Be patient with yourself as you work through this. If your background is psychology, almost everything about this exercise will seem strange or foreign. But when you are done, you should also have an appreciation for the certainty that can follow from specifying your claims in a mathematical form. If you get really stumped, I have placed answers in the Notes section for this chapter at the end of the book.

Proving Hopfield Networks Converge

Let $f[i]$ represent the activity of position i of input vector $\vec{f}$ and let $f[i]$ be computed as

$$f[i] \rightarrow 1 \quad \text{if } \sum_j A[i,j] f[j] \geq 0$$

$$f[i] \rightarrow -1 \quad \text{if } \sum_j A[i,j] f[j] < 0$$

(Note that we are taking f as both the input and output of our network so there is no g. We are considering an auto-association. Also, we are using A for the weight matrix to keep our notation the same as J.A. Anderson and J. Davis (1995), in case you decide to consult this source.)

Let's define a function to measure the "energy" of the network. The idea of using energy comes from physics, but it does not have to be energy like the energy of an electrical output. We can call anything we want "energy." In physics, the energy is a square of some quantity, and that is the idea we will make use of. Our equation for the energy of our network is

$$E = -\frac{1}{2} \sum_{i \neq j} \sum A[i,j] f[i] f[j]$$

When attempting a proof it is always best to make sure that you are very clear on both your starting point, what you can assume to be known "for sure," and what your goal is. This is the destination of your proof. The procedure for proof is to go from the known for sure stuff to the goal, or claim, by a series of logical steps whose truth is not in doubt. You are showing by this procedure that your goal statement necessarily follows on from your initial, assumed as true or known to be true, postulates.

Our proof will show that use of the *asynchronous* updating rule always halts. To do this we will show that each updating step results in a reduction of energy. Since energy is a "square" it can never be negative. We can only go down in energy and we are bounded by the lowest that we can go, which is zero. Since our network is of finite size, there are only a finite number of states that we can occupy. If each time we move we either go down or stay the same, we know that eventually we will either hit a state from which no other state is lower, or hit zero. Our migration will stop.

Try to work through each of the following steps. I try to give you a hint as to what you should try and tackle with each step.

1. Focus on a single unit k and another unit j and write an equation for the terms of the energy function that only contains k and j.

2. Now make the traditional assumption that all connections are symmetric and rewrite your equation.

3. Using the statement above, write an equation for the terms of the energy equation that are dependent on k, that is, all the inputs and outputs of k, and only k.

4. You can rewrite this equation with "sigma" notation so that one of the terms can be written outside the $\sum$ sign. Rewrite the equation in that fashion.

5. State in words what is represented by the part of your equation which includes the $\sum$ sign and all that follows.

6. Assume that the activation updating rule results in your changing the value of $f[k]$. Define the following expressions for changes (or differences):

$$\Delta E = E[k](\textit{new value}) - E[k](\textit{old value})$$

$$\Delta f[k] = f[k](\textit{new value}) - f[k](\textit{old value})$$

Plug these equations into your prior equations for E and simplify to yield a concise equation for $\Delta E[k]$ in terms of $\Delta f[k]$.

7. If $f[k]$ does not change, then neither does the energy. However, if $f[k]$ goes from 1 to -1 or vice versa, the energy will change. Consider both cases and state what happens to the energy, and explain why.

If necessary, see note 1 for possible answers.

13.8   Summary

In this chapter we met the Hopfield network. Its importance for us is to see that not all networks are the same and that different networks may provide better or worse matches for the psychological phenomena we are interested in. The Hopfield network shows a nice relationship to the human phenomena of memory completion and has been used as a proxy for understanding the computational requirements of those processes. In addition, the Hopfield network has helped us to appreciate some general benefits to using computational approaches. We have seen how thinking abstractly and using geometric representations can allow us to prove things in a definite and concrete sense. We would not be able to do this if all we did was discuss our ideas in words. In particular, we have seen how commonsense statements, such as Hebb's learning rule, can be restated mathematically, and that this, combined with concepts from mathematics and physics, can be used for drawing specific conclusions about network activities and operations.

Part III

Probability and Psychological Models

Chapter 14

What Are the Odds?

Objectives

After reading this chapter you should be able to:

- understand the basic terms of probability theory;
- understand how probability relates to set theory;
- understand conditional probability and Bayes' rule; and
- understand the conjunction fallacy.

14.1   Overview

The next two chapters deal with probability and its application in computational modeling. In psychology and neuroscience it is common to treat probability and statistics as synonyms, but they are not. Probability is about mathematical theory, while statistics is the application of this theory to questions of data analysis. If you understood probability theory well you could, in principle, devise the statistical tests you would need for a particular problem. Our interest in probability is not about hypothesis testing. We are interested in probability because it deals with randomness, and randomness seems to be an inherent feature of our environment, our nervous system, and our behavior. Even in simple tasks, reaction time (RT) varies from trial to trial. We try to ignore that variability when we summarize RTs with the mean or median, but when we want to describe or model the process underlying the task, we want that variability to persist. Our model needs to reproduce the variability in a sensible way if we are to have a sensible model. Summarizing variability and incorporating variability into models are important roles for probability.

In this chapter we will introduce some of the mathematical concepts. In the following chapter we move on to consider some practical examples of how we can use probability.

14.2   Paradox and Probability: Sets and Urns

Do not ask, "Why urns?" It just is. Probabilists always have their arms elbow deep in urns, drawing out colored marbles.

Probability theory touches several different areas of mathematics. Although we will only need to use a few basics, we will not be able to fully understand our simulations without some exposure to larger, more complicated issues. We also need to expand our vocabulary and learn a little bit of the vernacular if we are to be able to read articles using these techniques.

We begin with considering some ideas of sets, and we will motivate our use of sets by considering an example where we draw colored marbles from an urn. Figuring out all the different ways of doing something, which is a common reason for urn problems (and throwing dice and drawing cards, two more favorite activities of probability theorists), is to motivate an exercise in *combinatorics*. Combinatorics is the area of mathematics concerned with counting things and the number of "combinations" they can make.

Imagine that you are faced with an urn that is known to contain 30 red marbles and also 60 marbles of another color. The other colors are either yellow or black. How many are yellow and how many are black is unknown, but it is known that they total 60. Now imagine that you have the following choice: either I will pay you $100 if you draw a red marble, or I will pay you $100 if you draw a black marble. Which option do you prefer? Do you feel better betting on getting a red marble or a black marble?

Now imagine that you are faced with a second similar urn that is set up in exactly the same way. This time the bets are as follow: I will pay $100 for either a red or yellow marble OR I will pay $100 for either a black or yellow marble. Which of these two bets would you prefer to make? Take a moment and reach a decision for each scenario before reading on.

This scenario is an example of Ellsberg's paradox (Ellsberg, 1961). Most people in the first scenario prefer to bet on red. This implies that the value of the red choice is in some sense worth more to them, that is, p(Red) > p(Black). In the second scenario, most prefer the black and yellow combination, that is, p(Black) + p(Yellow) > p(Red) + p(Yellow), but since the number of yellow balls, whatever it may be, is the same, we can remove these (we may subtract whatever we want from one side of an equation as long as we subtract it from the other side as well). This leaves us with the conclusion that p(Black) > p(Red), contradicting what we apparently believed from our choice of bets in the first scenario.

Ellsberg's paradox relies on probability theory. Probability theory justifies the claim that the p(Black + Yellow) = p(Black) + p(Yellow). But our application of probability theory to human choices under uncertainty shows a paradox and is therefore a challenge to theories of humans as optimal rational decision makers.

14.3   Probability as Counting

Probability theory can be thought of as measuring the size of a set. What is the probability that a coin in my pocket is a nickel (5 cents)? That depends on the size of the set that is the set of all coins that are in my pocket and how many coins are in the subset of coins that are nickels and that are in my pocket. Those two numbers are counting measures. Their ratio is a probability. Below, I briefly consider these ideas, namely, sets and measures, more generally.

Set Terminology

Set theory is a subdivision of mathematics, and sets have allowed mathematicians to formalize their knowledge of many common mathematical concepts including probability, logic, computability, and even the concept of infinity (e.g., it allows us to prove that some infinities are bigger than others). Even though mathematical sets can be used for very complex exercises, they are basically an extension of our intuitive idea of a set gathered from real-world collections (like a dining room set).

The basic terms important for understanding sets are as follows:

Set: An unordered collection of elements.

Element: An indivisible thing.

Membership: Denoted by $\in$, it means is a member of or belongs to. For example, orange $\in$ Fruit.

Union: Denoted by $\cup$. Everything thrown together. For example, $\{1, 2, 3\} \cup \{3, 4, 5\} = \{1, 2, 3, 4, 5\}$.

Intersection: Denoted by $\cap$. Only those elements that are in both sets. For example, $\{1, 2, 3\} \cap \{3, 4, 5\} = \{3\}$.

Cardinality: This is the size of a set, and it is what we use as our counting measure. It is usually represented using the same symbol used to show absolute value ($|S|$). This makes sense when you think of absolute value as the "size" of a number; -3 is still three units big, the negative sign just says which way to go on the number line when we lay out the units.

Other concepts can be defined from combinations of these basic ideas.

14.4   Probability as a Measure of Set Size

Previously we mentioned the idea of a metric (see page 71). A related concept is that of *measure*. I have used this word a number of times, and you probably inferred its meaning from conventional uses. A measure tells you how big something is. A teaspoon is a measure and there are three teaspoons in a tablespoon. A mathematical measure is essentially the same idea. Where metrics quantify distances, measures quantify size.

> Individual outcomes, the elements of our set of interest, are often symbolized by a lower case omega ω, while the entire set of all possible outcomes is symbolized by a capital omega Ω.

Just as there is more than one kind of metric, there is more than one variety of measure (e.g., volume, area, Lebesgue). With sets we can often use the counting measure to quantify a set's size. The size of a set is the number of things it contains. To see how we can use this to derive a probability consider the trivial question: What is the probability of flipping a fair coin and having it land "heads?"

To answer this question we need to define a *probability space*. A probability space is a mathematical object that has three different parts. One part is the set of all possible outcomes. Another part is the measure that we use for quantifying the size of sets. And last we have a collection of all the subsets (we will call each of these subsets an *event*) that together comprise all the possible subsets of our set of all possible outcomes.* To figure out a probability, we compute the measure of our event of interest (the size of the subset of possible qualifying outcomes) and compare it to the size of the set of all possible outcomes. For the simple situation currently under consideration there are only two possible outcomes: head = H, or tail = T. The subset containing our event is $\{H\}$. It has measure 1. The measure of the set of all possible outcomes $\{H, T\}$ is two, and the ratio is $1/2$, thus our probability is 0.5.

To repeat, for the mathematician, probability is a measure on the sizes of sets. If that is too abstract for you then buckle up. For the mathematician a random variable is a function. Remember, functions are machines for turning inputs into outputs. The functions that are random variables take the abstract little entities that are our outcomes and turn them into real numbers on the number line. We can then define events by reference to these numbers. For example, an event could be the subset of all outcomes whose value after being crunched by a random variable function was between two values. Things like this are represented by notations that look like: $P(1 \leq X < 2) = |\{\omega \in \Omega \text{ s.t.} X(\omega) \geq 1 \text{ and } X(\omega) < 2\}|$. All this says is that our probability of observing some random variable having a value between 1 and 2 is equal to the measure of the subset of all possible outcomes that when run through the random variable machine X have a value between 1 and 2. Usually this complicated way of stating the obvious is not necessary, but it can be very helpful to return to this definition when considering complex cases just as it was useful to return to the definition of the derivative when trying to understand how we could numerically simulate simple DEs.

Exercise: Counting Probabilities

Demonstrate your knowledge of the counting measure of probability by computing the probability of two or more heads in a sequence of four coin flips. To do this, first write down the set of all possible outcomes from flipping a coin four times. Then count the size of the subset that specifies the event of interest.

Having done this, can you find a simple way, using the definition of probability, to prove what is the probability of getting less than two heads out of four flips? It may help to note that when two events are *disjoint*, which means that the subsets of their outcomes have no overlap (i.e., no shared elements), then the probability of the union of those events is the sum of the subsets.

14.5   Some Basic Relations of Probability

Our goal is now to work our way to Bayes' relation. Bayes' relation (sometimes elevated to Bayes' Theorem) is at the heart of Bayesian probability and Bayesian ideas are frequently

---

*I have simplified things somewhat. It could be worse.

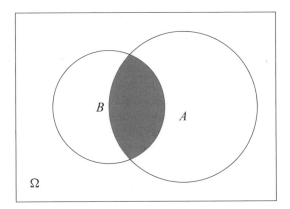

Figure 14.1   Joint and conditional probability — set view. The rectangle represents all possible outcomes. The event defined by A is the subset of outcomes for which A is true. Similarly for B. The overlap defines their *joint* probability and the ratio of the measure of their intersection to the measure of A defines the conditional probability of B given A.

invoked in neuroscience and psychology. We will first need a couple of additional definitions to establish this relationship.

Conditional Probability

When we say that something is conditional, we mean that it depends on something else. A child gets their allowance if they clean their room. The allowance is conditional on the clean room variable being TRUE. The notation for conditional probability typically uses a "pipe": "|". It is defined as

$$P(B|A) = \frac{P(B \cap A)}{P(A)}$$

To continue with our set-based view of probability, the equation of conditional probability means that we compare the measure of the subset of outcomes that are in both subsets B and A divided by the measure of the subset of outcomes that belong to the subset after the pipe, in this case A. You can also think of this visually, as in Figure 14.1.

Exercise: Compute a Conditional Probability

Demonstrate your understanding of the formula for conditional probability, by computing the probability of getting two or more heads in four flips given that there cannot be two heads in a row. The use of the word "given" is a common equivalent to the phrase "conditional on." It may be helpful to actually write out all the possible ωs and circle the subsets defined by the events.

Bayes' Rule

Bayesian probability is commonly used in psychology and neuroscience, but it is used in two largely different ways. One way that Bayesian probability is used is to expand the types of statistical tests that are employed when performing data analysis. This is often referred to as *Bayesian inference*. The other way that Bayesian probability is used is as a model for how *rational* actors use information.

In the method of *maximum likelihood* we try to figure out what is the most likely underlying hypothesis that would explain the data we observe. What we do with Bayesian probability is to expand this calculation to weight the possible hypotheses by how likely we thought they were before we observed any data.

Imagine that you see a cloud on the horizon. It is a dark cloud, the kind you would normally associate with rain. How likely is it that it will rain? What if you are in Saudi Arabia? What if you are in Britain? Your answers should be very different in the two locations. Rain is much more likely in Britain, and therefore your *posterior* estimate of rain should be greater when you are in Britain, even when observing the same cloud. This is the intuition behind Bayesian probability. Observations and their implications are combined with prior estimates.

As a formula Bayes' rule is

$$P(H|O) = P(O|H)P(H)/P(O) \qquad (14.1)$$

where the O represents our observations and the H represents our hypotheses. Note that which one is on top, the O or H, flips between the right and left hand side of the equation. We are interested in how our belief in the various hypotheses changes given our observations. To determine this we can multiply how likely the observations would have been assuming particular hypotheses (this term is sometimes called the *likelihood* and may be written $\mathcal{L}(O,H)$) by how likely they were to start with (this is called the *prior*). What we get out of this calculation, since it comes after we modify the prior, is the *posterior*.

Frequently, one may see statements of Bayes' rule that look like

$$P(H|O) \propto P(O|H)P(H)$$

Note that we do not have an equals sign, but a sign for "proportional to." When using Bayes' rule in practice we are usually trying to estimate the probability of our hypothesis given some data. The data do not change, so the $P(O)$ is the same for all estimates of the parameters of H. Therefore, the ordering of all the posteriors does not change simply because we divide them all by the same constant number. Our most probable values for H will still be the most probable, and so we can often ignore the term $P(O)$.

Bayes' rule is basically an instruction on how to combine evidence. We should weight our prior beliefs by our observations. It is important to remember what the Ps mean in the equation. These are distributions, not simple numbers but functions. This means that if our prior belief is very concentrated, and our likelihood very broad, we should (and the equation determines that we will) give more weight to the prior (or vice versa). We weight the evidence based on its quality. Much work in psychology is devoted to determining if this optimal method of evidence combination is actually the way humans think.

If you needed to determine $P(O)$ how could you figure it out? You could simply sum up all the possibilities for the terms you know. The $P(O)$ is equal to Σ all possible Hs $P(O|H)P(H)$.

14.6   Humans Are Not Rational

While Bayesian models are common, and there are many areas where near optimal behavior is observed, there are a number of observations that challenge the claim that humans are probabilistically sophisticated. In fact, we can easily be shown to be inconsistent. The Ellsberg paradox above is one example of this, but there are many others. One of the benefits of having some familiarity with the language of probability is that it allows one to construct probabilistic models, but another advantage is that it gives one the basis for constructing and evaluating experiments designed to test the ability of humans to reason under uncertainty. A famous example of this comes from the *conjunction fallacy* (Tversky & Kahneman, 1983).

Exercise: Conjunction Fallacy

Poll a group of your friends on the following question:
   "Linda is 31 years old, single, outspoken, and very bright. She majored in philosophy. As a student, she was deeply concerned with issues of discrimination and social justice, and also participated in anti-nuclear demonstrations."
   Which is more probable?

1. Linda is a bank teller.
2. Linda is a bank teller and is active in the feminist movement.

Many people will choose bank teller and feminist. Consider this response from the point of view of probability, sets, and counting. For the sets of all people and all occupations there is a set of events that correspond to bank teller and to feminist. Since not all bank tellers are feminists the intersection of the subsets feminist and bank teller must be no larger than the subset of bank teller alone. Thus, the size (measure) of the conjunction bank teller *and* feminist is less than bank teller by itself. Thus, the probability of the first statement is larger than the second. So why do people routinely pick the second?

Some people argue that the usual interpretation of the word "and" in spoken English is commonly taken to mean "or", that is, that Linda could be a feminist and have some occupation, a bank teller and not a feminist, or a bank teller and a feminist. Can you see why this interpretation would eliminate the fallacy using the rules of probability learned so far?

There is a large body of research following up on the observation of the conjunction fallacy. One popular account holds that the conjunction fallacy arises from humans equating the probability of an outcome with its *typicality*: the more typical something is, the more probable we estimate it to be. We feel that for someone with Linda's earlier social preferences, the characteristic of being a feminist is more typical, and so we rate it as more probable (for a recent discussion of the conjunction fallacy see Tentori et al., 2013). For developing computational modelling skills it is not critical what the answer is to the conjunction fallacy. What is critical, is that it is only from our familiarity with the axioms of probability and what these actually mean mathematically that we can perceive human responses as a possible fallacy. Without this computational vocabulary we cannot detect the paradox nor design experiments or models to explain it.

14.7 Conclusion

This chapter introduces some of the mathematics behind probability calculations. Most of the time we can view probability as the size of sets. Random variables and distributions can be viewed as functions. From these basics we can evaluate the evidence that humans are optimal reasoners or that they are sub-optimal. We can use this information to develop experiments and we can use these ideas to inform computational models. In the next chapter we will use these ideas to develop an example model: reaction time as a random walk.

Chapter 15

Decisions as Random Walks

Objectives

After reading this chapter you should be able to:

- understand the concept of a random walk;
- appreciate the relation between random walks and reaction time; and
- use the EZ-diffusion model to fit reaction time (RT) data with a computational model.

15.1 Overview

Up until Chapter 14 we were concerned with deterministic systems. In a deterministic system everything is *determined*. Nothing is left to chance. If you run your Hodgkin and Huxley model with the same input two times you will get exactly the same output both times. In a deterministic system the output is determined exactly by its input. This contrasts with a probabilistic system where the output is determined by the input only approximately. There is some degree of unpredictability. We can describe the output by a probability distribution. Our introduction to some of the mathematical terminology of probability was in Chapter 14.

Many theorists hold that including probability in a model of neuroscientific and psychological phenomena leads to a more accurate reflection of empirical findings. Although deterministic systems offer the advantages of transparency and concreteness, these will only take us so far. We expect a regularity between input and output, but we do not expect natural outcomes to be duplicated every time input states repeat. Whether a deterministic model is good enough depends on the scientific question the model is intended to address.

A common example of an area where determinism is felt to be inadequate is in the modelling of RT. Even when we reduce an RT task to its bare minimum, if we have an experimental participant push a button in response to a single, predictable flash of light, we will see that the participant's RTs will vary. This is why we need probability. The RT we observe is a function of the input, but it is subject to random variation.

In this chapter we will see how random processes can still give rise to predictable trends. We will look at a specific example, the random walk, that is often invoked when modelling RT. We will then write a simple program to measure RT. This will allow us to grow our programming skills, and it will give us data that we can use for developing a probabilistic model of RT that fits the data to parameters in a random walk model.

15.2   Random Walks

A random walk is well described by its name. Imagine that prior to taking a step you flip a coin. If it is heads, you turn around and take one step in the direction you just came from. If it is tails, you take another step in the direction you are facing. Because we are either moving forward or backward all our travel is along a line. This yields a one-dimensional random walk. Random walks do not have to be so simple, though. For example, the probability of going forward or turning back does not have to be equal, and we do not have to limit ourselves to one dimension. We can imagine the map of a city and use randomness to decide the way we go at intersections. Even though the process that generates random walks is random, essentially a coin flip, it does not mean that our aggregate progress in unpredictable. In the following exercise we see what kinds of information we can predict from the structure of a random process.

> **Exercise: Average Behavior of a Random Process**
>
> Where will you be *on average* for a one-dimensional random walk if you have equal probabilities of going forwards and backwards?
>
> We can answer this question analytically, but the benefit of developing our programming skills is that we do not have to worry about how to solve such problems. As long as we can describe them procedurally we can simulate and observe our answer.
>
> For a spreadsheet simulation of a one dimensional random walk:
>
> 1. Create the necessary column headings. You will probably need some of the following: step size, location, coin flip.
> 2. Start at position 0.
> 3. Use the random number generator in your spreadsheet program (use HELP to look for something like rand()) to compute the outcome of a random coin flip.
> 4. Simulate a series of coin flips for the number of steps you want to take. You might find it easier to record the outcome of the coin flips as ±1 rather than heads and tails. It will be easier to accumulate the result as distance travelled.
> 5. Use the outcomes of the coin flips to update your position (just like you did for DEs, new position = old position + change in position).
> 6. Plot the results for several repetitions.
> 7. What do you observe generally?
> 8. What is the average position, and how did you compute it?

Proving the Expected Location of a 1-D Random Walk

Simulation will often be good enough for determining the tendency of psychological and neuroscientific models, but there will also be times when we want to know the "truth." To give us a little practice, we can examine how we might try to determine the expected position of our 1-D random walk analytically and make use of our newly learned notation for probabilities.

First, let us imagine that we have already taken a step. Where will we be after our second step? That will be determined by where we start from (the location after the first step) and whether our second step was in the positive or in the negative direction. We can write this as an equation:

$$Location_2 = Location_1 + P(h)*(+1) + P(t)*(-1)$$

When we write this equation we are including the uncertainty in our calculation. We use the probability of going in a positive (or negative) direction to weight a step in both directions. From this relation, we see that we need to know the location after step 1. We can write an equation for that (assuming a starting position of zero):

$$Location_1 = Location_0 + P(h)*(+1) + P(t)*(-1)$$

Notice that everything after the location term is the same in both equations. We can plug our equation for $Location_1$ into our equation for $Location_2$ and simplify:

$$Location_2 = Location_1 + P(h)*(+1) + P(t)*(-1)$$
$$Location_2 = Location_0 + P(h)*(+1) + P(t)*(-1) + P(h)*(+1) + P(t)*(-1)$$
$$Location_2 = 0 + P(h)*(+1) + P(t)*(-1) + P(h)*(+1) + P(t)*(-1)$$
$$Location_2 = 0 + \sum_{i=1}^{t} 0.5*(+1) + 0.5*(-1)$$
$$Location_2 = 0 + \sum_{i=1}^{t} 0 = 0$$
$$\implies E[Location_T] = Location_0 + T \times (P(h) - P(t))$$

In this simple case we could have just used the expected value of a series of fair coin flips to deduce that the expected location was zero, but this derivation shows us a very handy trick: *recursion*. In the intermezzo we will examine how to use recursion in a computer program.

We can tell several interesting things by looking at Figure 15.1. First, on average we expect to be near zero. However, despite this average expectation, for any individual realization and any one point in time, it is rarely exactly zero; this is the difference between average behavior and behavior for a specific example. Second, we can make an educated guess about what would happen if we continued for another 200 time steps. To do this, imagine all the five examples picked up and moved end to end. Consider the realization that was moving away from zero. This becomes the starting point for another realization. The new realization will stay on average near this starting point (just

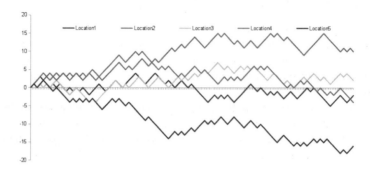

Figure 15.1   Five examples of a 1-D random walk. Each realization is different because of the inherent randomness, but at the same time we see that for many of the examples they hover close to zero. While two realizations drift away, one is to the positive side and one to the negative side. If we took the average of several realizations at each time step we would see how the mean would stay close to zero, but the variance of that estimate would grow with time.

as it stayed near its "old" starting point of zero), but it could go back towards zero or it could move even further away. If it did move further away, and we continued to run our simulation, there is an even chance it would move further away still. Although this reasoning is informal, we can surmise that there is a finite chance that, despite the average expected location being near the starting point, there is also a possibility of moving an almost infinite distance away from the starting point.

A 1-D version of the random walk is the simplest random walk there is, but even this simple version shows some complex and surprising behavior. Versions of the random walk in higher dimensions or with correlations among the steps can generate a rich array of dynamic behavior. In fact, random walks are used to model a number of biological phenomena. Einstein used the idea of a random walk to explain the phenomenon of Brownian motion, the observed jitteriness of grains of pollen suspended in a fluid as viewed by Brown through his microscope.[1]

The random walk, and the related idea of a diffusion model (Smith & Ratcliff, 2004), have been popular in explaining RT, a common staple of psychological measurement. Next, I will present some material on RT measurement and then I will introduce a simple interface for modelling RT from psychological experiments.

15.3 Measuring Reaction Time

RT is one of the oldest experimental measurements in psychology and neuroscience. Helmholtz can be considered the father of its use in both disciplines. In the late 1800s there was controversy over whether nerve conduction velocity would be physically measurable. Some scholars believed that nerve transmission would be nearly instantaneous, including one of Helmholtz's teachers, Johannes Müller. However, Helmholtz used a simple apparatus with a frog to stimulate a nerve and measure muscle contraction. By moving the stimulating electrode he could vary the distance from the stimulus point to

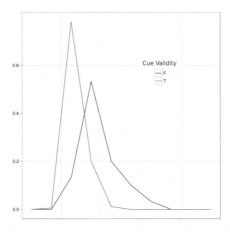

Figure 15.2   RT Data from Posner Task. The RT distributions for validly cued and invalidly cued trials are shown. The RTs for invalidly cued trials are slower on average. These data were collected using the program in the Intermezzo on page 137 that immediately follows this chapter.

the muscle. By comparing the difference in the time between stimulus and contraction, and the distance difference, Helmholtz could compute the conduction velocity.[2]

Given that the time taken by the nerves to conduct a message was long enough to be measurable, it was a short conceptual leap for early psychologists to hypothesize that the time taken to propagate a thought would also take a measurable amount of time. Then, by a careful partitioning of the different parts of a behavioral task, one could isolate cognitive operations and measure the RT associated with each part.

Early practitioners of mental chronometry were Donders and Wundt.[3] In their day, the measurement of precise millisecond-magnitude RTs required cutting edge technology in timing, and no psychological laboratory of the first rank could be without its Hipp chronoscope.[4] This was an unwieldy instrument that required frequent calibration and careful maintenance, yet it was able to achieve timing accuracy equal to that of today's commonly used computers. This is mostly due to the fact that using a computer to present visual stimuli is, practically speaking, limited by the screen refresh rate, that is, how long the computer allows itself to overwrite what is currently on the screen with new material. However, this timing accuracy and precision is greater than most human psychophysical procedures require. While the Hipp chronoscope was an expensive and rare instrument, computers are common, and their power puts in the hands of any computer owner the ability to do their own psychophysical experimentation. Further, the programming techniques we have seen so far can be easily adapted to allow us to program our own simple tasks.

15.4   Testing Models of Reaction Time

A characteristic of RT data is that these are not normally distributed. Here "normally" means that these do not have a normal or Gaussian distribution. Gaussian distributions are the familiar bell-shaped curve used for grades. However, the Gaussian is not the only probability distribution to have a bell-shape.

One reason that we know for a fact that an RT distribution cannot be normally distributed is that RT distributions are bounded by zero (the RT must always be positive). On the other hand a Gaussian distribution can be any value from $-\infty$ to $+\infty$. More importantly, most RT distributions are not symmetrically shaped. They tend to be right skewed. This means that the distribution is not symmetric around its peak because there is a *tail* of long RTs (Figure 15.2).

Exercise: Are RTs Normally Distributed?

Using data you collected or downloaded, plot a histogram. See if you agree that RT distributions are not symmetric. If RT distributions are not symmetric, which side of the RT distribution, that is, those times less than the mode or greater than the mode, has the longer tail?

Although the normal (or Gaussian) distribution is expressed as a somewhat complex equation, it can be seen to emerge naturally as the accumulation of Bernoulli random variables. A Bernoulli random variable is a variable that can take only one or the other of two possible outcomes, for example, left or right. This can be demonstrated by mathematical proof, but there are also very nice practical demonstrations, including the *bean machine*.[6] Invented by polymath Sir Francis Galton (a cousin of Darwin), it shows how the normal distribution emerges automatically from a series of left/right random decisions.

RT data are central to many psychological experiments. There have been many efforts to model RT data. Some models are descriptive and others are mechanistic. The descriptive models may describe a probability distribution from which, hypothetically, the RT data are drawn, and then they fit the data collected to this distribution. Mechanistic models on the other hand propose the steps in the process that make up the RT task and look to reproduce the empirical distribution from these assumptions. An important use of computational models is exploring how variations in experimental conditions are predicted to change results. This may only be possible with a mechanistic model. As stated above, one popular mechanistic conception of RTs in simple decision tasks is as a diffusion to bound (Ratcliff & McKoon, 2008). The diffusion process is a random walk, and variations of this approach are now widely used to explain decision making both at the level of humans and at the level of neurons (Gold & Shadlen, 2007).

Random Walk Models of RT

The diffusion model is a widely applied model of RT, but it is mathematically complicated with a number of parameters. Recent investigators have tried to simplify the diffusion model to make it more computationally tractable and to make the underlying logic more apparent. We can use a simple version to model a simple decision process as a diffusion to a barrier. In an alternative forced choice experiment, like the one that we programmed on page 137, we can imagine that our response is contingent on accumulating a certain amount of evidence. It is only when we have gathered sufficient evidence that we can

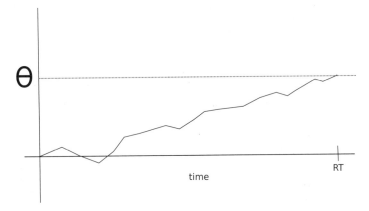

Figure 15.3   Idealized version of the random walk model of RT. Evidence accumulates in random increments until it reaches a specified threshold. The time until the barrier is reached constitutes the RT that will be observed behaviorally.

make our response. Thus, the RT measure includes the time to make a motor act, which should be constant, and the more variable time to reach the point of deciding to push the button "now."

In a two-alternative forced choice task we could easily propose two separate barriers, one for each alternative, but we will make it even simpler and propose only a single barrier. As we have stated earlier, it is best to start as simply as one can, and only add elaborations when required by a poor fit with data or strong theoretical assumptions.

Our model of a simple decision will have two conceptual pieces. We will have a particle that is migrating up and down as the result of random incremental steps. In general, the particle will migrate in a particular direction. This reflects the fact that there is some evidence for a particular alternative. The magnitude of this overall trend to migrate towards the barrier is called the *drift rate*. The second component of the model is the distance to the barrier that we use to satisfy our need for evidence. This distance from the start to the barrier is represented by Θ, where Θ represents the threshold (Figure 15.3).

This simple model provides three things that we can easily change. We can adjust the drift rate. This would seem to relate to the quality of the evidence. If the light is on and we are wearing our glasses, we recognize our friends quickly (large drift rate), but if we are in dim light with dirty lenses, we may not see our friends as fast (small drift rate). The step size discretizes the process for us. And the distance between our starting point and the barrier could represent our criterion. If I am looking for a tiger in the jungle, I may set my criterion low. A few false alarms is better than being eaten. In other situations, I may want to be very stringent before I decide something is present; maybe mistakes cost me money?

As you can see from the preceding, there are some obvious analogies between the pieces of the random walk drift to threshold model and our ideas about the important factors in a simple decision. If we had an experimental manipulation that we postulated affected one or another process, we could collect data and compare the fits of RT to such a model. If the parameter that was related to our putative process changed with the experimental manipulation, we could take this as partial confirmation of our theoretical ideas.

Exercise: Are Random Walks Good Models of RT?

We explore this question by adapting some ideas from our earlier coin flip exercise. We need to specify a mean drift rate and a parameter for step size. We will do this by specifying that the random steps are drawn from a normal distribution with a given mean and variance. If the mean is slightly positive the random samples we take from that distribution will also tend to be positive. Adding a series of generally positive numbers together will yield growth.

For our proxy measure of RT, we will count how many steps, or random numbers, it will take for us to reach our threshold. We will also specify the threshold. We will then repeat this process many times, as if we had multiple trials or multiple participants in an experiment. Then we can make a histogram from our simulated RT data and compare it to human performance.

1. Create a spreadsheet with a column for "parameters." Specify a μ (mean) and a σ (variance) for the step sizes. Specify a Θ for the threshold.
2. Create a column for your random numbers. To make a normally distributed variable a "standard normal" variable, you first subtract the mean and then divide by the standard deviation. Therefore, to give a standard normal variable a particular mean and standard deviation, you reverse the process: multiply by your sigma and then add the mu.
3. Some spreadsheet programs do not have a built-in function to generate normally distributed random numbers. They all have the ability to generate a number between 0 and 1, usually with a function called rand(). If you can do that you can use two of them to make a standard normal variate with: `=(SQRT(-2*LN(1-RAND()))*COS(RAND()*2*PI()))`. This transformation is called the Box–Muller transform.
4. In the adjacent column calculate the cumulative sum.
5. In the column adjacent to that, check to see if the cumulative sum has passed your threshold. A way to get the RT from this is to do the checking with an `if` function that puts out a 0 for false and a 1 for true. Then at the bottom use a `countif` to find the number of zeros. That will be your RT.
6. Lastly, do this a whole bunch of times. Beware that any time you update any value in the spreadsheet all the `rand()` functions will update. Therefore, with a spreadsheet implementation you may have to keep track of all the individual trial RTs manually. There is not a trivial way to do this over and over to capture the results in a spreadsheet implementation.

If you find the spreadsheet approach limiting, you can try writing your own program to perform the repeated "trials" as a loop. The following is one example:

Listing 15.1   A simple Python model for simulating data

```
import random as random
import matplotlib.pyplot as plot
mu = 0.25
sigma = 0.25
thr = 10
trialNum = 1000
rts = []
for i in range(trialNum +1):
    start = 0
    timer = 0
    while (start < thr):
        myrndnum = random.normalvariate(mu,sigma)
        start = myrndnum + start
        timer = timer + 1
    rts.append(timer)
plot.hist(rts,20)
plot.show()
```

Although there is a certain cost to getting started in programming and leaving behind your familiar platforms, the eventual benefits in terms of time and clarity can be much larger.

Are Random Walks Good Models of Evidence Accumulation?

As alluded to above, in many psychological experiments the stage between stimulus presentation and motor response can be described as a process of evidence accumulation. The random walk framework grafts easily onto such experiments. Neural and psychological processing of sensory information lead to a noisy accumulation of information. When the evidence has reached a point where it is "enough," the person decides on their answer and makes a report that might be spoken or could be a button press.

In a situation where we are fairly certain what is going to happen, we can imagine that the threshold for a decision moves down closer to the starting value of information. When we are certain of what is going to happen we are inclined to a particular response before we are even shown the stimulus. We do not require much evidence to confirm our suspicions. This then leads to a shifting of the threshold (or equivalently that we start higher up from the baseline).

Which parameter should change in that case?

With a specification of the drift rate, threshold height, and some knowledge about how noisy the process is we can test models of RTs in a particular experiment. Compare the setting of the Posner cuing task (Posner, 1980). With a validity of 80% we are fairly confident that we know where the target will appear. Therefore, we require less evidence before making our response than when the cue is invalid. If you have RT data for validly and invalidly cued trials in a Posner cuing task, you can test this idea that cue validity effects are mediated by the quantity of evidence necessary for a response, and that the benefit is not seen by changes in the efficiency of the evidence accumulation process.

Fitting RT Data to Random Walk Models

Classroom Exercise: What Is Different about Validly and Invalidly Cued Trials?

- What are the features of the RT data collected behaviorally that differ between valid and invalid cued trials?
- Which features of the random walk model of RT do you feel would best explain these variations?
- Could you distinguish changes at the level of thresholds or accumulation rates from histograms or statistical analyses of these data?

The Ratcliff model is mathematically complex. If that complexity is necessary, so be it, but it may not be. We should try simple versions of the random walk model to see if they are adequate to test our ideas. The simpler the model we can use, the more people will be able to follow the work, and the more transparent will be the reasons for any effects we observe.

If fitting RT data to models becomes a major part of your research program then you should give careful consideration to developing a familiarity with the full diffusion model. However, for many purposes a simpler approach suffices. We will use the EZ-diffusion method of Wagenmakers et al. (2007).

The idea for this spreadsheet implementation came from Tim Martin, Kenneshaw State University.

The EZ-diffusion model provides the two core features discussed above: a parameter for drift rate and a parameter for the threshold. In addition, it has another feature: non-decision time. This relates to the fact that in any RT task there is some obligatory "dead-time" that is constant across a condition because it relates to activities that are not subject to change by experimental manipulation. For analyzing our RT data, we will not be concerned with estimating this decision time, but will focus on the drift rate (denoted v in the Wagenmakers paper) and the separation of our two decision boundaries from the starting point (denoted a). The derivation of the equations that are used to fit the data is given in Wagenmakers et al. The equations are reproduced here. To estimate the quantities v and a from data we need to know the variance of RTs and the probability of being correct.

For fitting the model to these data statistics we use the following formulas:

$$v = \text{sign}\left(P_c - \frac{1}{2}\right) s \left\{ \frac{\text{logit}(P_c)\left[P_c^2 \text{logit}(P_c) - P_c \text{logit}(P_c) + P_c - \frac{1}{2}\right]}{VRT} \right\}^{\frac{1}{4}}$$

$$a = \frac{s^2 \text{logit}(P_c)}{v}$$

$$\text{logit}(P_c) = \log\left(\frac{P_c}{1 - P_c}\right)$$

A	B	C	D	E	F	G	H	I	J	K
	MRT	VRT	PC		MRT	VRT	PC	drift rate	boundary	NDT
1	0.274	0.0058	0.993		0.274	0.0058	0.993	0.44489	0.11137	0.15058
1	0.385	0.00966	0.958		0.385	0.00966	0.958	0.32202	0.09711	0.24688

Figure 15.4   Spreadsheet with fitted data. Here, 200 trials of RT data were fit with the EZ-diffusion algorithm. What is the basis, based on these data, for the difference between valid and invalid trials? The valid trials are in the top row. How might you have guessed this?

Figure 15.5   The columns used as intermediate steps in the fitting are demonstrated.

where s is a scaling parameter set by convention at 0.1, VRT is the variance of the RT data, and P_c is the probability of correct responses. These last two are computed from the empirical data.

Exercise: Fitting Data with EZ-diffusion

Create a spreadsheet that has columns for the RTs and that computes the variance of the RT and the probability of being correct and that inserts these values into the above formulas. You can program the formulas into your spreadsheet (Figure 15.4) or you could write a simple computer program.

Compare the estimates of drift rate and boundary separation for the valid and invalidly cued trials and discuss whether you feel your observations and model results fit with our original hypothesis that the effect would be mediated by changing the distance to the threshold.

15.5   Conclusion

In this chapter we have examined a specific example of how probability enters into the kind of data we record in neuroscientific and psychological experiments, and how probability can be included in models of our data.

The use of probability in our modelling allows us to capture the variability seen in real data. More than just providing verisimilitude, we can also use this variability as a source of new methods for modelling cognitive processes. From these models we can then compare and contrast experimental conditions at the level of the pertinent cognitive processes.

A prominent use of probability ideas has been in the modelling of RT. While RT models can be abstractly considered as data-fitting (Figure 15.5), they can also be viewed as representing the summation of cognitive processes that take a finite amount of time and which need to be executed to a stage of completion before we can generate a behavioral report. We can extrapolate back from RT data to models and from models to conclusions about cognitive processes.

Chapter 16

Intermezzo: Programming Psychophysical Experiments with Python

16.1 Writing Python Programs for Research

In the intermezzos we have gradually developed some familiarity with the methods and terminology of computer programming, and we have had an introduction to this through the use of Python. The Python computer programming language is an example of an interpreted, imperative language. Python has become very popular in recent years. A by-product of this popularity has been the development of a number of Python packages that support psychological experimentation and computational modelling. Remember, a *package*, sometimes called a module or library, is a collection of computer code and functions that are gathered together. They are usually grouped by area of application or because they perform similar functions. Python packages are often written in the Python language itself. This means you can use your knowledge of Python to see what exactly an imported function is doing and how it is doing it. Some packages are *wrappers* that are designed to give access in Python to functions written in another computer language. While the quality of Python packages is generally high, a downside to the language's popularity is that it is also a tool of hobbyists. A package found on the internet may have been written by an amateur like yourself. You should always do some research on the provenance of a computer programming library before you use it in a research or professional application. In general, the large Python user base means that most common packages have been well evaluated and do what they are supposed to.

Links to obtaining the Python language itself can be found at www.python.org. Some Python packages that are useful for research include:

Numpy and Scipy: Two popular packages that perform a number of numerical and scientific calculations.[1]

Matplotlib: A high-level plotting library.[2]

Brian: A neural network simulator.[3]

PyNN: A simulator-independent language for building neuronal network models.[4]

DataViewer3D – DVD: A neuroimaging data visualization tool.[5]

VisionEgg: A package for vision research experiments.[6]

PsychoPy: A package for psychology experiments.[7]

OpenSesame: A graphical, open source package for simple psychological experiments, for example, questionnaires or RT measures.[8]

16.2   The PsychoPy Library

We will use the PsychoPy package to build a simple tool for measuring RT. This program can be used to produce the data for modelling RT developed in Chapter 15.

Project: A Python Program to Measure RT

This project has several steps, and many readers may find it challenging. Do not despair. Be patient. Seek help. Be persistent. It gets easier with practice.

First, you need to install Python and the PsychoPy library. There are a number of ways to get Python. You may in fact already have Python installed on your computer. But the need to install additional, necessary packages can be difficult for newcomers. You may find it easier to get started with Python programming if you install a freestanding version with the necessary libraries included. The PsychoPy download page includes links to freestanding versions for the common operating systems, and provides detailed instructions for the "do-it-yourself" types and for more experienced users.[9] Note that these downloads can be large (> 100MB; keep this in mind for planning when and where you download it).

After obtaining PsychoPy you need to begin using it. I recommend the *coder* environment. PsychoPy comes with two ways to write the code for experimental programs. The *builder* method allows a GUI drag and drop methodology. It can seem a friendlier way to get started, but that ease is deceptive. You will not really know what is happening behind the curtains, and your progress will grind to a halt the first time you try to do anything non-standard. The coder allows you to do exactly what you want, and to blend your program with other Python language packages that may not be part of your PsychoPy installation.

In any programming task the most important step occurs before you actually begin typing your code. You need to develop design specifications. We will be programming a Posner cuing task (Posner, 1980). Before we start, we need to decide on the general structure of what your program will do. This planning stage can be as simple as a block and arrow diagram outlining the logical flow of your program on a piece of scratch paper. You will find it easier to write a sensible program if you first have an overall view of the project. For the Posner task I developed the following specifications:

1. Have a fixation spot appear in the center of our screen.
2. Have an arrow cue appear at the center. It points to the right or left with 80% accuracy. If the arrow points to one side, 80% of the time the target will be on that side.
3. Have a target appear on the right or left.
4. Detect a button press indicating that our participant detected the target.
5. Repeat until we have gathered 200 trials.

6. Save our data. From the data file we want to know whether the cue was valid or not, where the target appeared, how long it took our participant to respond (the RT), and whether the trial was correct or incorrect.

The next step is to convert our design into code. When you open PsychoPy it may begin in the GUI/builder mode. Close that and open the Coder View (found under the View menu). This gives you a blank page. Starting with a blank page is the most intimidating part of coding, and few programmers have to deal with it. More typically programs are written by adapting or expanding existing code. For example, after you get this version to run, you can adapt it and change it to suit your evolving needs. Start small and check the correctness of your code frequently.

> For a real experiment you would want to add additional checks to make sure that everything was working and being saved as you intended; my goal here is only to get you started.

Listing 16.1 A first pass

```
from psychopy import visual , core

expWin = visual.Window(size = (400 ,400))

core.wait(2.0)

core.quit()
```

This code snippet is actually an executable program. To see this for yourself, open a new file (under the File menu) and enter the above lines of code. Click the green RUN button. Save the file with a name and in a location you can find again. I called mine `posner` and put it on my Desktop. If you have installed PsychoPy correctly, and you do not have any typos, then a small gray window will open on your computer screen, stay open for two seconds, and then close. You have just written a Python program!

As this book is not a manual on Python programming, my comments are very brief, and we go rather fast. My goal is to develop your confidence. If all you do is type in what I have written, you will start to see the structure of the program.

In the code snippet above we tell Python that we want to get two pieces of PsychoPy. The `visual` piece lets us draw things and make a window. The `core` piece lets us do timing and gives us procedures for opening and closing things like files easily.

Once we can demonstrate that we have a functioning set-up by executing the snippet of code above, we can start filling in the blanks. We know that we will need some variables to specify things like trial number and validity. In addition, we will need something to keep the data that we collect. I will use empty lists for this purpose because they are simple.

Listing 16.2 Some details

```
from psychopy import visual , core
import random as random
```

```
maxTrials = 5
validity = 0.8

rt = []
tn = []
cueside = []
valid = []
correct = []

fix = "+"
arrows = ["left","right"]

expWin = visual.Window(size = (400,400))
fixspot = visual.TextStim(expWin,pos = (0,0),text = fix)
fixspot.draw()
expWin.flip()
core.wait(2.0)

core.quit()
```

I now run this again and make sure there are no errors. Check the correctness of your code often. It will make it easier to find the inevitable bugs. If you write too much between tests, and something doesn't work, you will have trouble locating the error.

Note that in this version of our program I have imported an additional Python package that is not part of PsychoPy. The `random` package has functions for generating random numbers. We use it to make the trials less predictable for our participant.

Note that I used a small number for my `maxTrials` variable. I will of course want more, but for testing purposes a small number is better. I do not want to have to do 200 trials just to verify that things are working. The empty lists that I am going to use for my data collection are indicated by the use of square brackets.

Something else that this version of our RT program shows us is how things get written to our computer screens. Most computers have two buffers for storing what gets written to the screen. In this sample of our code, we have created the plus sign we will use as a fixation spot. We put it in the center of our screen. Then we *draw* it. Drawing is a function that all our visual objects can do. Even if we do draw the object we won't be able to see it if that is all that we do. Drawing puts the information into a back, or hidden, buffer. It is only by "flipping" the two buffers of our window that we will bring the back buffer forward to the front where we can see the results of what we have done. Every object has to be drawn *and* the window flipped if we are to see it.

The next code extract is the full program, and you can see how it is all put together. If you manage to copy things correctly this program will run and you can use it to collect RT data for use in the model fitting exercise of Chapter 14.

Listing 16.3   The final version

```
from psychopy import visual ,core ,event
import random as random
```

```
maxTrials = 200
validity = 0.75
fixTime = 0.25
arrowTime = 0.5

rt = []
tn = []
cueside = []
valid = []
correct = []

targSide = 'z'
fix = "+"
arrows = ["<",">"]
targetSymbol = "#"


#Making our windows and stimuli
expWin = visual.Window(size = (400,400),fullscr = 1)
fixspot = visual.TextStim(expWin,pos = (0,0),\
                                text = fix)
leftArrow = visual.TextStim(expWin, pos=(0,0),
                                text = arrows[0],\
                                    height = 0.2)
rightArrow = visual.TextStim(expWin, pos=(0,0), \
                                    text = arrows[1],\
                                    height = 0.2)
target = visual.TextStim(expWin,pos = (0,0),\
                                text = targetSymbol, \
                                height = 0.4)
expTimer = core.Clock()


for i in range(1,maxTrials+1):
    fixspot.draw()
    expWin.flip()
    core.wait(fixTime)
    if random.random() < 0.5:
        leftArrow.draw()
        cueside.append("L")
        targPos = (-0.5,0)
    else:
        rightArrow.draw()
        cueside.append("R")
        targPos = (0.5,0)
        targSide = 'slash'
```

```
        expWin . flip ()
        tn . append ( i )
        core . wait ( arrowTime )
        if  random . random  ()  <  validity :
            valid . append ("T")
        else :
            valid . append ("F")
            targPos  =  ( targPos [0]*(−1) ,  targPos [1])
            if  cueside [−1]  ==  "L":
                targSide  =  'slash '
            else :
                targSide  =  'z '
        target . setPos ( targPos )
        target . draw ()
        expWin . flip ()
        expTimer . reset ()
        buttonPress  =  event . waitKeys ()
        print ( buttonPress )
        rt . append ( expTimer . getTime ())
        if  ( valid [−1]  ==  "T"):
            if  ( buttonPress [−1]  ==  "slash"  and  \
                    cueside [−1]  ==  "R")  or  \
                    ( buttonPress [−1]  ==  "z"  and  \
                        cueside [−1]  ==  "L"):
                correct . append ("T")
            else :
                correct . append ("F")
        else  :
            if  ( buttonPress [−1]  ==  "slash"  and  \
                    cueside [−1]  ==  "R")  or  \
                    ( buttonPress [−1]  ==  "z"  and  \
                        cueside [−1]  ==  "L"):
                correct . append ("F")
            else :
                correct . append ("T")



f  =  open ("./ posnerData . txt " , 'w')
f . write ("TN\tCue\tValid\tReaction  Time\tCorrect\n")
for  i  in  range (0 , maxTrials ):
    f . write ( str ( tn [ i ])  +"\t" +  cueside [ i ]  +  "\t" +  valid [ i ] \
                +  '\t ' +  str ( rt [ i ])  +  '\t ' \
                +  correct [ i ]  +  "\n")
f . close ()

core . quit ()
```

Once you have demonstrated that you can produce a functioning program, change something just to prove you can. Alter the number of trials, or change the identity of what is shown on the screen. PsychoPy allows you to use images and not just text. Look for information on the `visual.PatchStim` object.

16.3   Conclusion

This intermezzo was a sort of culmination of our contact with the Python language. From an elementary beginning of learning about a few basic programming constructs such as loops and conditionals we progressed to learning about a function. Now we can see how it can all be put together into a practical program that we can actually use for something. In later parts of the book we will look at other varieties of programming languages called *functional* languages.

Part IV

Cognitive Modelling as Logic and Rules

Chapter 17

Boolean Logic

Objectives

After reading this chapter you should be able to:

- understand the basic concepts of propositional logic;
- understand how it differs from predicate logic; and
- understand how Boolean functions implement some of these ideas.

17.1 Overview

Our travels so far have progressed from deterministic to probabilistic. We have modelled at the level of individual neurons with DEs, the level of neurons and small networks, and psychological measures like RT. Now we expand to the level of a deciding, cognizing agent. Many of the models for this level of psychology have adopted the position that a person is a rational actor. Rationality is a *normative* concept. By normative it is meant that it is the way that people *should* behave. Whether they do or do not behave that way is an empirical question. One division in this field of research is between those who focus on adapting their models to capture human departures from rationality and the research groups interested in describing intelligence as an ideal. These latter groups may look to human cognition for inspiration, but they do not feel constrained by human limits.

The mathematics at the heart of much of this research and many other threads in the general area of artificial intelligence (AI) agents is *logic*. In fact, some variants of AI presume that a particular variety of logic, first-order logic or *the predicate calculus*, is *the* way to model the mind, and that it is *the* basis for general intelligence.

In this chapter we review the mathematics behind logic. In particular, I concentrate on introducing the vernacular and notation. This introduction is necessary because this technical terminology places a large barrier between the user and some fairly straightforward ideas. If I use the term *modus ponens* you may not know what I am talking about. If I say that $A \wedge (A \supset B) \rightarrow B$ you may also be a bit puzzled, but you could reasonably wonder why either bit of arcana is necessary if all you want to do is to be able to conclude B is true, whenever you know that A implies B, and that A is true.

Of course, to logicians these phrases are not arcana but the terminology of their science. Logical terms are the agreed-upon conventions of a field. They speed communication, and they make explicit ideas that can easily become muddled when stated in a less explicit fashion. The critical point is that these Latin phrases and formulas are usually translatable into ideas and statements that we are familiar with.

Just as one benefits from knowing a few basics about DEs before modelling with integrate and fire neurons, a knowledge of some of the mathematical ideas of first-order logic will improve our ability to model with programs like ACT-R or NetLogo.

17.2   Origins of Mathematical Logic

AI is a recent science, but the logic that underlies it has ancient origins. We might guess this from the choice of philosopher featured in this famous syllogism:

- All men are mortal.
- Socrates is a man.
- Therefore, Socrates is mortal.

The syllogism is a logical structure where a necessarily true conclusion is deduced from a prior series of postulates. The syllogism had its origins with Aristotle, tutor of Alexander the Great of Macedonia and intellectual heir of Plato, who was himself a disciple of Socrates.

Logic's classical forms became rather ossified. An Aristotelian approach was standard throughout the Middle Ages. The relationship between logic and mathematics was recognized, but the path to treating logic mathematically was not clear. Boole's mathematizing of logic can be compared in importance to Descartes' algebraizing of geometry. As Descartes demonstrated a correspondence between algebra and geometry, Boole did the same for logic and mathematics. Both developments allowed for a more rapid advancement by giving mathematicians the justification to step back and forth between domains and use whichever was most helpful in proving their theorems.

The era of Boole begins logic's release from artificial paradoxes produced by the vagaries of language. We can ask what in the syllogism above it means to be "mortal?" How do we decide who Socrates is? These details are important for particular applications, but they are not essential for the argument viewed generally. By substituting symbols for wordy statements we can make the assertions less ambiguous. We can then focus on the relations among our propositions. To apply logic to our personal circumstance we will still need to decide how to map our specific circumstances onto the agnostic symbols of logic, but eventually we will be able to determine if our conclusions are logically justified. There is a risk when one focuses on logic as symbol manipulation. When symbols are considered apart from their semantic content, there is the risk that the whole exercise becomes sterile and loses its relevance for deciding human dilemmas.

George Boole (1815–1864)

Mathematical logicians argue about whether George Boole should be regarded as "founder." I have chosen to focus on Boole because the adjective *Boolean* is so common in computer science. Another reason for awarding Boole founder status is that his interest in symbols and their transformations was motivated by an effort to develop a theory of "thought," a motivation that is at the heart of AI. So, if he is not the founder of logic, he is at least the Patron Saint of AI.

Boole was born in 1815 to a family of very modest means. His father was interested in scientific and technical advances, and belonged to a cooperative that pooled resources to provide books and materials for education. Booles Senior and Junior collaborated on their own investigations and self-educating.

George Boole is described as an active and curious youngster. He was delighted at age 10 to be given a Latin grammar, and taught himself that language along with Greek. Eventually, though not as a child, he went on to learn other languages. With his interest in, and talent for, education, he found work as a teacher at a local school. To increase his income so he could contribute to the family's support, he opened his own day school.

Boole published widely, including in the *Proceedings of the Royal Society*.[1] Though he did not have a formal academic degree, his talent was recognized. When the Queen of England organized universities in Ireland, Boole was appointed to a position in mathematics.

For Boole, the connection between algebra and logic was a long time coming. There were 20 years between the first idea and "*A Mathematical Analysis of Logic*" published in 1847. Boole later published a fuller and better effort as "*The Laws of Thought*." Both of these books are available for free download through Project Gutenberg.[2]

Boole's idea was that scholastic logic, the logic of Aristotle, could be improved by a different symbolic treatment and through the introduction of transformations. For Boole, symbols such as $x, y,$ and z represented classes of objects, for example, flowers or men. In addition, there were operations, $+$ and $\times$, that operated on these classes. There was also the identity sign ($=$), and 0 and 1 were used to represent "nothing" and the "universe."

From these beginnings you will get that x is all things x. Since 1 is the universe, $(1 - x)$ becomes the complement of x, that is, all things in the universe take-away x, or stated yet another way, all things that are not x. This means that we can see the $-$ sign as meaning negation (other symbols used for negation are $\neg$ and $\sim$).

In many ways, the basic rules for Boole's logic are the same ones we learned for our secondary school algebra. One exception is $x^2 = x$. This is Boole's Law of Duality. If x is all things x and $-x$ is all things not x, then we can see that by the rules of conventional algebra we would have $-x \times -x = x \times x = x^2$. However, something cannot simultaneously be both a thing and the negation of that thing. Therefore Boole constructed his alternative definition. He used multiplication as,

(Continued)

(Continued)

basically, the intersection of two classes as things, for example, $x \times y$ is the class of things that are x and that are also y, and thus $x \times x$ is x.

This is the barest of introductions to Boole's ideas, but it shows how Boole foresaw the use of symbols to represent classes and signs, and that he recognized the value of utilizing an algebraic approach to demonstrate something intended to approximate the laws of thought. Claude Shannon, the founder of information theory, is said to have been partly spurred on in his researches by recognizing that there was a correspondence between electrical switches and Boole's truth functions. An excellent introduction to Boole and his ideas is found in Gasser (2000). That is where most of the information in this section was taken from.

17.3   There IS More Than One Type of Logic

In some cases we know, in others we believe, that something is true and something else is false.* We commonly refer to both types of things as facts. What we would like to have is a procedure to follow that would allow us to augment our current set of facts by bootstrapping from the set of things we currently take as given. This, in a nutshell, is the activity of the logician: to provide us with a justified recipe for expansion. As you might imagine, there is more than one way that we can set about this task.

The basic building blocks of logic are those items that can be either true or false. For example, the *statement* that today is a sunny day could be true or false. Such statements are only a subset of all sensible, allowable sentences. If I ask you to give me a route to Waterloo, Ontario, I have asked a sensible question, but the question "Can you tell me how to get to Waterloo?" is not a statement that can be regarded as either true or false. It is not a logical *proposition* even though it is a well-formed English sentence.

The statements that can be regarded as either true or false are the atoms of logic. They can be compounded and they can be placed into sets: Today is a sunny day. Today is a Tuesday. Today is the first day of Fall. Just because items are placed in the same set does not mean they all have to be true.

Logic enters into deliberations on truth and falsehood when we try to determine whether a new statement is true or false from the characteristic of other supportive statements. If you accept as true that the number x is even, and that the number x is prime, then you can deduce whether the statement that $x = 44$ is a true statement. You can also use those *premises* to support the claim that there is only a single integer for which x is true. Note that the logical conclusion depends on the assumption that the premises are true (or false). We can make any assumptions that we choose, even those that are known to contradict the "real world." Thus, saying that something is logically true does not mean it is factually true. The latter depends on the empirical evidence for the propositions.

---

*An excellent source for reviewing the material in this chapter is to be found in Galton (1990).

Table 17.1   Connectives for propositional logic.

∨	or
∧	and
~	not

Table 17.2   Truth table for "And."

A	B	A ∧ B
T	T	T
T	F	F
F	T	F
F	F	F

Propositional Logic

Propositional logic deals with statements and propositions. For example, the statement "It is sunny" may be true or it might be false, but it is only one or the other.

Or is it? What if it is partially cloudy? Does that count as sunny? These vagaries of language are part of the reason that logicians prefer to use symbols to represent statements like these. Logicians are interested in general rules about statements, and not so much in the truth or falsity of particular statements.

While the English statement "It is sunny" may be ambiguous, the statement "It is A" is not. It is not ambiguous because by definition A is something that can only be in one or the other of two states called *true* and *false*. You can see why, when a computer programmer uses a value (like the ones used in conditionals; page 49) that can only be either true or false, it is called a "Boolean variable" or even just a "Boolean".

In propositional logic the symbols representing true and false statements are combined with other symbols (Table 7.1). These *connectives* are sometimes called *truth functionals*.

> To convince yourself why logicians resort to abstraction try to come up with five non-trivial statements that can only be true or false. See if others agree with you.

We can evaluate whether two different sentences are *equivalent* (≅) or one *entails* (⊨; this symbol is sometimes called "turnstile") another. A simple, though tedious, method for doing this can be to use *truth tables*. For example, the truth table for ∧ is seen in Table 17.2.

In a truth table, we write out all the possible combinations of our symbols. Here A and B can each be true or false. As the number of symbols grows, so does the length of cases you have to consider. It can get very big, very fast. That is why computers can be a particular help in constructing and filling in these tables. Computers are good at these sorts of repetitive tasks. They are also good for checking if the lines are consistent. In this table we see that the "And" connective, symbolized by a wedge (which I think of as looking sort of like a letter 'A', the first letter of "And"), is true only when both of the things it connects are true. Otherwise it is false.

Exercise: Truth Table Construction "Or"

Construct the truth table for "Or" (symbolized by an upside-down wedge or 'V').

You might find this assignment difficult. It turns out we have to be clear what we mean by "Or." In Chapter 11 we met two different kinds of "Or" functions. In English, or is inclusive. If you ask me if I went to the movies OR I went out to dinner, I can truthfully say yes if I went to the movie AND went out to dinner. The alternative, the *exclusive or* ($\bigoplus$) is only true if I went either to the movies or I went to dinner, but not if I went to both.

Exercise: Truth Table Construction "Exclusive Or"

Construct the EXCLUSIVE-OR truth table and compare it to the AND and OR truth functionals. Can you also construct the NOT AND?

If you need to remind yourself what the symbols mean see Table 17.1 and the paragraph that follows.

The symbols for entailing and being equivalent are not truth functionals or connectives. They are statements about the relations between two logical propositions. It might be that whenever one statement is true, a second statement is also true. This means that the first entails the second. For two statements to be "equivalent" the entailment has to go both ways. Not only does the first being true mean the second will be true, but also it requires that if the second is true the first will be true. When statements are equivalent, they are both basically saying the same thing, and we can substitute one for the other.

Exercise: Demonstrating Entailment and Equivalence

We will use the truth table method. First:

1. Begin your truth table by writing down all the combinations of the truth or falseness of an "A" and a "B" proposition.
2. Next to them, in the same table, write down the corresponding true and false statements for both $A \lor B$ and $A \sim B$.
3. Rewrite the true/false states of B to the right of what you have just put down.

Questions:

- Does $(A \lor B) \land (\sim B) \models B$?
- Is $(A \lor B) \land (\sim B) \cong B$?

The logic of propositions is basically the logic of Boole. It deals with statements that can be true or false. It deals with statements where the truth, falseness, and equivalence of combinations are determined by connectives and the elemental pieces. There is a

Table 17.3   Quantifier symbols for predicate logic.

| ∃ | Existential quantifier | "there exists" or "there is" |
| ∀ | Universal quantifier | "for every" or "for all" |

great deal more to propositional logic than what I have presented here, but this should show you the relationship between these ideas and cognitive modelling.

Predicate Logic

Take the sentence, "No one can be a Boston Red Sox fan and a New York Yankees fan." (Feel free to substitute your favorite rivals, e.g., Manchester City and Manchester United.) Though this may feel like a statement you could make in propositional logic, it is not, and you can prove this to yourself by trying to write it down using symbols for true/false statements and the connectives introduced above.

What we seem to be doing in this statement is negating a statement about whether any one individual can be a fan of both teams. We have two statements: "is a fan of Red Sox" ∧ "is a fan of Yankees." We want to say that the ∼ (not) of that conjunction is true. But what exactly are we negating?

The transition from propositional logic to predicate logic (also sometimes called predicate calculus or first-order logic) is largely the work of Gottlob Frege. This variety of logic became popular among mathematical logicians in the early 1900s. The most dramatic innovation for the predicate calculus was the introduction of *quantifiers*. These quantifiers allow us to make meaningful statements about particulars. For example, we can say that there exists a person, and that the statement about that person being a fan of the Yankees is true, and that the statement about them being a fan of the Red Sox is true, and that the negation of the statement that there exists such a person is false. As Table 17.3 shows, the mathematicians were running out of symbols when they got this far and re-purposed some letters for their new intentions.

Predicate logic deals with statements about *classes* that are often defined by *properties*. This gives logic a connection to set theory, which we also discussed as a basis for probability theory (see Chapter 14). For example, we have the class of all people that are baseball fans. This is a subset of the set of all people. Predicate logic makes statements about the properties of elements, of objects, of a set, or of a class. It uses variables to represent elements of those sets, and it also has components for specifying the relations between elements and classes.

In predicate logic, lower case letters are the tradition for specifying putative individual elements (e.g., a) and capital letters are used to specify the class from which they come. In addition, upper case letters are often used for functions like the "isa" property: "isa" is just short hand for "is a." So if Albert is a baseball fan, we could use a capital "B" for "isa" baseball fan. Thus B(albert) or, better, B(a) to specify the function that maps our individual, Albert, to either true or false depending on whether he is, or is not, a baseball fan. For a Red Sox fan test we could use R and Y for the Yankees. Then to be a fan of both, $R(a) \wedge Y(a)$ would have to evaluate to true. Our original statement could now be written something like

$$\forall f \in F \sim (R(f) \wedge Y(f))$$

Is this an improvement? That depends. If you are talking to your neighbor, and he is not a logician, it is probably not an improvement. But if you are trying to be precise and clear and definite, then using a precise language with precise symbols is an improvement. It avoids the ambiguities of colloquial phrases, and it is more general. Even though we have specified our functions R and Y as having something to do with baseball fandom, they could really be anything. If we knew something about formulas that look like this then we would not only be able to evaluate statements about baseball players, but also we could evaluate statements about any problem that could be formulated with the same structure. Once we develop a formal vocabulary with specific rules, we can write a computer program for it, because computers are better than we are at the consistent, prolonged, repetitive application of rules.

As we will see shortly, many cognitive architectures make use of production rules and predicates. These are essentially statements about "things" and assert some property about them. We have two elements to worry about: the property and what it applies to.

A predicate is something we are familiar with from our intermezzo on "if" statements (page 49). A predicate is something that evaluates to true or false. "John is a baseball fan" has an object to which it refers, *John*, and we do not mean just any John, we mean a very specific John, and the predicate is: *is a baseball fan*. This predicate applied to this object is either true or false. While my illustrations so far have all applied to one object, we can specify relations between objects. "John and Jane are siblings" asserts a relationship between John and Jane. It may be true or it may be false, but it is a sensible and permissible predicate.

The predicate logic is basically a language. Just as English has words that have certain roles and a grammar that specifies the permissible ways to combine words based on their types, so logic has symbols (words) that have a syntax (grammar) that specifies the permissible combinations. One can say things that are grammatical, but nonsense, in both English and logic. It is also true that one can sometimes say things that are sensible, but not grammatical. This gives us some intuition for the difference between *valid* statements and *sound* statements. The former follow the rules, but may or may not be true. The latter are both valid and true.

Caution: Material Implication

> "Impenetrability! That's what I say."
> Humpty-Dumpty

It is common to see people in mathematics use a rightward-pointing arrow and to hear others, usually not logicians, say it means "implies." But to paraphrase Humpty-Dumpty, when logicians use a right arrow it means just what they say it means, neither more nor less.

Exercise: What Is the Meaning of Material Implication?

This exercise looks at the meaning of *material implication* and how it differs from our conventional use of the term "implies."

- In $A \rightarrow B$, assume B is true. What can we conclude about A; must it be true? False?
- In $A \rightarrow B$, assume B is false. What can we conclude about A; must it be true? False?
- How do your conclusions differ if the $\rightarrow$ is replaced by $\iff$?

The forward-pointing arrow ($\rightarrow$), but also, sometimes, the "subset" sign ($\supset$) or even a double-lined arrow ($\Rightarrow$), is usually read as "implies" or "if – then". As the preceding exercise shows, the meaning in logical parlance is not exactly the same as most of us would infer if we heard the word "implies" used in conversation. However, it is this "if – then" interpretation that unites predicate logic with the production systems that are the basis of many cognitive models and architectures. These form the basis for the chapter on ACT-R (page 173).

17.4 Summary

In this chapter I have provided a high-altitude flight over the land of Logic. I have intended to show that logic is not a single thing, but rather is a term that refers to a collection of rule-based systems. Logic is intended to state how we can rationally extrapolate from some statements to other statements. To control for the ambiguity of everyday language, most logical systems rely on abstract characters for their simple statements and use symbols to characterize permissible operations. While George Boole is the father in spirit and ambition for using logic to describe the language of thought, the form of logic most often used for cognitive modelling is the predicate logic of Gottlob Frege. Its innovation is captured in the pleasant-sounding phrase: existential quantification. In the following chapters, we will see how these ideas can be exploited as a base for modelling high-level cognition. We will also see that these ideas are not limited to modelling high-level cognition, but that they can also be exploited for modelling, at a high level, systems of cognitive agents.

Chapter 18

Intermezzo: Computing with Functional Languages

18.1 Functional Programming

In earlier interludes I wrote about imperative languages and presented examples of Python and Octave programs and scripts.* Imperative programming languages are languages organized around a sequenced set of instructions. There is another variety of programming language called *functional*. The criteria that make a computer programming language a functional language are subjective, but emphasize computing as the evaluation of functions and programs as elaborate function compositions.

This may become clearer after a few examples. If I want you to take a number, double it, square it, and then subtract 5, I could write an imperative program along the following lines.

Listing 18.1 Pseudocode imperative program

```
def compMath (x) =
    y = 2 * x;
    z = y * y;
    return (z −5)
```

This program performs each of the steps that we specified, in order, and uses a series of local, temporary variables to store the result. It is a perfectly good program, and would do what we specified. In this regard, functional programming can be regarded as a choice of "style." And a functional programming language is a programming language that supports that style.

Listing 18.2 Pseudocode functional Program

```
dbl  x  = x * 2
sqr  x  = x * x
sub5 x = x − 5
compMath x = (sub5 . sqr . dbl) x
```

---

*The difference between programs, code, and scripts is not crisp. Writing instructions to a computer is coding. If it is a brief set of instructions that runs and then quits, it is probably a script. If executing the code results in an autonomous computer operation that accepts further instructions from a user, and concludes when the user instructs it, then it is probably a program.

There are some interesting comparisons between this pseudocode and our imperative pseudocode above. First, we seem to be using the same syntax for defining functions in the functional example as the imperative code uses for the assignment of variables. Where the imperative code specifies y = 2 * x for a variable assignment we have the same sort of appearance for our dbl x = x * 2. Functional programming languages make little distinction between functions and data. Sometimes people will even advertise this fact by saying that for a functional programming language functions are data.

In an imperative language we feed a variable to our function and we get its output. But the functions in our functional example seem to take other functions as arguments since we have them all lined up in a single row with no intervening variable. We only have the little dot (.) in between them. This dot represents function composition. What our functional example does is compose our simple functions into one large function.

However, this example is a little artificial. You could view the functional version of compMath as really the same thing as the imperative example, but disguised by some new syntax. Let's try to make the idea of functions as data more explicit.

Listing 18.3   Pseudocode functional program: functions as data

```
sqr x   = x * x
dblf f = f . f
fourthPow = dblf sqr
```

I have used our sqr function again from above, but added two new functions. Look carefully at the dblf function. It is a function that takes another function and composes it so that it will be applied twice. Then to get the fourth power of a number I only need to apply dblf to sqr. But notice, too, that there is no variable here. In a sense, I am saying that whenever my program reads fourthPow it can substitute its definition, and the same for dblf and so forth. This continues until there is the most elemental expansion possible, which if I type in fourthPow 3 will print 81, because 81 is equivalent to fourthPow 3.

This can be a lot to get one's head around if one has experience with traditional languages. However, it really is no different from what you do in a spreadsheet program. You define a cell to have a certain function (e.g., = C1 * C1). This example is like our sqr. The representation that gets printed to the screen changes whenever you update the value in cell C1 of your spreadsheet.

18.2   Advantages of Functional Programming

Provability

In general, the advantages of functional programming relate to style, conciseness, and ease of understanding. Functional programming languages do not allow programming things that would be impossible in imperative languages, with a few technical exceptions. A pure functional language may make it possible to prove, in the mathematician's sense of the word prove, things about programs because some functional languages obtain a referential transparency, but most non-computer scientists will not find this much of a practical advantage.

Access to Innovation

Because functional languages are research tools for the computer science community, they often incorporate new ideas and innovations that will then be adopted by mainstream languages. For example, some functional languages developed techniques of "garbage collection" that are now standard in many languages. In the early days of programming, programmers specifically allocated memory to a process or data, and then when they knew that the program would be done needing the data, they specifically instructed the program to free up the locations in computer memory so that the storage could be used for something else. We generally do not need to do this anymore, in part because our computers have much more memory, but also because computer languages and the compilers and interpreters that support them have gotten better at figuring out themselves when they no longer will need a particular piece of data and they collect and discard the "garbage" and free up their own memory. Again, although this is an advantage, it is not unique to functional languages. And many of the innovations that appear in functional languages are not necessarily critically linked to their "functional" nature and are rapidly exported to other languages like Python and Java that are widely used in professional and enterprise environments.

Shorter Code Is Better Code

The real advantage in using a functional language lies in the fact that it may be a more natural way of expressing the idea that is being programmed. Thus it may be easier to say something in a functional programming language (and, vice versa, there are some things that seem kludged when expressed functionally, because they are naturally serial and imperative; with practice the latter exceptions become increasingly rare).

The greatest advantage for functional programming languages seems to be their conciseness. Functional programs often enable one to program more with fewer lines of instructions. The result is often more readable by a human being (the computer couldn't care less). Since shorter code is easier to read and figure out, it may lead to a shorter development time. It is also easier to come back to a short program after a period of weeks, months, or years, and remember what you were trying to do. If your program does not work as expected, hunting through fewer lines of code for a bug is a big benefit.

18.3   Functional Programming Languages

While the label is somewhat arbitrary, the list of functional programming languages frequently includes Lisp and Haskell.

Lisp(s)

LISP is an old language created in the 1950s. It dates back to the early days of computer science, and many of the innovations we see today in computer programming have their origins in this language. It is a language that has some fanatical adherents and that seems to have favored the lone wolf over the collaborative committee. An example of the fanaticism is that Lisp-ers argue over whether the program name should, or should not, be spelled with all capital letters. As an example of their independent streak there are numerous flavors of the language and various compilers. This variety can be a bit bewildering. Lisp features in our discussion of ACT-R, and so will not be considered further here. A good, modern introductory book to the Lisp language is the one by Barski (2010).

Another example of the independence of Lisp programming advocates is that there are dialects of Lisp. Some of these dialects have been developed with an educational goal in mind. These dialects, Scheme, which is now Racket, can be an excellent introduction to the Lisp style since they come with support for student learners. An example of the passion of the Lisp programmer can be seen in the evolution of Scheme to Racket.[1]

Haskell

This is my favorite programming language. It is uncompromising in its functional orientation, and it supports all the tools from basics to complex constructs. It is forthright in acknowledging its grounding in category theory and the lambda calculus, none of which needs to be known to make productive use of the language. It allows one to perform the eminently practical or esoteric. It can be used in an interactive mode or in a compiled mode. It allows a literate programming style or a traditional programming style. And the user community is extremely generous with their time in supporting novices.

Despite my quoting all these lines of praise, Haskell is not the main language I use to get things done. Most of my programming is done in Python, because there are already excellent libraries to support doing psychophysical experiments in Python, and I can leverage that work. When I want to do data analysis, I often use R because it is the statistician's language. New methods are implemented for me by experts. Haskell is the language I use when I want to enjoy programming, rather than when I need to be programming. For those younger than me, it would be an excellent first language. Unlike the other languages mentioned, Haskell's academic base means it is a rapidly evolving language. Though there are standard libraries, they can change frequently. The maturity of Haskell is reflected in some new, excellent resources for learning the language and for getting things done. Three excellent books are those by Hutton (2007); O'Sullivan, Stewart, and Goerzen (2009), and Lipovaca (2011).

18.4   Summary

In summary, the advantages of using a functional programming language are as much aesthetic as practical. You will write shorter programs, and that will make their maintenance easier. You will probably write more readable code, and that can speed development. But you will not find that you write code that does things a Java or Python program cannot.

Chapter 19

Production Rules and Cognition

Objectives

After reading this chapter you should be able to:

- understand the relation between an if–then statement and a *production*;
- appreciate the history of the use of productions as models of human cognition; and
- implement a simple production system.

19.1 Overview

A major approach to the high-level modeling of human cognition is to view intelligence as a *production system*. Two of the most widely known general purpose models of AI, Soar and ACT-R, follow this approach. Our goal in this chapter is to examine what it means for something to be a production system, and then to look at how these ideas can be extended to become a model of how humans think and human brains work.

19.2 Productions

A *production* is an **if–then** rule. The "if" part of the production is called the "left hand side" and the "then" part is called the "right hand side." For example, "if it is raining, then we will go to the museum, but if it is sunny, then we will go to the park" are two productions.

Productions are applied to "stuff." As we saw in Chapter 17, the theorist often finds it better to think of logical constructs abstractly, without binding them to specific real-world examples or terms. However, we may find that we can gain some intuition by using concrete examples. In this example, we are binding some of the abstract symbols to statements about the weather.

Multiple productions can operate on the same "stuff." Here we test the left hand sides of our two productions with the same information: the weather. Although this example makes the productions mutually exclusive, this is not the general case. We could, for example, have a production "if it is raining, then we will go to the museum, and if it is raining, then get my umbrella." Now both productions will be invoked on a rainy day.

The part after the "if" statement is sometimes referred to as a predicate, a term that, as we have seen (page 49), also comes up when writing if statements in computer programs. A predicate is a statement that can evaluate to either true or false. In our example, one of the predicates is the statement that "It is raining." This statement can be true or false. Our productions apply when the predicate for the left hand side evaluates to true. This will occur when it is raining.

What Do Productions Do?

Productions "do" what is in their then statement. You may be better able to remember what a production is if you think about the similarity between the words production and producing. Productions produce behavior. If the left hand side predicate is true, then our production produces the right hand side result. For our example, this would mean that we go to the museum with our umbrella.

An important detail is that productions may compete, cascade, or represent alternatives. Although we permit multiple productions to simultaneously test themselves, some common cognitive architectures, like ACT-R, restrict themselves to only allowing one production at a time to execute.*

If we wish to limit the number of productions firing to a single one, and we admit the possibility that productions can share the same predicate, then we need rules for deciding which production has precedence. The rules for arbitrating between preferences and for assigning priorities usually come not from the system itself, or specific rules of logic, but from a deliberate (and sometimes arbitrary) decision by the cognitive modeller. Even in the case where the decision is made arbitrarily, it is at least concrete. Therefore, its implications can be studied.

One way that the productions can be assigned a precedence is to make the predicates more extensive. For example, we could change the two "raining" predicates as follows: if it is raining and I have my umbrella then go to the museum. And the other production could be changed to: if it is raining and I do not have my umbrella, then get my umbrella. Now, we will have a natural ordering of the two productions. First, assuming that we do not have our umbrella, and that it is raining, we will fire the production that gets our umbrella. Now this production will no longer fire because its predicate will be false, but the production for going to the museum will be invoked.

In this simple introduction, I have introduced some points we will revisit. When multiple productions have access to the same state information, they are allowed to test themselves simultaneously. As a result, multiple productions may have predicates that evaluate to true. While all the productions with predicates evaluating to true are eligible to fire, we only allow one production on each pass through the system to actually do so. This means our production *system* needs a procedure for adjudicating or prioritizing. After an action is taken, everything repeats. As a result of a production's firing, our

---

*It is also common to say that a production "fires."

system's state has likely changed. A new set of productions enters the next round of competition and a different outcome results.

19.3   History of Production Systems

As we have seen before, developments in computational modeling were dependent on developments in digital computing. The history of production systems as models for human cognition tracks the emergence of the digital computer as a research tool.

Early developments in computing involved both hardware and software: how to instruct the computer what to do. Early computer languages used instructions at the level of the machine's hardware. Relatively quickly it was realized that a better approach would be to make languages that were at a higher level and to have other programs convert the high-level instructions into the machine's instructions. Languages evolved to emphasize letting people specify what they wanted the computer to do in a way that was more logical than digital. A natural inclination in composing such programs was to give a series of imperative commands with some sort of logic to regulate switching (see page 49): "Do this first, then do this second ..." Or "*If* this is true do this," or "*While* this is true do this." These types of instructions, namely, for, while, if, then, else, are part of almost every computer language (see page 49). The fact that this type of instruction seems natural led to the suggestion that it was also a suitable way to think about how human minds organized and iterated to solutions.

Herbert Simon (1916–2001)

A prime example of a figure who blended interests in psychology, AI, and computing is Herbert Simon. All these fields claim him as one of their own. His career used an interest in decision making to link these diverse fields. His accomplishments were recognized with a Nobel Prize in Economics in 1978 and the Turing Award, the computing "Nobel," in 1975.

As we have seen in our earlier historical profiles, a willingness to cross disciplinary boundaries also contributed to Simon's success. His interests were diverse and spanned from music to symbolic logic.

Simon's professional career began in public administration, but early in the 1950s he met Alan Newell when they were both at the RAND Research Corporation in California. Both appreciated that they shared a common point of view. They understood that computers could be much more than mere number crunchers; computers were symbol processors. For this reason, Simon and Newell felt that computers could be useful for the study of human intelligence.

One of their early joint efforts was *Logic Theorist*, a computer program written as a theorem prover. Elements of their early ideas, and the origin of productions as models of thought, can be seen in their early collaborative article on a computational approach to general problem solving (Newell & Simon, 1961).

Their conception of problem solving can be viewed as an *iterative, recursive* search involving the applications of productions. In their analysis of human problem

---

solving, which preceded their computational program, they wrote, "We may then conceive of an intelligent program that manipulates symbols in the same way that our subject does – by taking as inputs the symbolic logic expressions, and producing as outputs a sequence of rule applications that coincides with the subject's" (p. 113, Newell & Simon, 1961).

This idea, that computation, as performed by people, is the end result of a series of discrete steps that are performed according to rules (rules that have an if–then structure), was around even before the construction of an actual practical digital computer. Alan Turing's famous paper (Turing, 1936) also conceives of computation as the application of specific rules based on a computer's (human or machine) state. The current configuration, whether human or the machine's, leads to specific actions being taken, and ultimately leads to a correct computation.

Simon demonstrated to his own satisfaction that the notions of human and machine computation were similar. One of the ways he did this was by having a series of human beings function as "subroutines" to correctly solve a logic problem. According to his daughter,[1] Katherine Frank, this took place over a Christmas Holiday with family members as the subroutines. This event may have been the basis for the famous Simon story that in January 1956 he entered a classroom and told the students that over the Christmas break he had built a "thinking machine."

Solving the Simon and Newell Problem

In their work, Newell and Simon compared human and computer problem solvers. Here is the problem they used. Care to try your hand?

(R *implies* NOT P) AND (NOT R *implies* Q), *derive* NOT (NOT Q AND P).

The available rules and a solution are shown in Newell and Simon (1961).

19.4 Production Systems

We know what early researchers thought a production system could do, but what, more precisely, is a production system and how do they actually get the job done? In this section we explore, and write the code for, a simple production system.

Exercise: Productions and Tic-Tac-Toe

The purpose of this exercise is to explore how a production is built, and how decisions are made for its application and sequencing. Before we begin worrying about how to implement this as a computational system, it will be helpful to get a less formal introduction. To do this, work alone or in a small group, and try and develop a production system for playing the game of tic-tac-toe.

The only input your rule-based players should have is the state of the board. Everything should follow unambiguously, that is, only one rule at a time is used to play the game to completion. Necessary rules should include understanding whose move it is and when the game is over. In addition, some strategic rules, and their relative priorities, should be provided.

It can be easier to fix the icon of the two players, for example, the human subject is always the "o" and the computer the "x." From this you can determine, by knowing if there is an equal number of "x"s and "o"s, whose play it is. It can also be relatively easy to determine if the game is over. Either all the squares are filled or there are three of a kind in a row somewhere on the board.

Setting priorities is hard. How do you decide what to do when there are rows on the board with two tokens of the same type? And how would you write a rule to capture the strategy of placing a token where it renders possible getting three of a kind in more than one way?

To see how well your production system of if–then rules completes the game, pit your version against someone else's set. You play the computer's role to figure out what rule applies, and to determine the outcome of the game.

As the tic-tac-toe exercise shows, it is non-trivial to specify a set of rules for playing even a simple game. The need to decide which production has the highest priority is a challenge. While most adults, and not a few chickens,[2] think tic-tac-toe is a rather boring game with little opportunity for strategizing, the design of a production system to play this game is a hard problem. If it is hard to design a production system for such a simple game, what does that say about the appropriateness of the production system structure as a model for human cognition?

> Does the need for a modeller to design the production system pose a problem for cognitive architectures? Is a cognitive model incomplete if the rules and their specification come from outside the system?

Coding a Production System

How production systems develop is an important research question, but even if the productions are given to us, their use in a simulation requires that they be translated into a computer programming language. For any non-trivial system it will usually prove impossible to understand how a system of productions will interact and what behavior they will produce unless we implement them as a computer program and execute the program on a particular problem.

The need for a dynamic and frequently updated environment makes a production system a challenge to implement in a spreadsheet. It can be done. But programming a production system in a spreadsheet requires the use of macros and the spreadsheet program's scripting language. Our reason for preferring spreadsheet implementations initially was that their simplicity allowed us to begin programming some of the previous methods in an easy fashion and with a low overhead for having to learn any formal computer programming language. For production systems that advantage is lost. If we are going to have to learn how to program a spreadsheet with a scripting language, we

Table 19.1   Production system for string reversal.

Prod'n no.	Input	Output
1	$$	*
2	*$	*
3	*x	x*
4	*	null & halt
5	$xy	y*x
6	null	$

might as well learn something of a more general purpose language, and we will do this in the next chapter.

In a prior intermezzo (Chapter 18), I introduced functional programming languages. One advantage of such languages is their support for recursion: a function operating on itself. The idea of recursion is popular in cognitive theorizing and modelling, and we can begin to get a feel for its power, and the challenges of converting a production system to computer code, if we implement a simple production system.

The Problem: Reversing a Letter String

String is a computer term for a list of characters. ['H','e','l','l','o'] is the string for "Hello". A single quote (') is often used for one character and double quotes (") for lists of characters, that is, strings (note: Python is an exception to this rule). It is also common for a computer language to use square brackets to delimit a list.

This problem comes from the Wikipedia entry on production systems.[3] Our goal is to take a *string* and reverse it. For example, we want today to turn into yadot. We want this to happen without user control. We should write a program that takes one string as input and produces it reversed.

Now simply reversing the order of characters in a string is not a hard thing to do in most computer languages. Many of them actually have a function called something like reverse that does exactly this. But our goal is not just to reverse the order of the characters, but to do it using the six productions in Table 19.1.

The entries in the table work as follows: you begin scanning the string from left to right. If you find a match (e.g., to match production rule 1 you need to find two sequential characters that are both $ signs), you then remove those two characters and replace them with a single *. For example, "tod$$ay" becomes "tod*ay" when production rule 1 fires. The order above is important as it is the precedence for our rules. Even if multiple rules apply, we only use the highest ranked rule. Then, after our productions "fires," everything begins anew. It is when a production scans to the end of the string without a single match that it returns a "null" result. That is, it has reached an empty string, a string with no characters: "". This means that the first production we will use on any new input is production 6. Production 6 is the only one that is looking for letters alone. The first step in processing "today" will yield "$today".

Recursion is reflected in the way that we continue to repeatedly call our production system on an entry string. We take the output of the first pass through our production system and make that the input to the next round of exactly the same function. We just keep on recursing until our system reaches a base case that signals termination.

Exercise: Understanding Productions

To demonstrate your understanding of this production system, describe what plays the role of:

- the "if" or predicate;
- the "then";
- the adjudication process.

Then, to demonstrate that you understand the procedure we want to follow, process "ABC" by hand, recording at each step which rule you used, and what the interim representation was.

19.5 Summary

Productions are if–then rules. If this occurs, then do that. Collections of such rules are called production systems and they are suggested to be a basis for intelligent thought. Production systems as an architecture for human cognition often limit each processing cycle to one production; this requires that the specification of the production system includes a basis for adjudicating between multiple rules when there are multiple rules with predicates evaluating to true. We have seen how it can be a challenge to both generate the rules and apply the rules. In Chapter 21, we will examine a particular cognitive architecture ACT-R that uses production systems as the basis for modelling human cognition.

Chapter 20

Intermezzo: Functional Coding of a Simple Production System

In Chapter 19 we saw the production rules for a simple system to reverse the characters in a word (page 166). In this intermezzo, we will look at how we could code this in a functional programming style.

20.1 A Haskell Implementation

Haskell, and other functional programming languages, can easily express the rules of a production system and structure them to generate a recursive evaluation. We begin by coding each of the rules. I present a relatively complete example of the different production rules, and then take you through an explanation of some of the different symbols and syntax used in the Haskell language. You might find it easier to skip to the text after this entry and refer back to the code snippet as you read.

Listing 20.1 Haskell production system code

```
module ProdSys () where


p1 :: String -> String
p1 inp = case inp of
  '$':'$':rest    -> '*':rest
  []              -> inp
  _               -> (head inp) : (p1 $ tail inp)

p2 :: String -> String
p2 inp = case inp of
  '*':'$':rest -> '*':rest
  []      -> inp
  _            -> (head inp) : (p2 $ tail inp)
```

```
p3 :: String -> String
p3 inp = case inp of
  '*':x:rest -> x:'*':rest
  []         -> inp
  _          -> (head inp) : (p3 $ tail inp)

p4 :: String -> String
p4 inp = case inp of
  '*':[] -> []
  []     -> []
  _      -> (head inp) : (p4 $ tail inp)

p5 :: String -> String
p5 inp = case inp of
  '$':x:'$':rest -> (head inp) : (p5 $ tail inp)
  '$':x:y:rest   -> y:'$':x:rest
  []             -> inp
  _              -> (head inp) : (p5 $ tail inp)

p6 :: String -> String
p6 inp = '$':inp


runPs :: String -> [String]
runPs mystr = fmap (\f -> f mystr) [p1,p2,p3,p4,p5,p6]

chngd :: String -> [String]
chngd x = (filter (/= x)) (runPs x)

testPs :: String -> Bool
testPs x = ((elem '$' x) || (elem '*' x))

prodSys :: String -> String
prodSys inputString =
  let candidate = head . chngd $ inputString
  in if (testPs candidate)
    then prodSys candidate
    else candidate
```

Types

The double colons (::) are Haskell syntax for expressing the type of a function. Haskell is a statically typed language, which means that the type of a function never changes.

Types are found in all computer languages. For example, "one" could have a type of string, whereas "1.23" might have a type of float or double. Different computer languages use different typing systems. Some computer languages are dynamic and allow the types to be figured out, and potentially change. For example, "1.23" could be treated in one part of our program as a character string for printing a number to the

Figure 20.1   A screen grab of my computer running the production system for which the code is shown in Listing 20.1 above.

screen, and in another part of our program it could be used as a number for multiplying something else. Haskell does not allow such dynamic use. Although it is optional, I have explicitly declared the type signatures in this code, so that you can see how a functional language maps easily onto our mathematical idea of a function as a machine for processing input into output. In our case it means that we put in a string and we get another string as output. The symbol → in Haskell tells us this is a function that takes in one type and outputs another. In our case the input and output types are both strings. Just like Python, Haskell uses the [ ] notation for a list. Thus [String] specifies a list where each element in the list is a string of characters. For each function definition, on the line immediately after the type definition, I define what the function is doing. This should look similar to the functions we are used to seeing from Python.

> In most computer languages decimal representations of numbers are referred to as floats. This is because of the way they are represented in a computer memory that only uses discrete zeros and ones. If a float has not just 16 slots for the number, but in fact has 32, the number is called a double, because it has double the precision.

Getting Haskell for Your Computer

This code can be executed. To do so, you will need to have Haskell installed on your computer.

You can download the Haskell Platform,[1] a Haskell system that is available for many operating systems. After you have done so, you launch the interpreter by running ghci from a terminal (this is the Cmd in Windows). You will need to load the program. The "path" you specify will depend on where you stored the source code (text file with the functions). You can see from Figure 20.1 how it works on my computer. Once you have done this you can use all the functions that are written in the source file. If you type the last one, prodSys, it will call itself recursively.

Without attempting a Haskell tutorial there are still a few points to emphasize because they help us see how to express a production system concisely. We can specify each rule individually, as I have done here, and then test them all at once when we run the production system (runPs).

Recall that all our production rules can test themselves for eligibility given the state of the system (in our case, our input letter string). Our code takes only the first one that has changed. This reflects the fact that we want our productions to have a built-in precedence. The highest applicable production in the ranking gets to fire. Also note that I have built in a simple test to see when we are done.

Each of my productions uses a particular style. Because it is so repetitive we can more easily understand our code. Each production looks at the input to see if it fits a particular case or not. For most of the rules we scan down the length of the string to its end (the empty string: []). If we do not reach the end, we slide down a character and call our function again, from inside itself! This is recursion. We have it here explicitly in our code; recursion is a common theme of cognitive architectures for generalized problem solving. Many computer languages require some fiddling to get a recursive function, but for Haskell it works "out of the box." Lastly, our productions have a case that is invoked when our if condition is met; we perform substitution on our string and leave the function. We use recursion again when we execute the function prodSys. Note that we include the function in its own definition. Until testPs fails, prodSys keeps on calling itself, like a snake eating its own tail.

> Do you understand why the last line in Figure 20.1 has "Britt Anderson" as both input and output? Is that a bug?

20.2   Summary

What we have done here is no different from what you did by hand at the end of the previous chapter. It merely shows how you can use a functional computer language to compactly represent a series of rules and then use recursion to apply them. For this reason, functional programming techniques are frequently used in programs simulating human cognition and in general purpose problem-solving programs.

Chapter 21

ACT-R: A Cognitive Architecture

Objectives

After reading this chapter you should be able to:

- understand the basic structure of an ACT-R program;
- understand how ACT-R programs are built out of productions; and
- use ACT-R and Lisp to build a simple cognitive architecture for playing rock-paper-scissors.

21.1   Overview

We have introduced logic, Boolean variables, and their use for creating if–then rules called productions. We even implemented a simple production system to see its operations in action. In the present chapter, we explore one of the most successful and fully developed applications of the production system approach to cognitive modelling: ACT-R.

21.2   A Full-Fledged Cognitive Architecture: ACT-R

Two of the best developed and most widely used cognitive architectures are Soar and ACT-R. The latter has been used extensively in psychology and is the one we will focus on here (Anderson et al., 2004). We will consider first what is meant by the term "cognitive architecture" and then examine how ACT-R relates to the production system ideas that we have introduced above. Then we will look at getting a working version of ACT-R installed on our own computer, explore an introductory tutorial, and build our own simple version of the rock-paper-scissors game in ACT-R.

> ACT-R stands for Adaptive Control of Thought - Rational.

Despite their similarities, Soar and ACT-R have a fundamental difference. Soar is about intelligence per se, intelligence stripped of its biological implementation. Biology may provide examples of intelligent systems, but for Soar the goal is to create a general intelligence, not to understand human intelligence. ACT-R is concerned with the latter task. Human data serve not only as the source of ideas for ACT-R, but also as important constraints. It is possible for ACT-R to be too intelligent. This is not true for Soar.

This distinction should not be overdone. Both Soar and ACT-R draw inspiration from Simon and Newell's early ideas about how to model general problem solving. While ACT-R's recent implementations put a great deal of effort into biological plausibility, the origins of ACT-R were more psychological than neurological (Anderson & Kline, 1997).

What Is a Cognitive Architecture?

The answer to this question lies in considering the conjunction of its elements. Architecture should bring to mind blueprints and building. It is a specification. It outlines what the pieces are and how they go together. But the term also has the connotation of physical components. Cognition brings to mind thinking; deliberating over facts; making decisions; solving problems.

Specifying a cognitive architecture requires that we give some details to both terms: architecture and cognition. To be an *architecture*, one has to declare what the components are functionally speaking. What are the processing elements? Are the processing elements the nodes of a connectionist network or are they the structures of a production system? Either answer is acceptable as an architectural specification. To be a *cognitive* architecture, one needs to specify what cognition means, or at least give a few well-chosen examples of the class. Commonly, these are higher order psychological concepts like memory or reasoning. When you specify both the domain of application that is cognition, and the mechanisms of execution that cognize, then you have specified a cognitive architecture. To reveal a little rhetorical flourish, a cognitive architecture is a specification for thought. ACT-R is motivated by this idea, which is why its creator, John Anderson, wrote a book called *"The Architecture of Cognition."*

A Brief Sketch of ACT-R

Currently, ACT-R is more noun than acronym. As you might imagine, before there was an ACT-R there was an ACT. The software for ACT-R is now up to version 6.0, and ACT-R has undergone a great deal of change over its 40-year life. Despite these changes, ACT-R remains consistent in some very important ways. ACT-R views knowledge as being largely of two types: declarative and procedural. This emphasis on procedural and declarative processes demonstrates ACT-R's origin as a model of human memory.

Declarative knowledge is facts and figures: for example, there are seven continents; $2 + 1$ is 3. Procedural knowledge is *how* you do something. It is the variety of knowledge that encapsulates productions, for example, if this is true, then you do that.

We know from studies of brain injury that focal cerebral damage can cause isolated functional impairments. This suggests that the brain is composed of modules that run in parallel, and this is a major architectural feature of ACT-R. There are component modules that encapsulate knowledge. And there are modules that perform functions to manipulate that knowledge. The modules are not arbitrary, but are specified based on empirical results in human psychology. The only modules we will deal with are on empirical results in human psychology. The only modules we will deal with are the declarative and procedural, but ACT-R has modules for vision and motor behavior, among others. The software that implements ACT-R is sufficiently flexible to allow for the development of new modules that users might need and can justify.

A by-product of the modularity of ACT-R is that there needs to be some way for the contents of the various modules to interact. ACT-R implements such a system via buffers. The contents of modules can be selected and placed into a module's specific buffer. The size of the buffers is specified in *chunks*, and the number of chunks per buffer is limited, motivated by the classic claim that human short-term memory can maintain 7 ± 2 items. While we can only keep a few items, or chunks, active in our working memory, that is, our declarative memory buffer, we can keep a virtually unlimited number of facts in our long-term store. ACT-R enforces the limits by tracking chunks, their types, and their contents. The contents of the various modules are parcelled into pigeon holes called *slots*.

The operations of an ACT-R simulation are cyclic. At any given time there is a goal and buffers of relevant modules are probed. Based on the contents of the buffers, the procedural system searches its library of rules for all applicable holdings. If the left hand side "if" statement matches, then the production is applicable.

After the matching step, the procedural system selects one production for "firing." If more then one rule is in the running, then there is a system of conflict resolution. When a production is said to fire, it means that the right hand side is invoked. The right hand side is the "then" part of the if–then rule. The contents of this if–then rule can be wide. The goal could be changed as a result of the production's action or requests could be made to various modules to change, or clear, their buffer contents. Once the production has completed its activities, the cycle repeats. Repetition continues until there is nothing left to do. In practice, the software that implements ACT-R limits these stages to a single step, a specified number of steps, or a specified period of simulated time (see marginal note).

> How long a computer program takes to complete is its *run time*. But the computer may have another "clock" that converts processing stages and operations into the amount of time that it is thought they would take if being performed by a biological system. This "time" is called *simulated time*.

Using ACT-R

To use ACT-R you have to get ACT-R. In this subsection we will examine how to get a working copy of the free ACT-R software. In fact, there are a few different flavors that you can try. There are versions of ACT-R written in the Java[1] programming language and the Python[2] language. Both versions are true to the spirit of ACT-R and represent faithful implementations that adapt to their respective programming languages. They are adequate for anything that a beginner would want to do, but neither is the canonical program. If you know either Java or Python, then you should consider starting with one of these versions and leveraging your existing expertise. If you know neither of those programming languages, you might as well download the original version.[3]

ACT-R version 6.0 is written in Lisp. Lisp is one of the oldest programming languages and has a long history of use by those interested in the computational aspects of cognition and AI. It is no more difficult to learn than any other language, and for the novice some things may be substantially simpler. However, because it comes from a tradition of hackers and free-thinkers the standardization and support are fragmented. Fortunately, you need to know almost no Lisp at all to begin to use ACT-R as a tool for exploration, but you would need to learn some Lisp to exploit the research potential of ACT-R.

You Need Lisp

Actually, you do not. ACT-R provides standalone versions that do not require you to have Lisp installed on your computer. Because of this, the stand alone versions are easier to install and to begin to use. But because they are incomplete, and because they shield you from the implementation, they do not give you the full power of ACT-R.

Computer-based experimentation requires that you be able to read the source code. You should never trust a computer model that does not make the source code publicly available. To be publicly available does not mean free. For example, code written in MATLAB will require a working version of MATLAB, which will cost you money, but a model written in MATLAB can still make its source files available for inspection.

Getting Lisp is not as easy as getting other programming languages because there is no single approved version. Fortunately, there is an accepted standard, and almost all modern Lisps respect this standard (ANSI). Consequently they are sufficiently inter-operable that you can compile and run ACT-R using any one of them.

Given Lisp's eclectic background, there is more support for *nix operating systems than for Windows or Mac OS X. This is because most Linux operating systems will have a package management system for the installation of software packages. Common Linux distributions are Ubuntu, Debian, and my favorite: ArchLinux. It is possible to set up a Windows or Mac OS X computer to also be able to run Linux, but while it may be easier to get Lisp installed on a Linux system, it is not easy and it will require patience and perseverance.

*nix is an abbreviation used for all Unix and Linux-like operating systems in all their various flavors. Not all of these have the nix suffix, for example, FreeBSD.

Which Lisp?

Steel Bank Common Lisp[4] and CLISP[5] are widely used Lisp versions that are freely available and will work well for you. They can be more convenient when paired with QuickLisp,[6] a Lisp library manager which simplifies getting and installing common Lisp packages for Common Lisp variants. However, if you do not have experience in doing these kinds of free-form installations, then I suggest you remember the old adage: you get what you pay for.

LispWorks is a for-profit company that maintains a version of Lisp that installs and works and comes with necessary libraries. It also offers support for its products. If you envision using Lisp for business or as a major part of a research platform, LispWorks would be an excellent choice. We can take advantage of the fact that the company behind LispWorks is a generous supporter of education and provides a free personal version. This program is limited in its capabilities, but it is an excellent platform for becoming familiar with Lisp without having to worry about installation or maintenance issues.

The LispWorks Personal version will be all that we will need for running ACT-R. The LispWorks Personal edition is found through the company's website.[7]

Installing LispWorks

You are looking for the Products tab on the homepage menu. This will direct you to the Personal edition. Find and download the version that is correct for your operating system (Windows, Macintosh, or Linux). You will have to fill out a short form notifying the company about who you are and the purpose for the download. You will need a license file that LispWorks provides. This is for your personal installation of LispWorks. You should not try to copy files from one user to another user; there is no real benefit to doing so, and if you do you risk making your installation fragile or unsuccessful. The installation is more complex for Linux users, but if you are using Linux, you are probably already familiar with the basic procedures for downloading and installing software.

Installing ACT-R

In what follows, I assume you are using LispWorks. If you have installed another version of Lisp, you will have to adapt these instructions to your configuration, or follow the instructions for your particular version on the ACT-R website.

To download ACT-R you need to go to the ACT-R homepage.[8] There is a menu item of *Software & Tutorials*. Clicking this link will bring you to the download page. There are "standalone" versions for both Windows and Mac, but you should not download these. The reason you got LispWorks running is so that you could use the full, unconstrained version of ACT-R. Download the source code zip file to get all the software and the reference manual and tutorial files.

This *.zip* file is a compressed file. It has been run through a program to make it smaller. Before you can use it, it has to be expanded. You do this with a program called unzip. You probably already have a version of this on your computer, though it may have a different name. When you download the file your computer will prompt you to see if you wish to extract the archive, or words to that effect. If it does, then you have a version of unzip. Save the unzipped version in a directory near your LispWorks installation. If this does not happen automatically, you will need to find and download a version of unzip.

Barriers to Entry

At this point, you might be wondering if all this effort is worth the trouble. That is a question that only you can answer, but it does raise an interesting point about the barriers to computational research in neuroscience and psychology. Nothing about the downloading and unzipping of software has anything to do with research into computational psychology. Yet, if you do not know how to do all this then you cannot get to the point where you can begin to use the tools.

(Continued)

(Continued)

While the procedures for getting and installing software are arcane, they are not intellectually difficult. They do however require practice. Whether you ever want to use ACT-R or not, learning how to acquire source software for installation is a good skill. It will serve you well, and it will open up the opportunity to use a variety of free tools. Most researchers working on computational procedures will make their software freely available, but since most research groups are small, non-commercial operations, they will typically do so in a way that the user will have to have some practical knowledge about how to acquire and install software from source. If you develop this knowledge, you will find a wealth of material available for your research, exploration, and teaching.

Hopefully the Box "Barriers to Entry" has inspired you, because if you want to use any of the graphical utilities that ACT-R provides, you will also need to have Tcl/Tk installed on your computer. Tcl/Tk is a scripting computer language and comes with a grocery cart of widgets

> You do not need to use the GUI to use ACT-R, but if you are a beginner, you will find this helps you to get started.

for building GUIs. You may already have this language installed on your computer. You can determine this by going to a command line and typing: `wish` (no pun intended). If a little blank window opens up, then you are good to go. If not, navigate to the Tcl/Tk homepage[9] and get the version needed for your system.

Getting Up and Running

In this section we walk through the basics, step by step, to get you started. Start LispWorks using the method appropriate for your operating system (see Figure 21.1). Then use the FILE menu to locate the LOAD option. This will open up a menu. Navigate to the directory where you saved the unzipped versions of the ACT-R download and locate the file: `load-act-r-6.lisp`. Click OK

> If you make a mistake typing something, LispWorks will spit out a long error message. To back out of this you can usually type :C 5 or whatever number LispWorks tells you will "Return to top level loop 0."

to load. Lots of things will happen. Take a moment to enjoy life in the Matrix. Then press the SPACE bar as instructed. Now open a command line (also called a *terminal*). You will have to use the `cd` command to change the directory to where you have ACT-R installed. Inside the ACT-R directory you will see sub-directories that include `.../actr6/environment/GUI`. The `...` will be different depending on where you installed the program. Now you type `wish starter.tcl` to launch the GUI support for ACT-R. Switch back to the big LispWorks window and type the command `(start-environment)`. Note the parentheses. These are necessary, and they are what makes you a Lisp programmer. Everything in Lisp is a list, even commands, which in this case is a list of length 1.

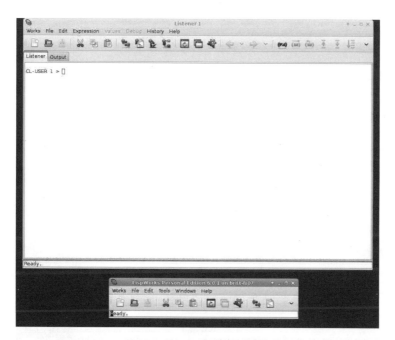

Figure 21.1   A screen grab of the LispWorks program after start-up. There are two windows that open up. You will use the larger one, and ignore the smaller.

You are now ready to run and execute ACT-R models. Several models come with the ACT-R installation. They are located in tutorial folders and come with documentation. The documentation explains the tutorials generally and helps you to develop your familiarity with the features and capability of the ACT-R platform. Figure 21.2 shows the LispWorks and ACT-R GUIs after I have loaded the addition model (use the same LispWorks Load option as before, but this time navigate to the tutorial folders).

Another Introduction to ACT-R: Counting

Exercise: Count with ACT-R

The best way to get a basic introduction to ACT-R is to start using it. The authors of the software have provided an elementary tutorial that covers the very basics.

- Load the counting model of ACT-R Tutorial 1.
- Run the model for 1 second of simulated time.
- Determine what number the model is counting from and what number it is counting to.
- Open up the source code file in any convenient word processor.

Remember, you can always look at the source files. Source files are text files. If you are confused or curious, look at the source. The Lisp code for the counting model is

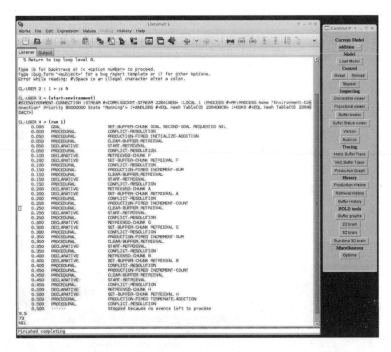

Figure 21.2   A screen grab of the LispWorks program after starting the ACT-R GUI and running the addition model provided in Tutorial 1. Note the use of the :c command to back out of an error and the (run 1) command to run the model. The long list following this command is called a "trace" and shows the various steps that ACT-R executed. The *verbosity* of this trace is under user control.

human readable and it uses words that make sense. You should remember this if you ever author your own programs. Take a little time and make thoughtful choices of variable and function names. Names that automatically suggest to a reader what a variable represents or what a function is doing can greatly improve the efficiency of your work and will make your code and your ideas more accessible to others.

The structure of the simple counting model is the same as the structure used for complex models. Elements of the model are *lists*. Sometimes these lists contain only commands, such as (clear-all). You can think of these models as a script. If you carefully typed each of these lines into the LispWorks command line one after another you could get the same result.

The outline of an ACT-R model is seen in this counting tutorial, and it provides some good lessons about programming in general. Usually you want to start with a clear workspace. No old variables or values are hanging about from a prior run or an earlier project. The counting tutorial author clears the workspace and uses the define-model command to, well, define the model. Parameters are set. These are like constants in an equation. They can determine fixed features of the model; like what types of items are to be held in declarative memory; chunk-types is the name for these constructs. To give an example in words: a dog is a species, a *type* of animal. Your own dog, Fido, is a particular dog, a particular animal that is of chunk-type dog.

Another part of an ACT-R model declaration is to add some facts to the declarative memory. Each of the facts has a name (like Fido ISA dog) and then a specification that the name *IS A* particular type. Next, we have the slots or pigeon holes for each example of our type with their value, for example, Fido ISA dog fur-color brown. You should note the similarity between the use of `isa` and our discussion of quantifiers in the introductory logic chapter (page 147).

After we are satisfied that we have an adequate list of declarative facts, we can specify the production rules. You know something is an ACT-R production rule if it starts with "p". After the p you can give a production a name. All elements before the "==>" comprise the *if* portion of our rule. Everything after is the *then* portion of our production. Lastly, we need a goal to get the model started. The goal is usually updated as the model proceeds. Goal declaration is done with the `goal-focus` command.

Exercise: Changing an ACT-R Model

Usually computer models begin with some prior work and proceed by incremental edits. To begin this process with ACT-R we will work with the count model.

First, edit the `count.lisp` file and make ACT-R count to 6. This is much easier than you might think.

Second, edit the `count.lisp` file and make ACT-R count to 7. This will require more work than counting to 6.

Third, if the first two assignments come easy, try making ACT-R count *down* from 7. This will require developing a new production, which the first two parts of this exercise do not.

ACT-R Reprise

We have spent time getting our environment organized. We have downloaded Lisp and ACT-R. We have unzipped and installed. Then we worked through a simple ACT-R script to see the main features of the language, and we edited an existing tutorial to begin to see how one might think about a cognitive model in ACT-R. Now, we can try to extend this effort by writing a simple model to perform a simple task. To do this we should remind ourselves that ACT-R is an architecture. It tells us how things can be built. According to ACT-R, cognitive models are built from productions. ACT-R also specifies how these pieces fit together and what functions and concepts are needed to be able to concretely program the instructions.

The ACT-R structure itself hides the arbitrary low-level aspects of a computer language. We do not need to know exactly what words are needed to store an item in computer memory, for example (this makes ACT-R a sort of domain- specific language embedded within Lisp). ACT-R gives us a higher order interface to a specific, non-arbitrary, hypothesis about how a cognitive architecture *should* be built.

ACT-R's architectural assumptions include, for example, that cognitive modules are encapsulated and that they include the functions of memory, vision, and motor acts. ACT-R hypothesizes that modules operate in parallel and communicate through size-limited buffers. Formally, a production rule system does not need any of these assumptions. These assumptions are what make ACT-R a particular hypothesis about how cognition works. It is the combination of a production rule engine welded to a modular chassis. The best way to evaluate the adequacy of this hypothesis is to use it as a basis for model building.

While ACT-R incorporates a number of assumptions and decisions about the structures and mechanisms essential for cognition, those assumptions provide general constraints. The assumptions limit the space in which we can search for a solution to a specific problem. That is where we, as users or modellers in the ACT-R framework, come in. We decide on the problem we wish to model, and we use our intuition and empirical data as the basis for conjectures on how a particular problem should be handled as a production system.

Then we build the model using the rules and pieces ACT-R gives us. ACT-R is like Lego. The pieces are generic, basic shapes. The pieces can be combined to build complex shapes. But the pieces are not much help in drawing the blueprints. Therefore, we do most of our thinking and planning before we begin to deal with specific decisions about the implementation. The success of our model as a model of human cognition will depend on how well the dynamics and performance of our model capture what is observed for real humans performing a similar task. If our model reproduces human performance, while at the same time respecting the constraints ACT-R imposes, then we will know that such cognition is possible in a production system framework. Since many other models have already done the same, this strengthens the claim that production systems represent a general solution to the puzzle of intelligence.

Playing Rock-Paper-Scissors with ACT-R

In this subsection we will try to use our basic familiarity with ACT-R to work through a problem not included in the tutorial set, but that is still elementary. We will play rock-paper-scissors (RPS).

Exercise: Code RPS Model in ACT-R

Building a model in ACT-R requires the following steps:

- Write out the specifications for what it is your model will need to remember to play RPS.
- Write out the productions your model will need to play RPS.
- When you are done, translate those statements into the language of ACT-R.

As the itemized list shows, model building proceeds from high-level descriptions to the lower level implementation. In addition, most programming is an iterative process. Code something, find bug, fix bug, repeat.

Coding is iterative in another sense too. It should start basic and gradually become more complex. Start with a fairly pedestrian implementation and use that to get a working prototype. Then refine this beginning version to be an ever better approximation to your goal. Lastly, when you have the full model running, compare its performance to appropriate empirical data.

An Example Approach to Playing RPS with ACT-R

In this section I lead you through my design. At each step I will explain my structure and demonstrate the incomplete version. You should try to complete each step of the modelling process yourself. Modelling is not a spectator sport, it is a practical competency, and it requires practice. Work slowly, completing each step before moving on. The bugs will not get easier to find when your code gets more complex. You want a clean, error-free execution of each step before proceeding to the next. I would encourage you to take minutes, hours, days, to try to make the next step on your own before moving on. If we disagree on how a step should be taken, do *not* assume you are wrong. There are a variety of ways to solve this problem. Mine is not necessarily the best. I chose it to be a simple and straightforward introduction.

To begin, open up a word processing program and save a plain text file with the name rps.lisp. Enter instructions to clear the work space.

Listing 21.1   Initialize

```
(clear-all)
```

How do I represent the pieces?   For my initial attempt, I have decided to let the game pieces be text strings. I know how to compare text strings in Lisp to see if they are equal. Using this simple approach lets me get started. Later on, I could decide to make the tokens of the game, the rock, paper, and scissors, their own types, but it is less frustrating if I do not have to go learning new functions before I even get started.

To decide whether a game is a win or a loss or a tie, I will need a function that takes in the two names for the tokens played by the two players, and that calculates the outcome. Try to write out a simple function in "pseudocode" that does this and then compare it to the Lisp function that I wrote below.

How do I tell who won?   To compare two text strings to define a winner we do not need ACT-R. We can write this in Lisp itself, and then call this Lisp function in our ACT-R production to get the answer.

Listing 21.2   Writing a Lisp function to judge the winner

```
(defun judge (p1 p2)
  (cond
    ((string= p1 p2) "tie")
    ((and (string= p1 "rock") (string= p2 "scissors")) "loss")
    ((and (string= p1 "rock") (string= p2 "paper")) "win")
    ((and (string= p2 "rock") (string= p1 "scissors")) "win")
    ((and (string= p2 "rock") (string= p1 "paper")) "loss")
    ((and (string= p2 "paper") (string= p1 "scissors")) "loss")
    ((and (string= p2 "scissors") (string= p1 "paper")) "win")
    (t nil)))
```

As this function shows, we can easily expand or adapt the ACT-R tools to suit our special modelling needs. defun is a Lisp keyword that lets us define a function which will have the name "judge" (see page 61 for a review of computer functions). The function accepts two inputs that have the names "p1" for player 1 and "p2" for player 2. string= is a Lisp function that tests whether two strings, a list of characters, are equal. We do a series of conditional tests to find the first condition that works. We also use the and function to see if both the first and second condition are true. And true to our Lisp environment we use lots of parentheses to say what goes with what. This function could be written much more compactly, but would it be better if it was compact? This function is fairly short and makes it obvious what is being compared even by someone not familiar with the Lisp language. Usually shorter is better, but not always. What you want is for your code to be clear. Remember that clever code is not always clear code.

Optional Exercise: Stretch Your Lisp Wings

Using the above function as a template, write a Lisp function to take two strings, any two strings, as input, and output whether they are or are not the same.

Write this in a file, load it into LispWorks, and then test it on the command line, for example, (judge "one" "two").

How do I define an ACT-R model?   We will use several keywords and begin with a comment. You can look up each of these keywords in the ACT-R help documentation, or you can do what I did and just copy them from someone else's code to get started and figure out if you need them later.

Listing 21.3   Declaring our model

```
;;; The ACT–R model

(define–model rps

(sgp
   :esc t
   :lf 0.05
   :v t
   :trace–detail low
   :er t
   :bll 0.5
   :ol t
   :act nil
   :ul t
)

(chunk–type name)
```

```
( chunk−type  name  slot )
( chunk−type  name  slot  slot  slot )
)
```

Lisp uses the ";" character for comments. Any following characters typed on the line after a semi-colon are ignored when Lisp reads the file. sgp is how we set ACT-R parameters. Just copy the ones that I have used here for now. Lastly, you will see three "chunk-type" statements. For my version of RPS, I need three types of chunks. I need to:

- describe the stage of a round of RPS;
- say where I am in the round; and
- indicate what all the parties are doing.

I have shown you where the name goes and how many slots I was planning to use. See if you can come up with your own schema, and then compare it to mine below. You will replace the word "name" with a good descriptive label for the chunk type, and then give individual names to the different slots that will help you remember what is supposed to be going there. Do not worry about whether we will pick the same words, but see how we compare in our intentions and the resulting structure.

What goes in memory?   Here is how I labelled my chunk-types

Listing 21.4   Chunk types

```
( chunk−type  stage )
( chunk−type  game  stage )
( chunk−type  trial  p1p  p2p  result )
```

I have chosen to create a series of chunks that will represent what stage I am at in the game, and another chunk that will carry and update that information. Lastly, I chose another chunk type that will contain the choices made by each of my two players and the result of the contest. Note that in ACT-R slots can be empty, so I can have a chunk of type trial and fill it in as play progresses.

Our next task will be to create the stages of our game. Initially it can be difficult to understand what a chunk-type is. Think again of animals. A dog is a type of animal, but my dog Fido is a particular dog. When we create the chunk-type stage we have created an ACT-R entity that is the type for all stages of the game (it is like the word "dog" in respect to animals). All the game stages will have a name and be an object of the chunk-type "stage". We add all these specific instances into the declarative memory.

Listing 21.5   Stocking declarative memory

```
( add−dm
  ( init  isa  stage )
  ( makep1move  isa  stage )
  ( makep2move  isa  stage )
  ( judge  isa  stage )
```

```
(record isa stage)
(quit isa stage)
(contest isa trial)
(g isa game stage init)
)
```

The first element of each of these little lists is the name that we assign to it. Then we use the keyword for ACT-R, isa to specify that it "is a" type stage. We can also fill up some of the available slots at this time if we choose, for example, by stating the name of the slot followed by the slot's value. Note that I created a chunk of type game with the name g and I put the value init into the stage slot.

What productions do we need?   While production rules are intuitively easy to under-stand, they present some challenges in practice because they use a specialized syntax. Recall that "==>" is the symbol that separates the if and then components. For each production we start with p init ... to declare a production and the name of it. We can use the same name for different types of things in ACT-R. For example, the string of characters "init" can refer both to a production and to a stage. Which "init" we mean will be deduced by our model depending on its context. The namespaces are local to the context where they are employed. Just because you can give the same name to multiple objects does not mean it is a good idea. It can make your code harder to understand and more difficult to debug.

In the *if* part of our production we need to specify which buffers should be checked and which conditions should be met. We can also create local variables that we can use inside a production to check or set the values of certain slots. We use buffername> to specify the buffer to check and we have a preceding symbol, "=", "-", or "+", in front of the buffer name. This can be made clearer by an example. Here is the code I used for the production that I envision initializing a round of RPS.

Listing 21.6   Initializing production
```
(p init
    =goal>
        isa        game
        stage      init
==>
    +retrieval>
        isa        trial
    =goal>
        stage      makep1move
)
```

In this production I query the goal buffer to see if it is contains a chunk that is an example of the chunk-type game and whether the slot named stage is present and contains a chunk with the name init. In ACT-R words that are not surrounded by quotes are expected to refer to the names of chunks. Later on you will see that the word "rock" is used rather than rock. I did this to make it easier for me to check equality, but in most instances it would be better to create a type of chunk to represent the tokens that could be played in the game and to check them as named chunks.

The *then* portion of this initial production purges the declarative memory buffer (known by the name *retrieval*) and recalls from memory a chunk of type trial. It then also queries the goal buffer and asks it to change the value of its stage slot to contain the chunk makep1move which is my name for the stage where player 1 makes a move. The only other prefix for a buffer that we have not seen in use is "-" which simply clears a buffer without writing anything into it.

Take a look at the next two production rules and then see if you can create productions for playing scissors and paper. The answers are available as part of the full code example in the Notes for this chapter. [10]

Listing 21.7   Two more productions

```
(p  getp1move
    =goal>
        isa         game
        stage       makep1move
    =retrieval>
        isa         trial
==>
    !bind! =p1choose (car
        (permute-list '("rock" "rock" "paper" "scissors")))
    =goal>
        stage makep2move
    =retrieval>
        p1p       =p1choose
)



(p  p2rock
    =goal>
        isa         game
        stage       makep2move
    =retrieval>
        isa         trial
        p1p         =p1p
==>
    =goal>
        stage       judge
    =retrieval>
        p2p         "rock"
)
```

There are a couple of new items in these productions. One is the use of words preceded and followed by exclamation points. The !bind! command is, as its name implies, used to bind something to the name of a variable, here p1choose by preceding it with the equals sign (=p1choose). This is where we use a simple Lisp function that chooses player 1's choice randomly from the three available choices. By entering the word "rock" twice on this list I make it twice as likely that rock will be chosen by player 1. This is obviously not player1's best strategy, because this biased play can be exploited by the second player to increase player 2's chances of success. But is it easy to get ACT-R to take advantage of this?

Exercise: Expanding Your Lisp Vocabulary

Find out what the Lisp commands car and cdr do and how they might be combined.

After we have gotten player 1's random, but biased choice, we store it in the variable named p1choose by prefixing the variable name with the equals sign. And then we use that variable to put the same value into a slot of the chunk which sits in our declarative memory retrieval buffer.

Note how our production that has player 2 playing rock advances the stage and sets player 2's choice.

Exercise: Player 2's Other Choices

Create the productions for player 2 to play scissors and paper, and think how it is that we can decide which of these productions will get played when.

Create the production for determining and recording the result of a trial. You will need to use the judge function created earlier.

Did I win? ACT-R does not have to work deterministically. That is, it does not have to pick the same production every time it faces the same set of conditions. Different productions can be randomly chosen. Also, the probability of a production can be set to determine how likely it will be chosen when multiple productions meet the "if" conditions. The probability of a production being chosen can also depend on how recently it has been chosen and how successful the outcome was when that production was used.

After we have finished a round, we will want to record an outcome and return to the initial stage. Here is how we can do this if player 1 won:

Listing 21.8 Production for recording a player 1 victory

```
(p record1Won
   =goal>
      isa        game
      stage      record
   =retrieval>
      isa        trial
      p1p        =p1c
      p2p        =p2c
      result     "loss"
```

```
==>
   !output!  ("P1  won")
   =goal>
       stage       init
)
```

Here we do not write the outcome to a file, though we could, but simply print out a message to the LispWorks console.

Exercise: More Outcomes

Create the two productions for recording whether there was a tie or player 2 won.

How to wrap it up? A mundane "halting" problem.   It can be convenient to have a production for exiting the cycle, though if you call the run function with a finite number your model will exit. In addition, it is often very useful to step through the model from the ACT-R GUI to observe each step in isolation and inspect the content of the buffers as the system is working. In this last snippet you will see the final things we need to do to write our ACT-R RPS model. We set the quit production, we manually assign different values to executing the productions that record who won, and we set the goal focus, which we need to begin, to our trial chunk.

Listing 21.9   Concluding the RPS model

```
(p  quit
   =goal>
       isa        game
       stage      quit
==>
   -goal>
)

(spp  record1Won  :reward  -1)
(spp  record2Won  :reward  1)
(spp  recordTie   :reward  0)

(goal-focus  g)
```

Even though our model has no choice what to do when it gets to the point of recording an outcome, the reward we have provided will be shared with all the productions that came before and led up to the ultimate reward. If player 1 is playing with a statistical bias then our ACT-R model should exploit this, because each time player 2 wins there will be a positive reward to share with the earlier productions. Since player 1 is playing rock more often than the other choices, the production for player 2 to play paper will get more reward than the others and should end up dominating player 2's selections. But will it work (see Figure 21.3)?

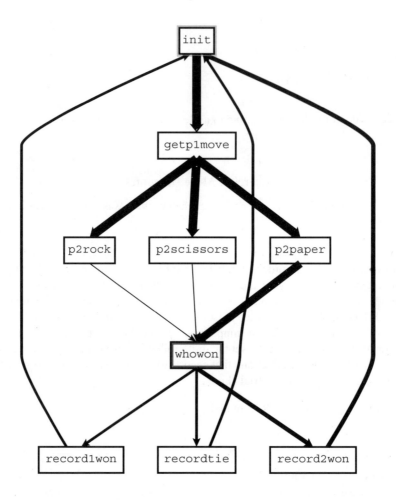

Figure 21.3   A plot generated from the ACT-R GUI that uses line thickness to show the relative proportion of trials that followed a particular route through the RPS production system. Note that the route showing that player 2 chooses to play paper most often and that it wins more than the other choices is demonstrated.

21.3   Summary

This chapter is a departure from our earlier chapters. Here we use an established cutting edge, cognitive modelling research tool. We were forced to this because there was no easier mechanism available to explore the production rule approach to cognitive modelling. As a bonus, this experience gives us a step up on being able to perform real research and helped us learn some basics about a common, popular functional programming language: Lisp.

In our exercises, we learned how to download and install software, and the basics of Lisp and ACT-R. We developed our skills at conceptualizing a cognitive problem and setting the outline for developing a cognitive model. We then stepped through the process of writing ACT-R code and ended up with a simple model for playing rock-paper-scissors. Such a first attempt could be the platform for a more detailed investigation of how humans learn to compete in simple two-player games. As such, it foreshadows the next chapter which looks at software designed for agent-based modelling.

Chapter 22

Agent-Based Modelling

Objectives

After reading this chapter you should be able to:

- understand what is meant by agent-based modelling;
- enumerate the components of an agent-based model; and
- implement an agent-based model using the NetLogo software.

22.1   Overview

A relatively new use of computational modelling in neuroscience and psychology has been the elaboration of an agent-based approach. The growth of this method directly parallels the growth of affordable, desktop computing power. We were always able to elaborate simple rules that we *thought* might *in the aggregate* yield emergent or complex phenomena, but we were not able to test our claims. Now, with cheap computing, we can use computational brute force to determine the answers. We program the individual behavior, and then we run numerous interacting versions of the same program and look at the overall behavior of the population of interacting agents.

It is obvious how such an approach could be useful to the social psychologist, but the benefits of an agent-based approach are not limited to that field. Any problem that can be posed in the language of autonomous interacting pieces can be studied with agent-based models. We should not conceive of agents as miniature people. Agents do not have to embody human goals or human abilities. We can associate our agents with animals, and then model butterflies flitting from flower to flower. An agent is just something that follows rules. Agency does not mean sentience or consciousness.

The ideas and tools of agent-based modelling can be used in a variety of settings and for a variety of questions. As an example of this approach, I will develop for this chapter an agent-based model of eye movements.

If your situation of interest involves a large number of items interacting or it needs to be repeated multiple times, then an agent-based model might be a useful approach. The real test of whether an agent-based model will be of use is whether you have a way to describe your system in terms of a small number of concretely specified actors.

In this chapter we will outline some of the ideas behind agent-based models and review some samples of their application. For developing our own agent-based model we will continue the example of Chapter 21 and learn how to use a freely available modelling package. NetLogo was developed for education, but it is very powerful, and it removes the need to worry very much about graphics, visualization, or developing GUIs for user interaction. Although it is programmed in Java it uses a Lisp-like syntax that will be similar to ACT-R's. Because of its prominence as an educational tool there is, relatively speaking, a large amount of tutorial material and examples are available. An excellent introductory text for NetLogo has recently been published (Railsback & Grimm, 2011).

22.2   History of Agent-Based Models

In many ways, the cellular automata of von Neumann presented in Chapter 11 can be regarded as the forerunners of the agent-based model. Cellular automata demonstrate the key features of an agent-based model, which include numerous entities operating under a small, specific set of rules and interacting in parallel to yield observations and phenomena on a larger scale.

Despite these roots, the language and popularity of the agent-based modelling approach date back only to the 1990s. Not surprisingly, this interest parallels the growth in power and the decrease in the cost of computer hardware. This growth was accompanied by a shift in the conception of an agent. For cellular automata, the rules were clear, concrete, and deterministic. As the idea of agents developed, agents began to be conceived of as little intelligences. Agents were imputed to have objectives, desires, beliefs, and intentions. It is easy to see how the value of this approach for the social sciences was quickly recognized.

Within this general approach there are different themes. In hindsight, work on *production systems*, formerly regarded as AI models, can be reinterpreted as agent-based models. Neural networks, too, can be rechristened as multi-agent systems. Another component of contemporary agent-based modelling is decentralization. By embedding the same agents in modified environments the effects of context can be studied.

Changes in computer science also impacted agent-based modelling. In the 1980s and 1990s there was a large emphasis on enlarging programming languages to include object-oriented programming support, for example, the C language was augmented to C++ and the latter grew greatly in popularity. Even the language of AI, Lisp, added an object-oriented model to its arsenal. With an object-oriented approach to programming, facts and procedures are grouped together into a computational "thing" called a *class* with individual members of the class referred to as *objects*. Just as a person has certain facts associated with them, such as their name, height, weight, age, and strength, they also have certain things that they know how to do, such as play the piano or throw a ball. Defining these facts and functions gives a specification of the human as object. Each individual is fitted out slightly differently. Our success at doing things like throwing balls depends on such factors as our height and weight and age and strength. In a computer program simulation of a human we can use this approach to compactly define our agent. Thus, along with the growth of computing power, the development of new software approaches facilitated the development of agent-based modelling and allowed non-computer scientists and non-programmers to more easily exploit these ideas.

Following these general developments, software platforms (essentially big programs with many supporting features) were written specifically for agent-based modelling. These platforms not only include the basics for specifying the agents, but also include facilities for viewing the agents and their activity graphically.

22.3   Components of an Agent-Based Model

The components of an agent-based model are becoming standard. In general, an agent-based model needs to have agents, links, and an environment. The agent is the computational unit that is given the rules for action. The links, also called relationships, specify how agents interact (e.g., compete or cooperate), and the environment provides the virtual space where these activities and interactions take place.

In general, the description of an agent is self-contained. A popular approach for conceptualizing the agent is the BDI approach where the **B**elief's, **D**esires, and **I**ntentions are specified. Beliefs refer to the agent's expectations about itself, its environment, and other agents, for example, how hostile are other agents likely to be? Desires can also be thought of as a goal, for example, to find food. Intentions are the plans for how the agent is going to go about accomplishing its desires given its beliefs.

22.4   Building an Agent-Based Model

While it is possible to implement features of agent-based models in a spreadsheet, the large number of actions taking place in parallel and the dynamics of the model make it challenging to do so. Either we implement every action by every agent one at a time, updating our spreadsheet as we do so, or we learn to use the spreadsheet's scripting language. In the first case, we lose the animation and dynamics of our simulation, which is an important source of information. In the second case, we have to program macros into the spreadsheet, usually by writing actual computer code. If we are going to do this, then the advantages of the spreadsheet, its simplicity and familiarity, are lost.

Therefore, we will use a friendly agent-based toolkit: NetLogo. This modelling platform has been around since 2000 and continues to be updated. It is frequently used in education settings, and there are good textbooks for guiding further learning. The NetLogo program uses its own programming language, but is written in Java. There is a large "commons" of models that provides numerous examples of how agent-based approaches can be used and how they are implemented.

22.5   An Introduction to NetLogo

Getting NetLogo

The homepage for NetLogo features the download links.[1] The download link (on the left) leads you to a page with a big **Download** button; click it and you will be led to the download page for the different operating systems. As of this writing, the current version is 5.0.1.

Because NetLogo is written in Java, it easily runs on all machines, but you need to have Java installed. For Windows and Mac OS X you will typically not need to worry about this requirement. If you work with Linux you will have to install a recent "JDK" (which stands for Java Development Kit) that your Linux distribution provides. This will almost certainly be available through the package manager for your distribution. It is possible that you will already have Java installed, because it is required by another application. Try NetLogo first, and only worry about Java if you cannot get NetLogo to run.

Test NetLogo

Assuming that NetLogo is installed, launch it using the method appropriate to your operating system. Click the FILE menu. One of the options will be MODELS LIBRARY. Click the little arrow next to SOCIAL SCIENCE to expand that menu. Select ETHNOCENTRISM by clicking it once. Now you will see a brightly colored illustration and a brief description. Below it is a button OPEN. Click it.

Now you have opened the model. All the buttons and displays are user programmable. For example, right-click the button GO with the two little arrows going in a circle (if you left-clicked it, just click it again and things will stop). Select the "edit" option, and you will see that the content of this button can be changed simply by typing. Currently it executes the "go" command.

If you want to see what the "go" command does, click the CODE tab which is a little under the ZOOM menu item. This will open a text editor that you can type in. It contains all the code for this model. If you search you will see a command that begins with "to go." This begins the "go" command. This procedure concludes where you see the word "end." This might look long and complex, but when you see what it is that the code does, you will realize that NetLogo is a very compact and expressive language.

To find out what the model is testing, click on the INFO tab (right next to CODE). This is also a window you can type in, but you first have to select the Edit button near the top. This is where you learn about the background to the model and the details of how the model operates. For right now, let's be impetuous. Go back to the INTERFACE tab. Click the SETUP EMPTY button once, click the GO button once, and watch the light show. When that gets boring, click the GO button again to freeze the simulation. Maybe now you will be more interested in reading what the model is testing, but before you do this, convince yourself that you cannot break anything. Move the slider buttons around, and then click GO again. It will look different, but it will run. To start over, just reopen the model.

Exercise: Exploring NetLogo Models

Search the model library for a model that appeals to you. Load it up, run it, and read the information so that you understand what the model is testing. Almost all the models will have sections on things to observe and things you might try changing. Explore the implications of your model by running it with altered settings. That is what models are for.

22.6   Making a NetLogo Model

NetLogo is a powerful and complex program. In this section we will construct a simple NetLogo model to demonstrate some of the features and capabilities of the system. The goal is to achieve sufficient familiarity with the structure and vocabulary of NetLogo so that you can evaluate and adapt models on your own. But first, we outline the relation between the vocabulary of agent-based models presented above and the commands of NetLogo.

NetLogo was inspired by a programming language called Logo. Logo had a small agent that moved around drawing. This agent was called a *turtle*. Therefore, in the NetLogo world, agents are called turtles. Turtles navigate around a world that is populated by *patches*. Collectively patches are the environment. Turtles and patches have characteristics that are built-in, such as their color and their location. Turtles and patches may also have user-defined properties. In addition, you can create different *breeds* of turtles and you can create links between turtles.

Everything in NetLogo is basically one of two different types of activities: NetLogo entities *do* things or they *report* things. We can instruct a patch or a turtle to tell us what color it is, we can tell a turtle to move somewhere in its environment, and we can tell a turtle to change some aspect of the patch it is on. Thinking in terms of real turtles and real patches of grass, we could imagine a command for the turtle to "eat." This would result in changing the patch variable describing how much grass was contained. Eating might also change the turtle's variable for energy level.

Select Your Problem

As we saw in Chapter 21, the first stage in any modelling problem is to develop a high-level description of the problem and the specifications for the model. For our sample model we will adapt a mathematical model of population movements to see if it can also account for eye movements in visual search. A value of abstraction is that we can leap levels: we can go from humans to eyes; we can shift the environment from New England to a computer-based search task.

Modelling Relocation

A common model for commuting and population movements is the gravitational model. The gravitational model relates the probability of relocating from one place to another as the product of the populations at each location (acting like mass in the formula for gravitation), and inversely related to the distance between them. Simini, González, Maritan, and Barabási (2011) propose another model. They propose what we might think of as a lazy algorithm. We go to the closest location that offers us something better than what we have.

How can we adapt this ideas to eye movements? When we search a scene for a hidden object, where we look depends on what we are looking for and the context in which the object is hidden. For example, when playing "Where's Waldo?" we look first for red and white striped objects.

In visual search, where we look is biased by the probability of recent events. For example, if we are cued to features of a hidden target, we prioritize those features when searching. Could the equations that explain human commuting apply to eye movements? If so, we would expect that we look at the nearest object that affords a greater likelihood of being the target than the object where we are looking now. We repeat until we view the target.

Exercise: Mapping Ideas to Software

Before we can simulate our eye movement model, we have to map our high-level description to software features. You might find some ideas for how to do this in the NetLogo dictionary and programmer's guide. There might also be ideas in other models. As an exercise, decide on your own or in small groups on answers to the following questions:

1. What NetLogo component is the agent?

2. What component of our eye movement model should we conceive of as "the agent?"

3. Given the pieces of a NetLogo model, how might we implement the objects of a visual search?

4. How can we have objects that are more or less likely to be the target?

Beginning our NetLogo Program

What are those lines starting with semi-colons? They are comments. Most computer languages use some character to allow you to add plain text statements to your code. These comments are helpful when trying to remember what the code is supposed to do, but do not add too many comments. They can actually obscure the code and make it harder to figure out what is supposed to be happening by camouflaging the lines of code within a nest of comments.

Once again, we will try to work our way through a simple example, and we will try to ease our entry by adapting existing code rather than starting with a blank piece of paper. If you find the Rumor Mill model in the NetLogo library, you will see that it is a fairly simple model. Open the code tab and copy it. Then go to the FILE menu, click "new", open the CODE tab (it should be blank), and place your copied code inside. Then go back to the FILE menu and "save-as" giving it a file name you can remember. You now have something to work with. NetLogo gives you a way to check if your code meets certain tests. These tests will assess if your code is correct enough to execute. It cannot check if your code is doing what you want, but it can check if your code will run. Click the CHECK button and you will see a yellow error message. This is because we have not defined "INIT-CLIQUE". "INIT-CLIQUE" is one of the slider bars for this model. We did not copy the commands for the slider bars. Therefore, we will get an error message. Since all we want from this model is a skeleton for getting started, this is not a critical error. The pieces we are interested in are the variables, procedures, commands, and reports. Anything that starts with a `to` is a command. The basic syntax is

```
to <ourFunctionName>

...stuff....

end
```

Where we replace `ourFunctionName` with the actual name of a function, such as `setup`.

Since we know how to spot functions in NetLogo, we also know how to spot variables. They are the pieces of code that do not begin with `to` but are followed by words sandwiched between "[" and "]". To get our skeleton ready to work with, remove all the text between the braces and between the function name and their end. If you have done it correctly, then when you hit the CHECK button, you will not have an error message, and the icon of the check mark will be colored gray.

> There are popular styles for function and variable names. The style that has no breaks and where each new word starts with an upper case letter (except for the first letter of the name) is called *Camel Case*. Another style is to replace spaces with underscores: our_function_name. However, this "_" key is not one I type often so I prefer Camel Case. Which style you use is mostly a personal or institutional preference. *No spaces* in function or variable names!

For our eye movement model, we will implement eye fixations as movements of the turtle. Our agent, the viewer, or at least their eye, will move from patch to patch based on rules we will establish. All patches will not be alike. Some will be background; we will color those black. Other patches will be red or green and will represent the objects that an experimental subject is searching through. One of those items will be the target. We will color this for our benefit with a different shade of red or green. To communicate that different colored objects have different values for attracting gaze, depending on whether that color has been "cued," we will set a variable that provides a numerical value for each colored patch.

The algorithm we want to implement requires that the search area, the world of our model, be broken up into regions. We will call them counties in keeping with the nomenclature of the article that inspired our model. In the present context it is just a mnemonic.

To get our model to work, we need to do the following steps:

- Figure out where we are looking now.
- Determine which of the objects in each county has the largest "value" for that county.
- Find the object that is nearest our current position and that has a greater value than the object we are looking at currently.
- Move to that object.
- Check if it is the target: if so, we quit; if not, we repeat the process.

Exercise: Creating a High-Level Specification

To see if you understand the algorithm at a high level, write down the specific details of how you would proceed through these steps, without worrying about concrete NetLogo code.

- What does it mean for a patch to have a value?
- What process will you use to identify the object with the maximum "value" for each county?

Developing the Details: A Walk Through Some NetLogo Code

Listing 22.1   Declaring variables in NetLogo

```
;;; Eye Movement Model
;;; Author: Britt Anderson

; global variables from eye movement model
globals [
    ngd         ; number green diamonds
    ctyPSz      ; county size in patches
    tClr        ; target color
    tClrInc     ; target color increment
    startx      ; starting x coordinate location
    starty      ; starting y coordinate location
    maxpm       ; maximum pick-me value
    turtN       ; number of turtles (i.e. eye-balls)
                ; we will create
]

; variables local to patches
patches-own [
    isDia       ; is this patch an object?
    isTarg      ; is this patch the target?
    cty         ; what is the county?
    pickMe      ; what is the pick-me value?
    visited     ; how many times have we looked here?
]
```

In this code listing I put identifying information at the top. This is not required. It is very helpful when you are going back to a file that you have not worked on in some time. I commented each of the two classes of variables that I will be using. The "globals" are those that can be seen anywhere in my program. The second classes are the names that I will be using for variables that are local to the patches. A patch can be a target (isTarg = True) or not (isTarg = False). Each patch will have an isTarg value, but none of the turtles will have a value for isTarg (note that this is a Boolean variable, as we discussed on page 49). I have commented each variable to remind me what they represent. I didn't realize I needed all of these variables when I started programming. For example, I didn't have a visited variable. The need for some of these variables only became obvious with testing. Don't feel bad if you didn't think of all of them, or you cannot guess what purpose they serve. To repeat, programs are often developed incrementally. Keep it simple to start, and add the elaborations as you need them.

Exercise: Fill in the Blanks

Here are some steps to continue your development of this model:

- Edit the code skeleton you have to include the name of the variables above. Check frequently to make sure that you have not introduced an error as you type. Save frequently.

- Create a category for turtle variables and enter the names `xjitt` and `yjitt`. We will use the values to offset our initial position slightly, so that we can more easily see how simulations run with multiple agents simultaneously.
- At the beginning of your `setup` procedure add `ca` and at the end add `reset-ticks`. These are common book-ends of a NetLogo procedure and clear all variables to start our set-up, and reset the clock timing our simulation.

The beginning of the set-up function should initialize our variables. Here are two examples:

Listing 22.2 Setting a Variables Initial Value

```
set  turtN  10
set  startx  max-pxcor  /  2
set  starty  max-pycor  /  2
```

We can use either a number or a mathematical expression for variables. The variable `max-pxcor` is a built-in variable that specifies the maximum x coordinate for the patches (notice the p as in **p**atch). To learn more about the dimensions of the NetLogo world, click back to the INTERFACE tab and click the SETTINGS button. While you are free to adjust these settings to your own preference, the code demonstrated here

> What is the result of this operation that we are performing on the maximum coordinates? If you cannot see the answer, make a little graph on some paper and plot the answer.

assumes that the world is 35 by 35 (note that since the numbering starts with 0, as is common in the computer programming world, the value of `max-pxcor` is 34). In this settings screen, place the origin of the world in the lower left, and turn off wrapping horizontally and vertically.

You will need two global variables that are not in the list above. The reason is we will use slider bars to control the values of these variables. Return to the INTERFACE tab so that you see the black, world screen (Figure 22.1). Click the BUTTON button and create a button for "Setup" and another for "go". For each of them, you will have to right-click the button itself to edit it. You can give the buttons whatever name you want, but the commands "setup" and "go" must be in the field on the right. If you wonder about whether you have done it correctly, open up another model from the library, right-click the set-up button for that model, select edit, and see how that model did it.

You will use the same procedure to create two slider bars that will control the global variables "nrd" (for the number of red objects) and "offset" which is the difference between the maximum value of the cued and uncued target categories (to simplify this exercise, we will assume that green is the cued color).

I have also created a graph for plotting how many of the objects have been visited and how many agents have yet to find a target. The method for producing this graph is not explained here, but it is not hard to do. You can probably guess. Or you could look at examples in the NetLogo documentation and models from the NetLogo library for ideas.

In our "setup" function we need to initialize our patches and our turtles. When we want patches to do something we `ask` them to do it, and the same for turtles. For example, to set all patches to some basic values I can do the following:

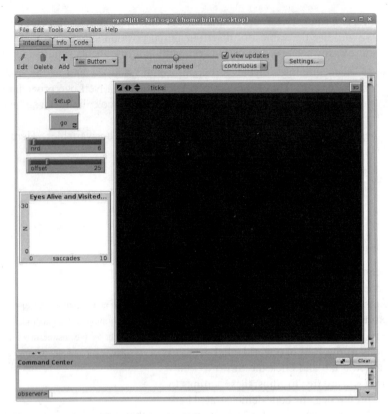

Figure 22.1   The NetLogo eye movement screen.

Listing 22.3   Initializing all patches

```
ask patches
  [
    set pcolor black
    set isDia false
    set isTarg false
    set pickMe −1
    whichCty
    set visited 0
  ]
```

In this code I ask each patch (`patches` is a special NetLogo word that refers to all the patches) to set its color to black. I tell it to say that it is not an object, nor is it a target. It has also never been visited. Initially, we give it a very low `pickMe` value. It is easier to set these variables for all patches and then overwrite the ones we need to change later. Notice that each of the expressions uses the keyword `set`. I have also asked it to set the value of its `cty` variable by running a function called `whichCty`. This is not a NetLogo function, but one that I wrote. You will need to add the `whichCty` function to the bottom of your CODE page. It looks like this:

Listing 22.4   The `whichCty` function

```
to  whichCty
    set cty (floor (pxcor / ctyPSz)) + \
    (floor (pycor / ctyPSz)) * (ceiling (max-pxcor / ctyPSz))
end
```

The `set` word is hidden in here. You could replace the use of the `whichCty` function with this line in your ask patches function and it would work just fine, but would you be able to understand what is going on as easily? I wrote `which Cty` as a separate function to keep things readable. Now when I look at the code I understand

> Do you understand how the `whichCty` function works to figure out which county a patch is in?

that I am computing which county a patch is in. That would not be so obvious by looking at the line which actually does the work. Later, if I want the details of how `whichCty` is calculating its value, I can look it up.

We use the `n-of` function to overwrite these default values and to create objects. We ask all the patches to pick a number (n) of themselves to be objects. NetLogo does this randomly.

Here is how I set the red objects:

Listing 22.5   Making the red objects

```
    ask n-of nrd patches [
      set pcolor 14
      set isDia true
      set pickMe random maxpm
    ]
```

I leave it as another exercise for you to do the same for the green objects. You will want to only pick patches that are black. Otherwise, you might replace a red one with a green one and your numbers will be off. To help accomplish this you might find it useful to use a selection of the patches by using the NetLogo keyword `with` as in `patches with [pcolor = black]`.

By picking one of the non-black patches you should be able to create the target patch. Then you can create the "eyes" that will search them.

Listing 22.6   Creating our searchers

```
    crt turtN
    [
      set shape "eyeball"
      set xcor one-of (map [? + startx] [-1 0 1])
      set ycor one-of (map [? + starty] [-1 0 1])
      set xjitt random-float 0.5
      set yjitt random-float 0.5
      pen-down
    ]
```

This function is similar to the others above. We use the `crt` to create our turtles, and we tell this function how many turtles we want. I use a variable. You might want to start with the explicit number 1 until you make sure things are working (again: start simple and elaborate on success).

If you really want the "eyeball" go to the TOOLS menu, select TURTLE SHAPE EDITOR, find the "eyeball" option, and import it.

I set the shape of my turtle to "eyeball". It serves no purpose. This is an eye movement task and it seemed fun. You can remove this line and you will have a little triangle icon as the default.

To begin you may want to set the initial turtle position to fixed patch coordinates. To do this set `xcor` and `ycor` to specific numbers, for example, 16 and 16. I have set up a little routine to jitter the starting position because we know real subjects would not have perfect fixation at the center of the screen, and because it will help to visualize multiple agents. The `pen-down` command means they will write their paths as they move.

The remainder of our model uses the `go` function. This critical function determines what happens when we run things. It needs to have reporter functions so we can find out what is going on. Reporter functions are functions that "report" on the value of things.

I have reporters to find out which patch in a single county has the maximum `pickMe` value, and a separate function that finds this value for all the counties (I broke them apart for readability, not because I had to).

To write these reporters I used a NetLogo function called `map`. This is a very important function in the world of functional programming languages like Lisp and Haskell (Python also has a variant). It is not special to NetLogo; `map` lets us do the same thing repeatedly, once we can figure out how to do it at least once. For example, if we had a function "square a number" we could do: "square a number" 2 -> 4. But if we "mapped" it, we could use our "square a number" on a list of numbers, like `map "square a number"` (list 1, 2, 3, 4) and get back (list 1, 4, 9, 16). If I have a function that works on one patch, I can `map` that function over the list of all counties. How do I know the list of all counties? I just ask the patches to tell me what county they are in (and delete the duplicates).

The reporter code needs to go at the bottom of the CODE tab and looks like this:

Listing 22.7   Reporting the patches with highest `pickMe` values

```
to-report maxPInCty [ctyN]
  let mic max [pickMe] of patches with [cty = ctyN]
  report one-of patches with [cty = ctyN and pickMe = mic]
end

to-report maxPInAllCty
  let patlst map MaxPInCty sort remove-duplicates [cty] of patches
  report patches with [member? self patlst]
end
```

Our most complicated function is the `go` function. It looks like this:

Listing 22.8 The go function

```
to go
  tick
  ask turtles [
    let fltlst filter [[pickme] of ? > pickme] sort maxPInAllCty with
    [distance myself >= 0]
    if not empty? fltlst
    [
      ;print [pickme] of first fltlst
      setxy [pxcor] of first fltlst + xjitt [pycor] of
      first fltlst + yjitt
      set visited visited + 1
    ]
    ifelse isTarg
    [die]
    [
      ask patches with [pcolor = 14 or pcolor = (14 + tClrInc)]
        [set pickMe max list
          (random maxpm - (visited * 10 / turtN)) 0]
      ask patches with [pcolor = 54 or pcolor = (54 + tClrInc)]
        [set pickMe max list (random maxpm + offset -
          (visited * 10 / turtN)) 0]
    ]
  ]
  print "green"
  print mean [pickMe] of patches with [pcolor = 54]
  print "red"
  print mean [pickMe] of patches with [pcolor = 14]
  if count turtles = 0 [stop]
end
```

The `tick` moves the clock. Since we want the turtles to do things, we `ask` them. In my function, I find the patches with the maximum `pickMe` for each county, and then I sort them by distance from the current turtle. This uses the NetLogo built-in function `distance`.

I take the list produced by these operations and I filter it (think coffee filter). This allows only those patches that have a `pickMe` greater than where I am currently located to make it through the filter.

> Filtering is another staple of functional programming.

Our algorithm only moves us when our eyes can find somewhere better to go, that is, some place with a higher value. Unfortunately, it is sometimes the case that there is nowhere better. This case complicates our code. I check for this case by seeing if my list of better places is empty. I only move if it is not.

If there are better spots, I go to the first one. I pick the first one, because I sorted the list by distance. I keep my jitter amount as I do so. Next, I ask if I landed on the target. If so, the turtle "dies" (a NetLogo term, not my choice). If my turtle is not dead, I keep on going. Each time that I move I randomize the value of `pickMe` for all the colored patches, keeping in mind that the range is different for red and green. Lastly, I print out some data as we are going along, mostly so that you can see how this can be done.

Exercise: Putting it All Together

Take all these pieces of code and glue them into a functioning, working, NetLogo model and run it. If you find that no matter how hard you try you cannot get it to work, the complete code for my model is listed in the Notes for this chapter. If you use it, do not forget to set the world coordinates properly yourself. You will still need to add the buttons and sliders.[2]

22.7   Running the Eye Movement Model

One of the advantages of having spent the time to build a model like this is that we can now utilize the model to see what happens when we change things (Figure 22.2). This is, to bring us back to the goals of modelling raised in Chapter 1, to explore the implication of model assumptions. Do you feel that this model looks like the gaze patterns of a human searching a visual display?

Exercise: Exploring Implications

Use the eye movement model to experiment with NetLogo and with agent-based modelling. Some things to explore are:

- Get more output. Can you capture statistics from this data? NetLogo has facilities for writing to files. Can you record the number of visits and the total ticks per turtle?
- How does search time and saccade number (in this case the same as number of moves) scale with the number of objects? How does this compare to visual search data with people?
- How does the preference for green over red influence search characteristics? For example, if the offset is 0 instead of 10 does that change search times in a way consistent with the human performance?

22.8   Conclusion

Agent-based modelling is a relatively new name for some old ideas. Its details are similar to those of neural networks and cellular automata: you use a collection of simple entities that compute locally, and then observe for emergent, or macroscopic, behavior. While the value of this approach has been realized for some time, the application to more complicated social scenarios has only been actively explored for about 20 years. In part, the application of agent-based modelling has been driven by the development of more powerful and cheaper computers. Desktop computers allow for individual researchers, even those without extensive computing experience, to quickly explore ideas. In addition, the development of specialized software packages to facilitate the use of these types of

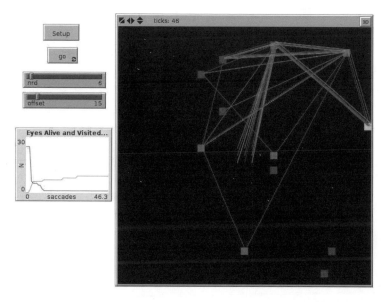

Figure 22.2   The "saccade" trace for 25 searches of the same display. Note that in this case all the high probability objects are visited at least once, but several of the low probability objects are not. Note that most of the searches move rather directly to the target, but that those that do not still seem to wiggle around in the same region. This figure appears qualitatively the same as an eye movement recording.

models has increased the accessibility of agent-based modelling to social scientists who previously might not have had the time to write customized code. As our example shows, these types of models reach beyond social scenarios. The ideas and the software developed for agent-based modelling can also be used for a wide variety of modelling projects.

Chapter 23

Concluding Remarks

For my conclusion, I would like to review my ambitions for the book. I feel that the time is ripe, and the tools available, for great advances in neuroscience and psychology. Computational approaches will be one of the principal methodologies that drive that advance. Thus, it was my intention to write a book that would help students to join this endeavor by convincing them that computational approaches are both useful and within their power. In addition, I wanted to provide basic lessons in their use.

To accomplish this aim, I discussed topics that spanned from the neuron to the rock-paper-scissors game player. I tried to show that the notation used for mathematics is just one more thing to memorize, like the names of the lobes of the brain; it is no more difficult and just as necessary.

I wanted people to see how today's powerful computers allow them to find answers with brute computational force. If they understand the definitions and basics of mathematics they do not need algorithmic subtleties. And to convince the doubters that they can program their computer to achieve these ends, we began with Excel and ended up with the cutting edge languages Lisp and Haskell. We then went beyond these general purpose languages to examine the use of very powerful programming environments for cognitive modelling: ACT-R and NetLogo. These exercises are complex, but will reward you with tools that you can truly use, unlike the more modest spreadsheet programs we began with.

Along the way, I have also tried to share some of the stories of the people who developed these areas. They have inspired me, and I see their stories as providing the blueprint for innovation and scientific success: be interdisciplinary; mix the empirical with the theoretical; enjoy what you do.

I have sprinkled together the psychological, mathematical, and computer programming facts in a way that I intended to preserve the flow, but which inevitably makes it harder to study each in isolation and depth. Because my ambitions were vast, but my patience and pages limited, the topics I covered were covered in brief. Large gaps are open between them. It is also true that in every instance I have stayed near the surface, and not developed the psychological themes or their corresponding models in depth. But you can now dig down deeper on your own.

Thus, I close the book as I began it, by emphasizing the word: introduction. Please regard this book as an *amuse-bouche* and not your *entrée*. Now that you possess these diverse and hard-earned competencies, you should feel confident going forward. If you do pursue any of these topics or exercises further, please share your results with me.

Notes

Chapter 1 Introduction

1. http://bluebrain.epfl.ch/cms/lang/en/pid/56882
2. http://www.nytimes.com/2008/12/05/us/05hm.html?pagewanted=all
3. http://www.ted.com/talks/lang/eng/henry_markram_supercomputing_the_brain_s_secrets.html
4. http://www.networkworld.com/news/2009/112409-ibm-cat-brain.html

Chapter 2 What Is a Differential Equation?

1. Comment on 2.4. One answer for Equation 2.1 would be $y = x$ since $dx/dx = 1$, but notice that $y = 2x$ is also a solution since $dx/dx = 2$. Often, solutions to DEs are not unique if you consider the constants, but since constants are not "interesting" we sweep that mathematical detail under the rug by using the symbol "C" and writing our solution as $y = Cx + C'$.
2. The idea of the infinitesimal distance, a distance essentially zero, but not zero, is not the modern basis for establishing the existence of derivatives. The modern derivation uses the concept of the limit, but the infinitesimal was good enough for Leibniz and Newton, the discovers of the calculus, and so it should be good enough for us to get started. Later, if you wish to use derivatives and DEs with more rigor, you will need to familiarize yourself with mathematical definitions for limits.
3. Sometimes you will see an equation with a derivative that is not on one side by itself. Often you can rearrange the equation, using the rules of algebra, so that it is. Sometimes you cannot. It might still be possible to find an *implicit* solution, but we will not pursue that here. Those equations are still DEs, though.

Chapter 3 Numerical Application of a Differential Equation

1. The damped oscillator is very similar to our original model. In this version we consider a damping term. To dampen means to decrease. This model assumes that there is a drag on our spring. Our model equation is: $a(t) = -Ps(t) - Qv(t)$. To adapt your original model to this damped version requires that you change only a single formula in your working spreadsheet (and that you add a spot for the new constant Q). Is it necessary for this model to oscillate, or can it smoothly decay? If so, what does the curve look like?

Chapter 5 Integrate and Fire

1. http://en.wikipedia.org/wiki/Action_potential
2. http://www.afodor.net/HHModel.htm.
3. http://lcn.epfl.ch/gerstner/BUCH.html.
4. http://www.afodor.net/HHModel.htm.

Chapter 7 Hodgkin and Huxley: The Men and Their Model

1. http://www.nobelprize.org/nobel_prizes/medicine/laureates/1963/
2. http://www.science.smith.edu/departments/NeuroSci/courses/bio330/squid.html

Chapter 10 Intermezzo: Interactive Computing

1. http://www.gnu.org/software/octave/

Chapter 13 Auto-associative Memory and the Hopfield Net

1. **Proving Hopfield Networks Converge**
Answers

1. $E(f[k], f[j]) = -\frac{1}{2}A[j,k]f[k]f[j] + -\frac{1}{2}A[k,j]f[j]f[k]$

2. $E(f[k], f[j]) = -A[j,k]f[k]f[j]$

3. $E[k] = \sum_{j \neq k} -A[j,k]f[k]f[j]$

4. $E[k] = f[k] \sum_{j \neq k} -A[j,k]f[j]$

5. $\sum_{j \neq k} -A[j,k]f[j]$ represents what we use to decide whether or not to change $f[k]$.

6.

$$
\begin{aligned}
\Delta E[k] &= E[k](\textit{new value}) - E[k](\textit{old value}) \\
&= f[k](\textit{new value}) \sum_{j \neq k} -A[j,k]f[j] - f[k](\textit{old value}) \sum_{j \neq k} -A[j,k]f[j] \\
&= (f[k](\textit{new value}) - f[k](\textit{old value})) \sum_{j \neq k} -A[j,k]f[j] \\
&= -\Delta f[k] \sum_{j \neq k} A[j,k]f[j]
\end{aligned}
$$

7. If $f[k] \to$ from 1 to $-1 \implies \Delta f[k] < 0$ and $\sum_{j \neq k} A[j,k] f[j] < 0$, then their product is greater than zero. Since there is a negative sign out front the whole thing will be negative. The alternative case has a similar logic. Since the updating is asynchronous, this logic holds for all updating. Since the number of the units is *finite*, there will be at least one minimum.

Chapter 15 Decisions as Random Walks

1. http://www.jstor.org/stable/2304386
2. http://www.nature.com/nature/journal/v464/n7289/full/464681b.html
3. http://psycnet.apa.org/psycinfo/2001-05332-006
4. http://www.psych.utoronto.ca/museum/hippchron.htm
5. http://en.wikipedia.org/wiki/Bean_machine
6. http://en.wikipedia.org/wiki/Bean_machine

Chapter 16 Intermezzo: Programming Psychophysical Experiments with Python

1. http://numpy.scipy.org/
2. http://matplotlib.sourceforge.net/
3. http://www.briansimulator.org/
4. http://neuralensemble.org/trac/PyNN
5. https://www.ynic.york.ac.uk/software/dv3d
6. http://www.visionegg.org
7. http://www.psychopy.org/
8. http://osdoc.cogsci.nl/about/
9. http://code.google.com/p/psychopy/

Chapter 17 Boolean Logic

1. http://royalsociety.org/
2. http://www.gutenberg.org/ebooks/15114

Chapter 18 Intermezzo: Computing with Functional Languages

1. http://racket-lang.org/

Chapter 19 Production Rules and Cognition

1. http://www.cs.cmu.edu/simon/kfrank.html
2. http://www.nytimes.com/2012/06/11/nyregion/chinatown-fair-returns-but-without
-chicken-playing-tick-tack-toe.html?pagewanted=all
3. http://en.wikipedia.org/wiki/Production_system

Chapter 20 Intermezzo: Functional Coding of a Simple Production System

1. http://www.haskell.org/platform

Chapter 21 ACT-R: A Cognitive Architecture

1. http://jactr.org/
2. https://github.com/tcstewar/ccmsuite
3. http://act-r.psy.cmu.edu/
4. http://www.sbcl.org/getting.html
5. http://www.clisp.org/
6. http://www.quicklisp.org
7. http://www.lispworks.com/products/lispworks.html
8. http://act-r.psy.cmu.edu/actr6/
9. http://www.tcl.tk/software/tcltk/
10. Complete listing of the RPS model:

Listing 23.1　The go function

```
(defun judge (p1 p2)
  (cond
    ((string= p1 p2) "tie")
    ((and (string= p1 "rock") (string= p2 "scissors")) "loss")
    ((and (string= p1 "rock") (string= p2 "paper")) "win")
    ((and (string= p2 "rock") (string= p1 "scissors")) "win")
    ((and (string= p2 "rock") (string= p1 "paper")) "loss")
    ((and (string= p2 "paper") (string= p1 "scissors")) "loss")
    ((and (string= p2 "scissors") (string= p1 "paper")) "win")
    (t nil)))



;;; The ACT-R model


(clear-all)

(define-model rps
```

```
(sgp
    :esc  t
    :lf  0.05
    :v  t
    :trace-detail  low
    :er  t
    :bll  0.5
    :ol  t
    :act  nil
    :ul  t
)

(chunk-type  stage)
(chunk-type  game  stage)
(chunk-type  trial  p1p  p2p  result)


(add-dm
  (init  isa  stage)
  (makep1move  isa  stage)
  (makep2move  isa  stage)
  (judge  isa  stage)
  (record  isa  stage)
  (quit  isa  stage)
  (contest  isa  trial)
  (g  isa  game  stage  init)
)


(p  init
    =goal>
        isa        game
        stage      init
==>
    +retrieval>
        isa        trial
    =goal>
        stage      makep1move
)


(p  getp1move
    =goal>
        isa        game
        stage      makep1move
    =retrieval>
        isa        trial
==>
    !bind!  =p1choose  (car  (permute-list  '("rock"  "rock"  "paper"  "scissors")))
    =goal>
        stage  makep2move
```

```
   =retrieval>
      p1p      =p1choose
)



(p  p2rock
   =goal>
      isa        game
      stage      makep2move
   =retrieval>
      isa        trial
      p1p        =p1p
==>
   =goal>
      stage      judge
   =retrieval>
      p2p        "rock"
)



(p  p2paper
   =goal>
      isa        game
      stage      makep2move
   =retrieval>
      isa        trial
      p1p        =p1p
==>
   =goal>
      stage      judge
   =retrieval>
      p2p        "paper"
)



(p  p2scissors
   =goal>
      isa        game
      stage      makep2move
   =retrieval>
      isa        trial
      p1p        =p1p
==>
   =goal>
      stage      judge
   =retrieval>
      p2p        "scissors"
)
```

```
( p  whoWon
    =goal>
        isa      game
        stage    judge
    =retrieval>
        isa      trial
        p1p      =p1c
        p2p      =p2c
 ==>
    !bind! =outcome (judge =p1c =p2c)
    ;;!output! =outcome
    =retrieval>
        result      =outcome
    =goal>
        stage    record
)


( p  record1Won
    =goal>
        isa      game
        stage    record
    =retrieval>
        isa      trial
        p1p      =p1c
        p2p      =p2c
        result   "loss"
 ==>
    !output! ("P1  won")
    =goal>
        stage    init
)


( p  record2Won
    =goal>
        isa      game
        stage    record
    =retrieval>
        isa      trial
        p1p      =p1c
        p2p      =p2c
        result   "win"
 ==>
    !output! ("P2  won")
    =goal>
        stage    init
)


( p  recordTie
```

```
   =goal>
      isa      game
      stage    record
   =retrieval>
      isa      trial
      p1p      =p1c
      p2p      =p2c
      result   "tie"
 ==>
   !output!  ("Tie")
   =goal>
      stage       init
)




(p  quit
   =goal>
      isa      game
      stage    quit
==>
   -goal>
)

(spp  record1Won  :reward  -1)
(spp  record2Won  :reward  1)
(spp  recordTie   :reward  0)

(goal-focus  g)
)
```

Chapter 22 Agent-Based Modelling

1. http://ccl.northwestern.edu/netlogo/
2. Complete Code for the eye movement NetLogo model:

Listing 23.2   The go function

```
;;;Eye  Movement  Model
;;;Author:  Britt  Anderson
;;;Date:  April  22,  2012

;global  variables  from  eye  movement  model
globals  [ngd
         ctyPSz
         tClr
         tClrInc
         startx
         starty
```

```
            maxpm
            turtN ]

;variables local to turtles
turtles—own [xjitt yjitt]

;variables local to patches
patches—own [isDia
             isTarg
             cty
             pickMe
             visited]


;every model needs a setup function
to set up
   ;now begin by clearing all variables
   ca
   ;color patches black unless they are diamonds
   ;if they are, color red and green, and pick the target
   set maxpm 60
   set ngd nrd
   set ctyPSz 5
   set tClrInc 13
   set startx max—pxcor / 2
   set starty max—pycor / 2
   set turtN 10
   ask patches
   [
      set pcolor black
      set isDia false
      set isTarg false
      set pickMe —1
      whichCty
      set visited 0
   ]
   ask n—of nrd patches [
      set pcolor 14
      set isDia true
      set pickMe random maxpm
   ]
   ask n—of ngd patches with [pcolor = black]
   [
      set pcolor 54
      set isDia true
      set pickMe random maxpm + offset
   ]
   ask n—of 1 patches with [pcolor != black]
   [
      set tClr pcolor
      set pcolor pcolor + tClrInc
```

```
    set isTarg true
  ]
  crt turtN
  [
    set shape "eyeball"
    set xcor one-of (map [? + startx] [-1 0 1])
    set ycor one-of (map [? + starty] [-1 0 1])
    set xjitt random-float 0.5
    set yjitt random-float 0.5
    pen-down
  ]
  reset-ticks
end ; this concludes a procedure


; now the function for what to do when turtles move
to go
  tick
  ask turtles [
    let fltlst filter [[pickme] of ? > pickme]
        sort maxPInAllCty with [distance myself >= 0]
    if not empty? fltlst
    [
      ; print [pickme] of first fltlst
      setxy [pxcor] of first fltlst +
            xjitt [pycor] of first fltlst + yjitt
      set visited visited + 1
    ]
    ifelse isTarg
    [die]
    [
      ask patches with [pcolor = 14 or pcolor = (14 + tClrInc)]
          [set pickMe max list (random maxpm -
          (visited * 10 / turtN)) 0]
      ask patches with [pcolor = 54 or pcolor = (54 + tClrInc)]
          [set pickMe max list (random maxpm + offset -
          (visited * 10 / turtN)) 0]
    ]
  ]
  print "green"
  print mean [pickMe] of patches with [pcolor = 54]
  print "red"
  print mean [pickMe] of patches with [pcolor = 14]
  if count turtles = 0 [stop]
end

; computes the county for a patch
; only apply to patches with diamonds
to whichCty
    set cty (floor (pxcor / ctyPSz)) +
        (floor (pycor / ctyPSz)) * (ceiling (max-pxcor / ctyPSz))
```

```
end

to-report maxPInCty [ctyN]
  let mic max [pickMe] of patches with [cty = ctyN]
  report one-of patches with [cty = ctyN and pickMe = mic]
end

to-report maxPInAllCty
  let patlst map MaxPInCty sort remove-duplicates [cty] of patches
  report patches with [member? self patlst]
end
```

References

Anderson, J. A., & Davis, J. (1995). *An Introduction to Neural Networks* (Vol. 1). MIT Press.

Anderson, J. R., Bothell, D., Byrne, M., Douglass, S., Lebiere, C., & Qin, Y. (2004). An integrated theory of the mind. *Psychological Review*, *111*, 1036–1060.

Anderson, J. R., & Kline, P. J. (1977). Psychological aspects of a pattern directed inference. *Sigart Newsletter*, *63*, 60–65.

Barski, C. (2010). *Land of Lisp*. San Francisco, CA: No Starch Press.

Catterall, W. A., Raman, I. M., Robinson, H. P., Sejnowski, T. J., & Paulsen, O. (2012). The Hodgkin-Huxley heritage: From channels to circuits. *Journal of Neuroscience*, *32*, 14064–14073.

Caudill, M., & Butler, C. (1992). *Understanding Neural Networks: computer explorations. Volume 1: Basic Networks*. Cambridge, MA: MIT Press.

Collobert, R., & Bengio, S. (2004). Links between perceptrons, mlps and svms. In *Proceedings of the twenty-first international conference on machine learning* (p. 23).

Craik, K. (1952). *The Nature of Explanation*. Cambridge: Cambridge University Press.

Ellsberg, D. (1961). Risk, ambiguity, and the savage axioms. *The Quarterly Journal of Economics*, *75*, 643–669.

Galton, A. (1990). *Logic for Information Technology*. Chichester: John Wiley & Sons, Inc.

Garrett, B. (2011). *Brain & Behavior: An introduction to biological psychology*. London: Sage.

Gasser, J. (2000). *A Boole Anthology: recent and classical studies in the logic of George Boole* (Vol. 291). Berlin: Springer.

Gerstner, W., & Kistler, W. (2002). *Spiking Neuron Models: Single neurons, populations, plasticity*. Cambridge: Cambridge University Press.

Gold, J. I., & Shadlen, M. N. (2007). The neural basis of decision making. *Annual Review of Neuroscience*, *30*, 535–574.

Griffiths, T., Chater, N., Kemp, C., Perfors, A., & Tenenbaum, J. (2010). Probabilistic models of cognition: Exploring representations and inductive biases. *Trends in Cognitive Sciences*, *14*, 357–364.

Hebb, D. (1949). *The Organization of Behavior: A neuropsychological theory*. Chichester: John Wiley & Sons, Inc.

Hopfield, J. (1982). Neural networks and physical systems with emergent collective computational abilities. *Proceedings of the National Academy of the United States of America*, *79*, 2554–2558.

Hutton, G. (2007). *Programming in Haskell*. Cambridge: Cambridge University Press.

Johnson-Laird, P., Byrne, R., & Schaeken, W. (1992). Propositional reasoning by model. *Psychological Review*, *99*, 418–439.

Kumar, S., Forward, K., & Palaniswami, M. (1995). An experimental evaluation of neural network approach to circuit partitioning. In *IEEE International Conference on Neural Networks*, *1*, (pp. 569–574).

Lipovaca, M. (2011). *Learn You a Haskell for Great Good! A beginner's guide*. San Francisco, CA: No Starch Press.

Mainen, Z., & Sejnowski, T. (1995). Reliability of spike timing in neocortical neurons. *Science*, *268*, 1503.

McClelland, J. (2009). The place of modeling in cognitive science. *Topics in Cognitive Science*, *1*, 11–38.

McClelland, J., Botvinick, M., Noelle, D., Plaut, D., Rogers, T., Seidenberg, M., & Smith, L. (2010). Letting structure emerge: connectionist and dynamical systems approaches to cognition. *Trends in Cognitive Sciences*, *14*, 348–356.

McClelland, J., & Rumelhart, D. (1981). An interactive activation model of context effects in letter perception: I. an account of basic findings. *Psychological Review*, *88*, 375–407.

McCulloch, W., & Pitts, W. (1943). A logical calculus of the ideas immanent in nervous activity. *Bulletin of mathematical biology*, *5*(4), 115–133.

Minsky, M., & Papert, S. (1969). *Perceptrons: An introduction to computational geometry*. Cambridge, MA: MIT Press.

Newell, A., & Simon, H. A. (1961). GPS: A program the simulates human thought. In *Lernende Automaten* (pp. 109–124). Berlin: Oldenbourg

O'Sullivan, B., Stewart, D., & Goerzen, J. (2009). *Real World Haskell*. San Francisco, CA: O'Reilly Media.

Posner, M. (1980). Orienting of attention. *Quarterly Journal of Experimental Psychology*, *32*, 3–25.

Railsback, S., & Grimm, V. (2011). *Agent-based and individual-based modeling: A practical introduction*. New Jersey: Princeton University Press.

Ratcliff, R., & McKoon, G. (2008). The diffusion decision model: Theory and data for two-choice decision tasks. *Neural Computation*, *20*, 873–922.

Rosenblatt, F. (1958). The perceptron: A probabilistic model for information storage and organization in the brain. *Psychological Review*, *65*, 386–408.

Rosenblatt, F. (1960). Perceptron simulation experiments. *Proceedings of the IRE*, *48*, 301–309.

Simini, F., González, M., Maritan, A., & Barabási, A. (2011). A universal model for mobility and migration patterns. *Arxiv preprint*, arXiv:1111.0586.

Smith, P., & Ratcliff, R. (2004). Psychology and neurobiology of simple decisions. *Trends in Neurosciences*, *27*, 161–168.

Tentori, K., Crupi, V., & Russo, S. (2013). On the determinants of the conjunction fallacy: Probability versus inductive confirmation. *Journal of Experimental Psychology: General*, *142*, 235–255.

Turing, A. (1936). On computable numbers, with an application to the Entscheidungsproblem. *Journal of Mathematics*, *58*, 345–363.

Tversky, A., & Kahneman, D. (1983). Extensional versus intuitive reasoning: The conjunction fallacy in probability judgment. *Psychological Review*, *90*, 293–315.

Von Neumann, J. (1958). *The Computer and the Brain*. New Haven, CT: Yale University Press.

Wagenmakers, E., Van Der Maas, H., & Grasman, R. (2007). An EZ-diffusion model for response time and accuracy. *Psychonomic Bulletin & Review*, *14*, 3–22.

Wolfram, S. (2002). *A New Kind of Science*. Champaign, IL: Wolfram Media.

Index